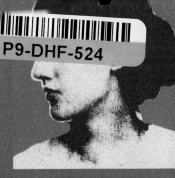

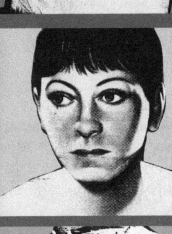

"I read a little from this book each day as there is so much information packed in here. I had no idea that the first recorded writer in human history was a woman! I am learning so much from this and it is written in a delightfully entertaining way. I am inspired!"

—Varla Ventura, author of *Sheroes*

"Enter into this fascinating world of women who are desperately in love with books. They are a diverse group of personalities who were at times ignored, banned and reviled by the public for their use of the written word. Becca Anderson offers some intriguing and entertaining profiles of women in the literary scene. They are listed in cool categories which include prolific pens, those whose books were banned, women who wrote from a different spiritual point of view and other interesting facts about women in the field of literature. Did you know that women were responsible for writing the Bible under the 'guidance' of Jerome? Are you aware of the prolific amount of prose penned by Barbara Cartland, Margaret Mead and Edith Wharton? These are just a few tidbits of information that will encourage you to read more and, hopefully, be inspired to pick up the pen yourself!"

—Autumn Stephens, author of *Wild Words from Wild Women*

"This book is a testament to the relationship and contributions of women writers, lest we forget their impact and inspiration. Becca paints portraits of women writers with her energetic and enigmatic words in an accessible and engaging manner. Please join me on this amazing journey through women's history—I know you will be as inspired by it as I have been."

—Ntozake Shange, author of *For Colored Girls Who Have Considered Suicide / When the Rainbow Is Enuf*

"So go on, do some guilt-free indulging in the pages of Becca Anderson's basket of literary bonbons. She has gathered a wealth of delectable stories in which to immerse ourselves, a bite at a time. Let's hear it for bibliophiles and book ladies—our richest yet most non-fattening vice."

—Vicki León, author of the *Uppity Women series*

THE BOOK
OF AWESOME
WOMEN
WRITERS

THE BOOK OF AWESOME WOMEN WRITERS

Medieval Mystics, Pioneering Poets, Fierce
Feminists and First Ladies of Literature
from Aphra Behn to Zora Neale Hurston

BECCA ANDERSON

Mango Publishing
CORAL GABLES

For permission requests, please contact the publisher at:
Mango Publishing Group
2850 S Douglas Road, 2nd Floor
Coral Gables, FL 33134 USA
info@mango.bz

For special orders, quantity sales, course adoptions and corporate sales, please email the publisher at sales@mango.bz. For trade and wholesale sales, please contact Ingram Publisher Services at customer.service@ingramcontent.com or +1.800.509.4887.

The Book of Awesome Women Writers: Medieval Mystics, Pioneering Poets, Fierce Feminists and First Ladies of Literature

Library of Congress Cataloging-in-Publication number: 2019944233
ISBN: (print) 978-1-64250-122-3, (ebook) 978-1-64250-123-0
BISAC category code BIOGRAPHY & AUTOBIOGRAPHY / Women

Printed in the United States of America

This is for Mrs. Evelyn Gammon

my late and great teacher who taught me to read in the first grade and made me believe in myself. I'll never forget the support and encouragement she gave me to pursue my dreams. I also dedicate this to every teacher, librarian, and volunteer who instills a love of books in their students.

and in memory of Richard J. Chin, my eternal inspiration

Table of Contents

Editor's Note
by Ntozake Shange, poet, playwright, and author

Women have shaped and inspired me my whole life, especially women writers, in whom I have found inspiration, hope, and camaraderie. One can never underestimate the power of women—they have motivated, stimulated, and encouraged since the first book was written. In fact, a woman may have written the first book! *The Book of Awesome Women Writers* explores in a compelling manner the fascinating history and work of the world's most beloved and influential women writers, without whom I never would have been a success.

As a curious and impressionable young girl, I was blessed with a mother who educated me about Black women writers. My mother shared her race records with me (similar to race books), which documented the traditions, achievements, and work of Black writers. I was especially inspired by Phillis Wheatley and Lucy Terry Prince, pioneering African American women and some of the first women writers in America—if not *the* first.

My mother also took me to see Lorraine Hansberry's *A Raisin in the Sun*—a pivotal and moving moment in my life which encouraged and nurtured my creativity. The work and courage of this successful woman of color, who shared her message with audiences all over the country (and later, all over the world), became the foundation upon which my creativity was developed.

I was moved in a similar manner while studying at Barnard, where I was introduced to Anna Akhamatova's Russian poetry and Virginia Woolf's *To the Lighthouse*. I was so taken with *To the Lighthouse* that it was the subject of my freshman composition; I argued that Woolf was writing about the choices a woman has to make. My professor wrote on my paper that it was about "the choices a person has to make," but, to me, it was specifically about the ensuing weight and consequences of those decisions. In *The Book of Awesome Women Writers*, Becca Anderson explores the complex life and work of both these mavens, along with the history and achievements of many other women writers.

In my senior year of college, Caroline Rodgers published a little paperback poetry book that changed my life and influenced my own writing—her stanzas were sculpted in such a way that they flowed like rivers—and that continues to be important to me today. I owe a great deal in terms of lyricism and syntax to Zora Neale Hurston, who along with Sonja Sanchez and June Jordan influenced my personal writing style.

I respected June Jordan, whom I met during college, because upon reading her work I was filled with delight—she tackled public issues through a female voice. That was and still is extremely important to me.

My first experience with writing came about because there were no Black women writing about themselves, the world, and politics—so we had to write it for ourselves. In 1967, my friend Tawani Davis and I approached Barnard for a grant because we noticed there was no published literature by women of color. With the five hundred dollar grant, we designed a magazine called *Fat Mama* that published drawings, pieces of music, and poetry by women of color. We had our first taste of self-publishing and loved it—we had the opening party at the African American Museum in Harlem.

While in graduate school, I was enchanted by Diana Lakoskey, Anne Petrie, Margaret Randall, and the narratives of Maya Angelou. Around this time, I discovered two works that changed my life, Susan Griffin's *Women and Nature* and Mary Daly's *Gyn/Ecology*, both of which I still rely on when I teach feminist literature and aesthetics.

Soon after *For Colored Girls Who Have Considered Suicide/When the Rainbow Is Enuf* was published, I encountered incredible hostility. When it opened, I was subject to much animosity from the Black male community, but I did experience the joy of reaching women (eventually reaching women all over the world). I now know that what I went through was worth it, for women globally have had the opportunity to perform *For Colored Girls* and it's been true for them—and that is an amazing phenomenon. I'm very grateful and humbled by it.

Today I am lucky enough to be constantly working with Black women writers—we read and critique each other's work and support each other. I am in a community of writers with the very women who have influenced me the most—Toni Morrison, Alice Walker, and Maya Angelou. I am truly blessed on this journey.

This book is a testament to the relationship and contributions of women writers, lest we forget their impact and inspiration. Becca paints portraits of women writers with her energetic and enigmatic words in an accessible and engaging manner. Please join me on this amazing journey through women's history—I know you will be as inspired by it as I have been.

Foreword by Vicki León
author of the Uppity Women series

With her new book, Becca Anderson has made it not only legitimate but cool to be book-mad. As a woman with a chronic case of bibliomania, I'm delighted to see we're out of the closet. Of course, it makes me anxious, too; will there be enough books for everybody, if, you know, all those other people become bibliophiles?

As a student of history, I've learned that we're in supremely good company. Ever since there have been books, there have been bookworms. That's more than four thousand years of voracious reading—and a lot of it accomplished by women. The making of books was a scary new technology: marks made on clay or silk or paper became time capsules of knowledge. They conveyed secrets. They ignored distances. No wonder that, early on, books became sacrosanct in ways we cannot even imagine.

From the earliest times, females honed in on the reading, transcribing, and authoring of books. Take ancient Mesopotamia, for instance. Although it made males quite testy, women occasionally became scribes. In fact, the earliest author we know of in history—male or female—was a priestess and poet named Enheduanna of Ur, whose work dates from 2500 BCE. Only boys were supposed to learn reading and writing. So many women managed to do so, however, that a distinctively female written dialect called *emesal* came into being.

Books in Mesopotamia were palm-sized or smaller, durable, and portable. They were made of clay and were able to be reused. They sound suspiciously like the smartphones and e-books of today, don't they?

With literacy came cupidity. Thousands of years ago, women lusted for books—and began to collect them. One of the earliest bibliophiles was— surprise—the world's most famous sex goddess and political schemer: Cleopatra the Seventh. At Alexandria, the Egyptian queen possessed a world library that was without parallel. A lifelong student of philosophy, she got a voluptuous enjoyment from reading. When Marc Anthony set out to win Cleopatra's heart, he knew just what to give her: the library at Pergamum in Asia Minor— the second most wondrous in the world. (It was, however, a nightmare to gift wrap.)

A few hundred years later, highly educated Roman women took part in one of Christianity's great literacy projects. Women like Paula and her daughter Eustochium spent thirty-five years translating the Bible into Greek and Latin under the direction of early Christian writer and glory-hound Jerome, who took all subsequent credit for the work of his corps of skilled female readers and translators.

On the other side of the globe, Asian women had been hip-deep in bibliomania since the eighth century, when a bright Japanese empress named Koken ordered up a print run of one million copies of religious verse—Asia's first block printing project.

From the eleventh through thirteenth centuries, a golden age of reading and writing bloomed among Japanese literati with women at its forefront. The hands-down superstar of the age was Murasaki Shikibu, whose psychological novel, *The Tale of Genji*, is now considered the world's first "modern" novel. As in Mesopotamia, the number of women involved in reading and writing reached such a critical mass that the phonetic Japanese writing system called *hiragana* came to be called "woman's hand."

In medieval times, nuns fought to save the collected wisdom of the world in permanent form. Although literacy took a nosedive among Europeans, here and there women still managed to read, write, and collect books; Eleanor of Aquitaine, for instance, and Heloise, the nun whose hots for Abelard overshadowed her love for books. There were lesser lights we haven't heard much about, too, like Mahaut, the French Countess of Artois. Glamorous Mahaut traveled with sixty horses, forty servants, and her best illuminated books carried in special leather bags. One of her favorites was *The Book of the Great Cham*—the tell-all by Marco Polo.

So go on, do some guilt-free indulging in the pages of Becca Anderson's basket of literary bonbons. She has gathered a wealth of delectable stories in which to immerse ourselves, a bite at a time. Let's hear it for bibliophiles and book ladies—our richest yet most non-fattening vice. Thanks to women from Aphra Behn to Zelda Fitzgerald, we can enter the most magical looking glass of all: the bright world beyond the moment, the one we call "literacy."

Introduction

This book is intended to be a travel guide from the library to the Left Bank of Paris and back again. Moreover, it is a tribute to those solitary nuns who scratched out their feminist theologies in anchorite cells, to slave girls who composed classical poetry the equal (at least) of that written by their male contemporaries, to the biblical "J," and to Saint Jerome's nameless army who wrote and translated the Bible we know today. It's a gift of gratitude to the defiant dames who survived rejection letters, bad reviews, and jail time, a big bouquet to the first novelists, pioneer poets, and innovative intellectuals who hosted salons. From the mass-marketed darlings of the mystery world and the romance writers who steal our hearts to the bravehearted who find themselves banned and blacklisted into obscurity, this collection of profiles offers a look at the price women have had to pay to be creative, to be political, and to break new ground. Their surviving, and in some cases ongoing, work continues to affect people worldwide. A great book or poem is, at its zenith, an expression of the divine. For you, for me, for the women portrayed here, to read and to write is to live!

If you ask a distinguished writer the secret to great writing, they will often tell you that reading is the best thing you can do to advance your craft. By reading, absorbing, and paying close attention, you will learn so much about what works in writing. Even more importantly, you will discover what does not work and avoid it thereafter. J. K. Rowling, who went from being an impecunious unknown to one of the wealthiest women in the world thanks to her successful Harry Potter series, admits, "I don't believe in the kind of magic in my books. But I do believe something very magical can happen when you read a good book." Joyce Carol Oates reveals a hint of her approach to craft in her reverie on reading: "Reading is the sole means by which we slip, involuntarily, often helplessly, into another's skin, another's voice, another's soul." Many an awesome woman writer is a voracious reader who learned much about craft and excellence from exemplars of the same.

My great hope is that YOU are inspired by these women, their personal stories, and the stories they tell in their writing. Whether you aspire to change the world with your poetry, strive to write the truly great American novel, or perhaps forge new worlds and galaxies with your speculative fiction or fantasy series, you, my dear, can do all of that and more. I would love nothing more than to craft another volume including you, dear reader. You can also nominate anyone you think should be included in future volumes; please find the nomination form in the back and do be in touch. We would love to hear from you.

Stay awesome,

Becca

CHAPTER ONE

....

First Ladies of Literature
Mothers of Invention

Hats and pen caps off to these pioneers who paved the way for every woman who followed in their courageous footsteps. Here are stories of their struggles, unmitigated moxie, and unbridled determination to express themselves and share their views with readers. No fainthearts, these women survived jailing, name-calling, and, cruelest of all, having their reputations and accomplishments hidden for decades and even centuries. In addition to the women profiled here, let's also salute Lady Murasaki Shikubu, the first novelist of any gender, whose novel, *The Tale of Genji*, depicted court life, love, and adventure in eleventh-century Japan.

The literary laureates are rousing as well, slowly but surely knocking down barriers and opening minds in their wake—and, in this category, let us not forget to acknowledge brilliant Marguerite Yourcenar, the first woman "immortal," who in 1980 was elected to the French Academy by secret ballot over the objections of one member who memorably claimed, "The Academie has survived over three hundred years without women, and it could survive another three hundred without them." Aphra Behn, Charles II's spy, dared to write for a living and expected to be paid for it. (Her work also went unacknowledged for three hundred years as a precursor to the novel.) From Saint Jerome's uncredited nuns who really "wrote" the Bible to poet-slave Phyllis Wheatley, these first ladies of literature deserve credit for showing us that real inspiration can come only from being true to yourself at any cost.

ENHEDUANNA *sacred poet of Sumeria*

Any discussion of breakthrough writers must surely begin with Enheduanna, the first recorded writer of either gender. Born into the royal family of Sumeria in the area that in the modern world is known as southern Iraq, she served as high priestess to the moon god and goddess, Nanna and Inanna. Her poem-hymns were written in cuneiform on clay tablets, and they escaped the fate many other documents of the time suffered: disintegrating into forgotten dust. Her portrait, carved on a limestone disc, was discovered in an excavation of the ancient city of Ur.

Her greatest work is the "Hymn to Inanna." It is difficult to know whether she employed poetic license when she describes being sent into exile during a time of political upheaval. Readers can't help but notice that the poem "Nin-me-sar-ra" describes how Enheduanna's prayers to the moon god Nanna went unanswered and how Nanna's daughter, the moon goddess Inanna, came to her aid, exacting justice and restoring her to her rightful place as priestess. More than four thousand years old, the poem is simple, powerful, and beautiful.

> *Let it be known! That this is not said of Nanna, it is said of you—his is your greatness. You alone are the High one.*
>
> Enheduanna

THE MUSES *the nine Greek goddesses of the arts who inspire artists*

Calliope, the "Fair Voiced," is the eldest of Muses and presides over epic poetry.

Clio, the "Proclaimer" and the muse of history, carries a scroll of knowledge.

Erato the "Lovely," with her lyre, rules over love poetry and mimicry.

Euterpe, the "Giver of Pleasure," plays a flute. Her domain is music.

Melpomene, the "Songstress," wears the mask of tragedy, over which she presides.

Polyhymnia is "she of many hymns." Wearing a veil, she is the muse of sacred poetry.

Terpsichore, "the Whirler," has the domain of dance.

Thalia, "the Flourishing," wears the mask of comedy and is the muse of both comedy and idyllic poetry.

Urania, "the Heavenly," is the astronomer's muse; she wears a crown of stars and foretells the future through astrology.

The Three Fates determine all our destinies: *Clotho* spins the thread of life, *Lachesis* chooses the length and outcome, and *Atropos* cuts the thread of life.

MARGERY KEMPE *medieval autobiographer*

Margery Kempe herself is the best source of information on her life, having written her autobiography—the first of its kind in English—in the fourteenth century. Born in 1373, she was the daughter of the mayor of the town of Lynn in Norfolk, England. She married late for the times—at twenty—and got pregnant right away. While undergoing a wretchedly long and painful labor, she went mad and became violent, tearing at her own flesh, shrieking, having visions of devils, and screaming obscenities about her husband, her neighbors and friends, and herself. She claimed to be calmed down when Christ himself appeared to her in a vision, and indeed, she returned to her life as a wife and mother and bore thirteen more children.

Margery Kempe was profoundly changed, however, by her vision and decided to dedicate her life to Christian mysticism, as she continued to experience visitations and fits of weeping. She undertook a journey to the Holy Land, traveling alone from England across the continent to the Middle East. Her religious intentions meant nothing to those she met along the way; she was treated horribly and was called a whore and a heretic. She was jailed for her efforts and forced to defend herself with no help. Her recollections of the time depict a woman heeding a calling, torn between her love of Christ and her love for her family.

Despite all her tribulations, she managed to live a long life. Unable to write herself, she worked with hesitant scribes to compose her life story. Called *The Book of Margery Kempe*, this literary treasure was lost for nearly five hundred years. Thankfully, a copy was rediscovered in 1934, and Britain's first autobiographical text is again telling the story of this extraordinary, ordinary housewife and mother.

> *And sometimes those that men think were revelations are deceit and illusions, and therefore it is not expedient to give readily credence to every stirring.*
>
> Margery Kempe

APHRA BEHN *living by the pen*

It is amazing that the name of Aphra Behn, England's first professional woman writer, is not better known. While a handful of her contemporaries—Anne Finch, the Countess of Winchilea, and Margaret Cavendish, the Duchess of Newcastle—wrote for the entertainment of a small circle of friends, Aphra Behn was paid for her work and undertook it as her profession. Her circumstances were far different from those of such courtly ladies, as well. She was a widow of modest means and used her talent to survive.

Behn's parentage is unclear. We know she was born in 1640 and traveled with her foster family to Surinam in the West Indies. Some biographers say she was involved in a slave rebellion in 1663. That same year, she and her family and fellow travelers were the first Europeans to visit a tribe of Indians in the West Indies. The following year, she returned to England and married a London merchant, Johan Behn, who died of the plague in 1665.

After the tragedy of her short-lived marriage, Aphra Behn needed an income and was fortunate to have an opportunity to enter King Charles II's private force of spies. "Such public toils of state affairs [were] unusual with my sex or in my years," she admitted. Behn was sent to Antwerp, where she proved to be a most able spy, but she did not receive her promised payment and was sent to a London debtor's prison in 1668. While in jail, she determined never again to subject herself to anyone's mercy and vowed to make her way independently and by her own wits.

She wrote her first play and saw it published partly because of the sheer novelty that she was a woman. The play, *The Forced Marriage*, was staged in London in 1670. From then on, Behn's progress was rapid. Her career as a professional playwright established, she wrote and published fourteen plays encompassing many styles from farce to drama, including *The Rover, Sir Patient Fancy, The City Heiress*, and *The Roundheads*. She also began publishing poetry and comic verse. Always skirting the edge of controversy, she wrote some very sensual poems which shocked the readers of the day and prompted Anne Finch to comment, "a little too loosely she writ." Criticism of her work fell consistently into one of two extremes of either wild praise or scorching criticism and often focused on her femaleness: the "body of a Venus and the mind of a Minerva," the "English Sappho," or cruelly, "that lewd harlot."

Behn's response was to carry on, pointing out that the great male writers of the day suffered no public shame for their openly erotic references. When the London theater fell on hard times after the glories of the Restoration, Behn turned her hand to writing prose fiction: *Love Letters between a Nobleman and His Sister*, published in 1684, followed by *The Fair, Jilt, Agnes de Castro*, and her opus, *Oroonoko*. Written in 1688, *Oroonoko* was loosely autobiographical, a retelling in a fictionalized version of her journey to Surinam as a young woman and her protest against slavery. This account is widely regarded as the first novel in English literature.

Sadly, a mere year after her triumph, she passed away, ill and impoverished. She continued to suffer denigration after her death by many who disapproved of her fiercely independent spirit. But Behn blazed the trail for every woman writer to come after her. Three hundred years later, Virginia Woolf penned this homage: "All women together ought to let flowers fall upon the tomb of Aphra Behn, for it was she who earned them the right to speak their minds."

> *I'll only say as I have touched before, that plays have no great room for that which is men's great advantage over women.*
>
> Aphra Behn

APHRA BEHN *The first female professional writer in the English language*

LADY MARY CHUDLEIGH

A contemporary of Aphra Behn, Lady Mary Chudleigh wrote a verse response to British minister John Sprint, who in 1700 wrote *The Bride-Woman's Counselor*, which instructed women to love, honor, and obey in no uncertain terms. Chudleigh wrote, in verse, a series including *The Female Advocate; or A Plea for Just Liberty of the Tender Sex* and notably *Married Women and the Ladies Defense; or the Bride-Woman's Counselor Answered*. John Sprint was indeed resoundingly answered with Chudleigh's beautifully wrought feminist rhetoric scorning the tacit rules that kept women "Debarred from knowledge, banished from the schools, And with the utmost industry bred fools," entrapped in the "mean, low, trivial cares of life." She exhorted women to "read and think, and think and read again." Sadly, we know very little of her life except that she married Sir George Chudleigh and lost her children at very young ages. Her poems were crafted skillfully and with a keen intelligence and courageous idealism. Writing in 1700 and 1701, Lady Mary was well ahead of her time.

Wife and servant are the same, But only differ in the name.

Lady Mary Chudleigh, *To the Ladies*

CHRISTINE DE PISAN *the first woman writer to be published in English*

In the same way that, according to Virginia Woolf, English women writers are indebted to Aphra Behn, Italian women writers, including Nobel laureate Grazia Deledda, are indebted to Christine de Pisan. Three hundred years before Aphra Behn set pen to paper, de Pisan was earning her way as a writer.

Born in 1364, she was the daughter of a scientist and scholar, Thomas de Pisan, a Venetian court-appointed astrologer to the French king Charles V. Her girlhood saw a rare advantage for Christine: a classical education. She loved France and claimed it as her heart's home. Her father saw to it that she was educated as well as any man, and Christine learned French, Latin, arithmetic, and geometry. She married Etienne du Castel, who was nine years her senior, at fifteen. In three short years they had three children, and du Castel died around the time of the third baby's birth. At barely nineteen, Christine de Pisan was left to support her children and several hapless relatives, and did so with her talent for prose and poetry.

She claimed to write constantly, noting "in the short space of six years, between 1397 and 1403…fifteen important books, without mentioning minor essays, which, compiled, make seventy large copy-books." Among her books are a biography of Charles V, another on Philip of Burgundy, and *Le Livre de Paix*. In the latter, an instruction on rearing princes and a rebuttal to the bestselling "bible of courtly love," *The Romance of the Rose*, de Pisan sought to repair a woman's reputation that had been ruined by the popular epic poem.

After a writing career that lasted twenty-nine years, Christine retired to a convent. In 1429, just before her death, she wrote a book honoring Joan of Arc. It was, wrote Vicki León in *Uppity Women of Medieval Times*, "the only French book ever written about the Maid of Orleans in her lifetime."

While she was alive, Christine de Pisan received unstintingly positive reviews for her work and was compared favorably to Cicero and Cato. Her work stands the test of time. In 1521, *Le Livre du duc des vraies aman* was published in England as *The Book of the Duke of True Lovers*, the first book by a woman published in English. Her *City of Women* was rediscovered in the twentieth century and is taught in literature courses worldwide.

ANNE BRADSTREET *Pilgrim's Progress*

Fifty years before Aphra Behn shocked English society, Anne Bradstreet wrote the first book of poetry published in the American colonies. Upon arriving with her family in 1630, Anne Bradstreet saw the raw new America as an opportunity to create a new way of being: "I found a new world and new manners, at which my heart rose," she wrote.

She was at once a pioneer and a typically religious member of her Puritan community. She had come from a privileged background afforded her by her father, Thomas Dudley, who ran the estate of an earl of Lincoln. Anne Bradstreet was allowed to visit the earl's library freely, and she took full advantage, reading religious texts, poetry, and classics exhaustively.

In 1628, she married Simon Bradstreet, a graduate of Cambridge who worked as a steward for the earl. Anne's husband was nine years older than she and equally educated. Life on the earl's estate was filled with ease, comfort, and security, but that soon changed. The devout religiosity of the Dudleys led them to believe they should prove their devotion to God through trials and tribulations. These they found in plentitude in the New World. The whole family moved lock, stock, and barrel to the Massachusetts colony, where Anne's father and husband both served as governors. They suffered from the cold, malaria, starvation, and the harsh, unforgiving climate of this savage new world.

Part of the Puritan ethos included stringent second-class status for all women, for it was God's will that a woman should be subordinate, a constant helpmate to man, and humble, with no personal ambitions. In these circumstances, writing was dangerous. In 1645, Massachusetts governor John Winthrop lamented the sad straying of "a godly young woman" who was mentally unstable and who in a weakened, fallen state, gave "herself wholly to reading and writing, and [had] written many books." He had banished Anne Hutchinson seven years earlier for daring to interpret religious doctrine in her own way.

But Anne Bradstreet's brother-in-law John Woodbridge didn't hold to the belief that women couldn't have their own intellectual lives. He had Anne Bradstreet's poetry, collected in *The Tenth Muse*, printed in London, where it had proved to be highly "vendable," according to London booksellers. Woodbridge provided a foreword to the book making clear that it was "the work of a woman, honoured and esteemed where she lives, for…the exact diligence in her place, and discreet managing of her family occasions, and these poems are but the fruit of some few hours, curtailed from her sleep and other refreshments."

A devoted mother, Anne Bradstreet gave birth to eight children, and in her role as helpmate, she saw her husband rise to considerable prosperity and power in the colony. With little time to rest or write, her literary output ceased. She suffered from continuing symptoms of the smallpox she had contracted as a child and died in 1673.

Though she was forgotten for centuries, twentieth-century poets, particularly Conrad Aiken and John Berryman, have recognized her contribution in various tributes. Adrienne Rich demands her genius be honored: "To have written… the first good poems in America, while rearing eight children on the edge of the wilderness, was to have managed a poet's range and extension within confines as severe as any American poet has confronted."

Fool, I do grudge the Muses did not part
Twixt him and me that overfluent store....

From the Prologue, Anne Bradstreet

MARY MANLEY *the first bestselling woman author*

It is amazing that Mary Manley is not better known; she was the first British woman to have a career as a political journalist, the first female author of a bestseller, and the very first woman to be jailed for her writing. Born in 1663, she was ahead of her time in her advocacy for women's rights and her willingness to take risks with her own comfortable life to fight for these rights. Manley decried the inequity that saw women punished for acts any man could freely engage in. Her greatest passion was that women should as writers have equal opportunity with men.

She herself was prolific, authoring short stories, plays, satires, political essays, and letters. She replaced Jonathan Swift of *Gulliver's Travels* fame as the editor of the Tory paper, the *Examiner*, yet she remains relatively unknown, while he has a permanent place in the canon and is widely read and widely taught. Swift's achievements seem Lilliputian in comparison to Mary Manley's feat.

Her bestselling satire, *Secret Memoirs and Manners of Several Persons of Quality of Both Sexes from the New Atlantis, an Island in the Mediterranean*, was aimed at the opposition to the Tory party, the Whigs. The poison prose swiftly hit its target. Manley and her publishers were thrown in jail, and the adage about any kind of publicity—even bad publicity—being good held true. Readers bought the book in droves to figure out who the real people were behind the thinly veiled biographical sketches. Clever lass that she was, Manley's absolutely public *Secret Memoirs* included much to titillate and tantalize, including Corinna, the maiden who staunchly refuses to get married, and a mysterious lesbian group called the Cabal.

As a challenge at the height of her fame, Mary Manley described herself as "a ruined woman," and in a fictionalized autobiography revealed her betrayal and entrapment into marriage to a cousin who took her money and ran. Inspired by her father, a writer who held a high office, Mary wasn't ruined at all, but was a huge success as a writer who chose lovers of standing as peers and lived life on her own terms. Before there was J.K., Danielle, or Nora, there was Mary! This seventeenth-century virago paved the way for Joe Klein's bestselling political satire, *Primary Colors*, and for every female who ever mounted the bestseller list.

> *She who has all the muses in her head, wanted to be caressed*
> *in a poetical manner.*
>
> Mary Manley from *Secret Memoirs*

LUCY TERRY PRINCE *pioneer and poet*

As one of the first Black American poets, Lucy Terry has yet to receive her due. She was born in 1730 in Africa. After being kidnapped as a baby, she was brought to the colony of Rhode Island by slavers and was purchased at the age of five by Ensign Ebenezer Wells of Deerfield, Massachusetts, to be a servant. Wells had Lucy baptized on June 15, 1735, at the insistence of his mistress, during the "Great Awakening," an effort to root Calvinism in New England. As many Black people in America as possible were baptized in this mass conversion effort.

Little is known of her life until age sixteen, when she was inspired to poetry by the bloody massacre of two colonial families by sixty Indians in "the Bars"—a colonial word for "meadow"—an area outside Deerfield. George Sheldon, a Deerfield historian, declared Lucy's ballad, "The Bars Fight," to be "the first rhymed narration of an American slave" and believes it was recited and sung by Lucy. He further describes it as "the fullest contemporary account of that bloody tragedy which has been preserved." While the original document has been lost, it was passed down in the oral tradition and printed for the first time by Josiah Gilbert Holland in 1855.

PHILLIS WHEATLEY *the muse of Africa*

While Lucy Terry Prince remains fairly obscure, Phillis Wheatley has been acknowledged for her role as one of the earliest women writers in America. She is, in fact, generally regarded as the first Black woman writer, and, after Anne Bradstreet, the second woman writer in America. A poet, her verse expresses guarded pride about her "sable race" and includes a subtle treatment of the subject of slavery, though her letters expressed her strong feelings about it. She called herself "Africa's Muse" in her *Hymn to Humanity*.

Her story and Lucy's began the same way: Phillis was kidnapped by slave traders in Africa as a child, and, along with as many as eighty other young girls, she was transported by ship from Senegal, brought to the port of Boston, and sold into slavery in 1761.

Phillis' fortunes were a bit better than those of many others as she was purchased by a kind-hearted woman, Susannah Wheatley, who took pity on the forlorn child wrapped in a dirty scrap of carpeting. Phillis's price was a bargain; the Wheatleys, guessing her to be around seven years old because of missing front teeth, took her into their home on King Street and gave her their last name, as was the practice with slaves.

The Wheatleys noticed how curious and alert Phillis was and judged her to be of exceptional intelligence. When she tried to write on the wall, their teenaged daughter, Mary Wheatley, started to teach Phillis in earnest. At the end of a year's time, Phillis was reading and writing with ease and had also learned, according to her master's recollection, a "little astronomy, some ancient and modern geography, a little ancient history, a fair knowledge of the Bible, and a thoroughly appreciative acquaintance with the most important Latin classics, especially the works of Virgil and Ovid." Phillis became, again in his words, "one of the most highly educated young women in Boston," and went on to study and translate Latin. Indeed, one of her interpretations of a Latin tale by Ovid was published.

She also liked to compose verse and loved the brilliantly crafted poetry of Alexander Pope, whom she took as her model. In 1767, fourteen-year-old Phillis wrote the first of many occasional poems, "To the University of Cambridge," thirty-two blank verses of counsel for college boys. The Wheatleys proved to be generous to the girl and encouraged her to pursue her poetics, providing her with paper and pen in case of sudden inspiration. Phillis had a delicate constitution and was only allowed to perform light chores such as dusting and polishing.

One of her occasional poems, "On the Death of the Reverend Mr. George Whitefield," brought her to the eyes of the world when it appeared on a broadside printed in Boston in 1770, which was then reprinted throughout the colonies and in England. Her story was sensationalized as the work of "a servant girl…but nine years in this country from Africa." She was ushered into literary and social circles she would normally have been forbidden to enter, though because of her slave status, she was not allowed to dine at her hosts' tables.

In 1772, Phillis considered the prospects of collecting her poems into a volume, and the ever-supportive John Wheatley sent a manuscript and a letter of introduction and biographical information to Archibald Bell in London. Bell and the Countess of Huntingdon, to whom he had shown Phillis's poems, doubted that an African girl had really written the work and required the testament of no fewer than eighteen prominent Bostonians.

Meanwhile, Phillis's health weakened, and the Wheatleys reasoned that a trip abroad might bolster her. Accompanied by Nathaniel Wheatley, Mary's twin, who was on a business trip, Phillis set out to London, where she was an immediate cause célèbre, thanks to an introduction into society provided by the Countess of Huntingdon. She was fêted and flattered in a land free from slavery. According to one account, "Thoughtful people praised her; titled people dined her; and the press extolled the name of Phillis Wheatley, the African poetess." Her single published book, *Poems on Various Subjects, Religious and Moral*, came out in 1773 and was dedicated to none other than the countess. Complete with a portrait of Phillis holding a quill pen drawn by slave artist and poet Scipio Moorhead, it contained thirty-nine poems.

The following year, Susannah Wheatley, the only mother figure Phillis had known in the land of her captors, died. With the Revolutionary War impending, Phillis wrote a letter to General George Washington, who was impressed by the "elegant lines" of her missive and invited her to be received by him and his officers. When John Wheatley passed away, Phillis was set free.

She married a Boston grocer a month later, a handsome free black man who claimed to have worked as a lawyer and physician as well as merchant. His looks and talent are said to have led him to a degree of "arrogance" and "disdain" for work, which allegedly saw the newlyweds into poverty. Two of their three children died, and Phillis labored at a cheap boarding house to support herself and the remaining child. At thirty-one, she died, followed almost immediately in death by her child. They were buried together in a location that remains unknown. The last attention the "African poetess" received for her writing talent was for a poem she wrote about the death of her baby son, published in 1784 in the *Boston* magazine. This was one of several compositions from the last part of her life, all set to be published in honor of Benjamin Franklin, to whom she had dedicated the book. The manuscript disappeared along with all trace of Phillis Wheatley's work as a mature poet.

> *Imagination! Who can sing thy force? Or who describe the swiftness of thy course?*
>
> Phillis Wheatley

HARRIET E. ADAMS WILSON *provocateur*

Like many other literary women, Harriet Wilson was also left out of history books. She was the first Black woman to publish a novel in English and the first Black person, male or female, to publish a novel in America.

Sadly, we know precious little about this author. Harriet E. Adams Wilson is believed to have been born in Fredericksburg, Virginia, in 1807 or 1808 and trained in millinery as her trade; she was then deserted and left in poverty by her sailor husband, who impregnated her before the abandonment. Her son from this relationship, George Mason Wilson, died at age seven, a year after the publication of the one novel it is known that Wilson wrote.

Her groundbreaking work, *Our Nig*, a title deliberately chosen for its challenge and daring, was printed by George C. Rand and Avery of Boston. It is believed Wilson self-published *Our Nig* to prove a political point, as evidenced by the full title, *Our Nig, or, Sketches from the Life of a Free Black, in A Two-Story White House, North, Showing That Slavery's Shadows Fall Even There*, with the author credit to "Our Nig."

Our Nig was ignored by reviewers and readers and barely sold. Wilson's work was in the dustbin of lost history until Henry Louis Gates, Jr., discovered it and reissued it in 1983. Gates observed that the provocative title probably contributed to the novel's near oblivion. The plot, a marriage between a white woman and a Black man, would have alienated many readers.

> *Example rendered her words efficacious. Day by day there was a manifest change of deportment toward "Nig."*
>
> Harriet E. Adams Wilson

SARA TEASDALE *parting the shadows*

Poet Sara Teasdale, known now for the evocative intensity of her language, was brought up in the truest Victorian tradition in the late 1880s in St. Louis, Missouri. She was pampered and protected, but like a hothouse flower starved for light, felt smothered by her parents' watchful restrictions. Imaginative and sensitive, Sara found her only solace in writing. In 1907, when she was twenty-three, *Reedy's Mirror*, a St. Louis weekly paper, published her work for the first time.

By age twenty-six, she was desperate to break free of the hampering bonds of dependency on her parents. The only way she could manage this was to marry. She didn't find the prospects particularly appealing, but it seemed preferable to her stifling life at home.

Her hopes included a serious writing career, which she found incompatible with the role of wife and mother. When she discovered she was pregnant, she had an abortion and obtained a divorce, hoping for the independence she believed would foster her writing. This unfortunate series of events sent her into a depression and failing health. From that point on, she lived the secluded life of a semi-invalid.

Teasdale's beautiful poetry, bespeaking the secrets of the human heart, created an international reputation, beginning with her early *Love Songs*. Subsequently, she channeled her painful struggles for freedom from oppressive Victorian mores in *Flame and Shadow*. She won the highly regarded Columbia University Poetry Society prize, and in 1917 won the Pulitzer Prize for *Love Songs*, earning her place in history as the first poet to receive this prestigious award. Ultimately, the delicate despair described in her poems won out, and Sara Teasdale committed suicide in 1933.

> *O, beauty, are you not enough? Why am I crying after love?*
>
> Sara Teasdale, "Spring Night"

PEARL BUCK *pearl of great price*

Pearl Buck was born in West Virginia in 1892 to the Sydenstricker family, deeply religious people who dedicated their lives to missionary work. They chose to spread the word of Christianity in China, and Pearl spent a good portion of her girlhood there. She attended Randolph-Macon Woman's College in Virginia, but after she graduated hurried back to Asia with her teaching certificate.

She made her living as a teacher until she married John Buck, a fellow American and an agriculturist. They married in 1917 and lived in northern China among the peasants. The Bucks had one child, born mentally handicapped, and adopted another child during Pearl's tenure at the University of Nanking. In 1922, she started writing during the long hours she spent caring for her ailing mother. Her very first story was published in *Asia* magazine three years later. Pearl Buck returned to the United States to seek proper care for her daughter and studied for her master's degree at Cornell. Later, she taught at three different universities in China until anti-foreigner sentiments became unavoidable. While fleeing violence in 1927, Pearl lost the manuscript for her first novel. Still, she continued, publishing *East Wind: West Wind* in 1930, followed the next year by *The Good Earth*.

The Good Earth was a global phenomenon from the beginning; in 1932, it won the Pulitzer Prize. A stage play was also written, as well as a script for the Academy Award-winning film. Pearl Buck was a huge success and saw her book translated into dozens of languages and selling millions of copies. In 1935, she left her adopted country, divorced her husband, and returned to the United States. Soon after, she married her publisher, Richard J. Walsh, but that didn't stop her writing. While her success was generally more popular than critical, that all changed in 1938 when she became the first American woman to win the Nobel Prize. Buck was an amazingly prolific writer who once wrote five books in one year, penning more than eighty-five books in all. Her work includes plays, biographies, books for children, translations, and an autobiography as well as novels. She continued to write novels and articles through her entire life.

During the McCarthy years, she came under suspicion and was forced to write under the pseudonym John Sedges, but she never wavered in her essential beliefs of tolerance and understanding. She founded the East and West Association and was the president of the Author's Guild, a free speech organization founded in the 1950s. She also created an organization to care for orphaned children of Asian mothers and American fathers and adopted six such orphans herself. A champion of women's rights and rights for the mentally handicapped, she died of lung cancer in 1973 in her home of Danby, Vermont. She was a fierce crusader for greater mutual understanding for the people of the world, and with her Nobel Prize in Literature, she opened a new chapter for women in literature.

> *(I want to) write for the people...*
>
> **Pearl S. Buck, regarding her great novel** *The Good Earth*

GWENDOLYN BROOKS *poet of the Beat*

Gwendolyn Brooks has the distinction of being the first Black person to receive the Pulitzer Prize (for *Annie Allen* in 1950). One of the most innovative poets in the literary landscape of America, she was born in 1917 in Topeka, Kansas. Her family moved when she was young to the more urban city of Chicago, which imparted a street-smart influence that still informs her work. Brooks wanted to bring poetry to the poor Black kids of the inner city, and she attracted them with rapid-fire, tightly wound iambic pentameter that predated rap. In later life, she took a more radical bent, hooking up with the revolutionary Black Beat writer LeRoi Jones (now Amiri Baraka) and with Don L. Lee, and jumped into the causes of African Americans with both feet. She became a tough and angry Black Power poet, penning verses grounded in classical style deconstructed through the lens of her newfound racial awareness and commitment to cause. Forty years after her prizewinning feat, her poetry is still raw, fresh, and commanding.

> *I want to clarify my language. I want these poems to be free. I want them to be direct without sacrificing the kind of music, the picture-making I've always been interested in.*
>
> Gwendolyn Brooks

GRAZIA DELEDDA *songs of Sardinia*

While Pearl Buck and *The Good Earth* are household names, the Italian novelist Grazia Deledda is much less familiar. But she received the Nobel Prize for Literature twelve years before Buck and was a powerful voice among her people.

Born in 1871 in Sardinia, Deledda was a country girl who had little exposure to formal education. She did have access to books, however, and read avidly. She came from a troubled clan and was seemingly the only family member to escape illness or criminality; thus she ended up bearing the brunt of household chores and responsibility. Still, she managed to write in her precious spare time.

She married in 1900, and with her new husband moved to Rome, where she sought a broader readership for her work. She soon received approval from the critics and began writing intently, striving for excellence, writing what she knew best—stories of the life and passions of the peasants of Sardinia: in her words, a place of "myths and legends." Deledda was dedicated to her craft and produced a considerable body of work, including her favorite novel, *Canne al vento (Reeds in the Wind)*, the story of a dissolute family centered around the guilt of a servant, and *La Madre (The Mother)*, about the turbulent relationship between a mother and her son. In addition to her novels and short stories, she produced one volume of poetry, *Paesaggi sardi (Sardinian Landscapes)*, as well as a translation of Balzac and a nonfiction analysis of the customs of her native island.

She was awarded the Nobel Prize in 1926, the first Italian woman to be so honored. She died ten years later of breast cancer, but not before the publication that year of *La chiesa della solitudine (The Church of Solitude)*, a semiautobiographical novel about a woman who deals with her breast cancer diagnosis at the cusp of the twentieth century by keeping it a secret, with predictable human fallout; it was published in an English translation by E. Ann Matter in 2002. Her autobiography, *Cosima*, was published posthumously the next year.

LUTIE EUGENIA STERNS *librarian extraordinary*

In 1887, Lutie Sterns began teaching in the Milwaukee school system. She quickly became appalled at the paucity of books for her students and made such use of the public library for her kids that library officials offered her the job of superintendent of the circulation department. Lutie's passion for the public library system would lead her to travel the state indefatigably by train, boat, buggy, and sleigh, preaching the importance of public libraries, and according to legend, wearing out five fur coats in the process. This was no easy feat— Lutie had a bad stammer, but she cared so much for the cause that she wrote her speeches in such a way as to avoid the letters she had trouble with. Before she "retired" to campaign for women's suffrage and child labor protection, she had established 101 free libraries and 1,480 traveling libraries in the state of Wisconsin.

GABRIELA MISTRAL *voice of the people*

A poor, rural schoolteacher of mixed race, Gabriela Mistral went on to become the first Latin American woman to win a Nobel Prize in Literature. She was born in the Chilean village of Montegrande in 1889. Her mother, Petronila Alcayaga, was a teacher of Basque descent, and her father, Jeronimo Villanueva, also a teacher, was a poet of Indian and Jewish birth. Jeronimo was overly fond of wine and not quite so attached to his duties as a breadwinner and father; he deserted the family when Gabriela was three. As a schoolgirl, Gabriela discovered her call to poetry and tapped into her own stubborn independence, switching her birth name, Lucila, for her choice, Gabriela. As an adult, she also chose a fitting surname, Mistral, hinting at a fragrant Mediterranean wind.

Her first love was a hopelessly romantic railroad worker who killed himself when the relationship faltered after two years. Her first book of poetry, *Sonetas de la Muerta (Sonnets of Death)*, was written as a result of her sadness, guilt, and pain over the death of this man. In 1914, she received Chile's top prize for poetry.

In the '20s and '30s, she wrote many volumes of poetry, including *Desolación (Desolation)*, *Ternura (Tenderness)*, *Questions*, *Tala*, and a mixed-media anthology, *Readings for Women*. In addition to writing and teaching, Mistral felt a special sympathy for women and children and worked to help victims of World Wars I and II. She made social strides as an educator as well. She initiated programs for schooling the poor, founded a mobile library system, and traveled the world, gleaning whatever information she could to improve Chile's education system. In 1923, she was named "Teacher of the Nation." She became an international envoy and ambassador for her country off and on for twenty years, eventually serving in the League of Nations and the United Nations.

In the late 1920s, a military government seized power in Chile and offered Mistral an ambassadorship to all the nations of Central America. Mistral refused to work for the military state and made a scathing public denouncement of the government machine. Her pension was revoked, and Mistral had to support herself, her mother, and her sister through her writing. She lived in exile for a while in France, eventually moving to the United States, where she taught at the University of Puerto Rico and at Middlebury and Barnard Colleges.

In 1945 she received the Nobel Prize. Upon accepting the revered award, Gabriela Mistral, in her plain black velvet, made a sharp contrast with Sweden's dashing King Gustav. Pointedly, she didn't accept the prize for herself, but on behalf of "the poets of my race." Mistral died in 1957 and was mourned by her native Chile, where she was revered as a national treasure. She was the "people's poet," giving voice to the humble people to whom she belonged—the Indians, mestizos, and campesinos—and scorning rampant elitism and attempts to create a racial hierarchy in Europe and in her beloved Chile.

> *I consider myself to be among the children of that twisted thing*
> *that is called a racial experience, or better, a racial violence.*
>
> Gabriela Mistral

LORRAINE HANSBERRY *young, gifted, and Black*

Chicago native Lorraine Hansberry was born in 1930 to a politically aware and progressive family who knew that they had to work to make the changes they wished to see. But they paid a price. When Lorraine was only five, she was given a white fur coat for Christmas but was beaten up when she wore it to school. In 1938, the Black family moved to Hyde Park, an exclusive and exclusively white neighborhood. Lorraine's first memories of living in that house are of violence—being spit on, cursed at, and having bricks thrown through the windows. Her mother Nannie kept a gun inside the house in case it got any worse. An Illinois court evicted them, but her real estate broker father hired NAACP attorneys and had the decision overturned at the Supreme Court level, winning a landmark victory in 1940. He died at a relatively young age, which Lorraine ascribed to the pressure of the long struggle for civil rights.

Lorraine Hansberry's parents' work as activists brought them into contact with the Black leaders of the day. She was well accustomed to seeing luminaries such as Langston Hughes, Paul Robeson, and W.E.B. DuBois in her home. Educated in the segregated public schools of the time, she attended the University of Wisconsin at Madison before she moved to New York for "an education of another kind."

Throughout her life, she stayed dedicated to the values her parents had instilled in her and worked steadfastly for the betterment of Black people. At a picket line protesting the exclusion of Black athletes from college sports, Lorraine met the man she would marry, a white Jewish liberal, Robert Nemiroff. Lorraine worked for Paul Robeson's radical Black newspaper *Freedom* until her husband's career as a musician and songwriter earned enough to support them so that Lorraine could write full-time.

Her first play, *A Raisin in the Sun*, was a huge hit, winning the New York Drama Critics' Circle Award as Best Play of the Year in 1959. Hansberry was the youngest American and the first Black person to receive this prize. This proved to be a watershed event; after the success of *A Raisin in the Sun*, Black actors and writers entered the creative arts in a surge. Lorraine continued to write plays, but in 1963 was diagnosed with cancer. She died six years after winning the Drama Critics' Award at the age of thirty-four, tragically cutting short her work. Nevertheless, she made huge strides with her play, forever changing "the Great White Way."

> *Racism is a device that, of itself, explained nothing. It is simply a means, an invention to justify the rule of some men over others.*
>
> From *Les Blancs: The Collected Last Plays of Lorraine Hansberry*

SELMA LAGERLÖF AND NELLY SACHS *making history*

In 1909, Selma Lagerlöf became the first woman and the first Swedish writer to receive the Nobel Prize in Literature. The prize was awarded for her body of work, including the 1891 novel *To the Story of Gösta Berling* and the 1902 two-volume work of fiction *Jerusalem*, the chronicle of Swedish peasants who migrated to Jerusalem. Selma was the preeminent Swedish writer of her day and produced an impressive body of work: thirty novels and four biographical narratives. She wasn't content merely to be the most brilliant novelist of her age, however; she also worked extremely hard at obtaining the release of Jewish writer Nelly Sachs from a Nazi concentration camp. Sachs, inspired by her savior, won the Nobel Prize in Literature herself in 1966!

BARBARA TUCHMAN *trailblazer*

One of the most respected historians of the twentieth century and the only woman to win a Pulitzer Prize twice, Barbara Tuchman has written first-rate chronicles accessible to readers from every walk of life. The core of her theory of history is that true understanding comes from observing the patterns that are created through an aggregation of details and events. Tuchman has covered topics from the Trojan War to the Middle Ages, the leaders of World War I, and the United States' problematic involvement in Vietnam. All of her books are known for their narrative power and for her portrayals of the players on the world stage as believable individuals.

Born in 1912, Barbara Tuchman attended Radcliffe College and, after graduation, took her first job as a research assistant at the Institute of Pacific Relations in New York and Tokyo. She began writing articles for several periodicals and went on to work as a staff editorial assistant at the *Nation* and a correspondent for London's *New Statesman*. From 1934 to 1945, Tuchman worked for the Far East News Desk and Office of War Information. Here, she got firsthand experience of researching and writing about history as it happened.

Tuchman put this invaluable wartime experience to good use with her immense study of the pivotal events prior to World War I, *The Guns of August*, published in 1962. This thoughtful and thorough history of the thirty days leading up to the first global war spanned all of Europe, detailing the actions of key players in London, Berlin, St. Petersburg, and Paris. Her book was met with thundering critical praise and acceptance from popular readers and historians the world over—she received her first Pulitzer Prize for this powerful exposé.

Barbara Tuchman's other books include *A Distant Mirror*, which explores everyday life in fourteenth-century France, and *The March of Folly*, an analysis of four conflicts in world history that were mismanaged by governments, from the Trojan War to Britain's loss of her colonies to Vietnam. Her second Pulitzer Prize was for a biography of US General Joseph Stilwell: a probing look at the relations between China and the United States through the personal wartime experiences of Stilwell.

> *To be a bestseller is not necessarily a measure of quality, but it is a measure of communication.*
>
> Barbara Tuchman

RACHEL CARSON *"The Natural World...Supports All Life"*

World-famous pioneering ecologist and science writer Rachel Carson turned nature writing on its head. Before she came along, notes *Women Public Speakers in the United States,* "the masculine orientation [to the subject] emphasized either the dominant, aggressive encounter of humanity with wild nature or the distancing of nature through scientific observation." By creating a different, more feminine relationship to nature, Rachel Carson portrayed humans as part of the great web of life, separate only in our ability to destroy it. In a very real sense, Carson not only produced the first widely read books on ecology, but laid the foundation for the entire modern environmental movement.

Rachel inherited her love of nature from her mother, Maria, a naturalist at heart, who took Rachel for long walks in woods and meadows. Born in 1907, Rachel was raised on a farm in Pennsylvania, where the evidence of industry was never too far away. By the beginning of the twentieth century, Pennsylvania had changed a great deal from the sylvan woodlands named for colonialist William Penn. Coal and strip mines had devastated some of the finest farmland. Chemical plants, steel mills, and hundreds of factories were belching pure evil into the air.

As she grew, Rachel's love of nature took an unexpected turn toward oceanography, a budding science limited by technological problems for divers. The young girl was utterly fascinated by this biological science, and though she majored in English and loved to write, she heard the ocean's siren song increasingly. While studying at the Pennsylvania College for Women in the mid-1920s, she changed her major to zoology, despite the overwhelming advice of her professors to stay the course in English, a much more acceptable major for a young woman. Her advisors were quite correct in their assertions that women were blocked from science; there were very few teaching positions except at the handful of women's colleges and even fewer job prospects for women outside of academia.

However, Rachel listened to her heart and graduated with high honors, a fellowship to study at Woods Hole Marine Biological Laboratory for the summer, and a full scholarship to Johns Hopkins University in Maryland to study marine zoology. Rachel's first semester in graduate school coincided with the beginning of the Great Depression. Her family lost their farm, and her parents and brother came to live with her in her tiny campus apartment. She helped make ends meet with part-time teaching at Johns Hopkins and the University of Maryland while continuing her studies.

In 1935, Rachel's father suffered a heart attack and died quite suddenly. Rachel looked desperately for work to support her mother and brother, but no one would hire a woman as a full-time university science professor. Brilliant and hardworking, Rachel was encouraged to teach grade school, or better yet, be a housewife, because it was "inappropriate" for women to work in science.

Finally, her unstinting efforts to work in her field were ultimately rewarded by a job writing radio scripts for Elmer Higgins at the United States Bureau of Fisheries—a perfect job for her because it combined her strength in writing with her scientific knowledge. Then a position opened up at the bureau for a junior aquatic biologist. The job was to be awarded to the person with the highest score on a placement test; Rachel aced the test and got the position. Elmer Higgins saw that her writing was excellent, making science accessible to the general public. At his direction, she submitted an essay about the ocean to the *Atlantic Monthly*, which not only published Rachel's piece but asked her to freelance for them on a continuing basis, resulting in a book deal from a New York publishing house.

By now, Rachel was the sole support of her mother, brother, and two nieces. She raised the girls, supported her mother, and worked a demanding full-time job, leaving her research and writing to weekends and late nights. But she prevailed nonetheless. Her first book, *Under the Sea Wind*, debuted in 1941 to a war-preoccupied public. It was a completely original book, enacting a narrative of the seacoast with the flora and fauna as characters, the first indication of Rachel's unique perspective on nature.

Rachel's second book, *The Sea Around Us*, was a nonfiction presentation of the relationship of the ocean to Earth and its inhabitants. This time, the public was ready; she received the National Book Award and made the *New York Times* bestseller list for nearly two years. *The Edge of the Sea* was also very well received, both critically and publicly. Rachel Carson's message of kinship with all life combined with a solid foundation of scientific knowledge found an audience in postwar America. However, shy and solitary, Rachel avoided the literary spotlight by accepting a grant that allowed her to return to her beloved seacoast, where she could often be found up to her ankles in mud or sand, doing research.

As her popularity rose and income from book royalties flooded in, Rachel was able to quit her job and build a coastal cottage for herself and her mother. She also returned the grant money that had been given her, asking it to be redistributed to needy scientists. In 1957, a letter from one of Rachel's readers changed everything. The letter came from Olga Owens Huckins, who was reporting the death of birds after airplanes sprayed dichloro-diphenyl-trichloroethane (DDT), a chemical then in heavy use. Carson was keenly interested in discovering the effects of DDT on the natural habitat. Her findings were shocking; if birds and animals weren't killed outright by DDT, its effects were even more insidious—birds laid eggs with thin eggshells that broke before the hatchlings were fully developed. DDT was also suspected of being carcinogenic to humans.

Rachel vowed to write a book about the devastating impact of DDT upon nature "or there would be no peace for me," she proclaimed. Shortly after, she was diagnosed with cancer. Despite chemotherapy, surgery, and constant pain, Rachel worked slowly and unstintingly on her new book. In 1962, *Silent Spring* was published. It was like a cannon shot. Chemical companies fought back, denied, and ran for cover against the public outcry. Vicious charges against Rachel were aimed at what many of the captains of the chemical industry viewed as her Achilles' heel: her womanhood. "Not a real scientist," they claimed. She was also called unstable, foolish, and sentimental for her love of nature. With calm logic and cold reason, Rachel Carson responded in exacting scientific terms, explaining the connections between DDT, the water supply, and the food chain.

Ultimately, President John F. Kennedy assigned his Science Advisory Committee the task of examining the pesticide, and Rachel Carson was proven to be absolutely correct. She died two years later, and although her reputation continued to be maligned by the chemical industry, her books had launched a movement that continues to this day.

Perhaps if Dr. Rachel Carson had been Dr. Richard Carson, the controversy would have been minor.... The American technocrat could not stand the pain of having his achievements deflated by the pen of this slight woman.

Joseph B.C. White, author

BETTY FRIEDAN *mother of modern feminism*

In 1956, young housewife Betty Friedan submitted her article about the frustrations women experience in their traditional roles as housewives and mothers. She received rejections from *McCalls*, *The Ladies' Home Journal*, and every other publication she approached. The editors, all men in that day and age, were disapproving, going so far as to say any woman would have to be "sick" to not be completely satisfied in her rightful role!

But Betty knew that she and the millions of women like her were not sick, just stifled. Betty had put aside her dream of being a psychologist for fear of becoming a spinster, instead choosing to marry and work for a small newspaper. She was fired from her job when she got pregnant for the second time and began, like most middle-class women of her day and age, to devote herself full-time to the work of running a home and family, what she called "the dream life, supposedly, of American women at that time."

But, after a decade of such devotion, she still wasn't happy and theorized that she wasn't alone. A graduate of Smith College, she decided to poll her fellow alumnae. Most of her classmates who had given up promising careers to devote themselves to their families felt incomplete; many were deeply depressed. They felt guilty for not being completely content sacrificing their individual dreams for their families, each woman certain that her dissatisfaction was a personal failing. Betty called this "the problem that has no name," and she gave it one, "the feminine mystique."

Over the next five years, her rejected article evolved into a book as she interviewed hundreds of women around the country. *The Feminine Mystique* explored the issue of women's lives in depth, criticizing American advertisers' exclusively domestic portrayal of women and issuing a call to action for women to say no to the housewife role and adopt "a new life plan" in which they could have both families and careers. With its publication in 1963, *The Feminine Mystique* hit America like a thunderbolt; publisher W.W. Norton had printed only two thousand copies, never anticipating the sale of three million hardcover copies alone.

Unintentionally, Betty had started a revolution. She was flooded with letters from women saying her book had given them the courage to change their lives and advocate for equal access to employment opportunities and other equality issues. Ultimately, the response to Betty's challenge created the momentum that led to the formalization of the second wave of the US women's movement in 1966 with the formation of NOW, the National Organization for Women.

Betty was NOW's first president and took her role as a leader in the women's movement seriously, traveling to give lectures and take part in campaigns for change, engendering many of the freedoms women now enjoy. She pushed for equal pay for equal work, equal job opportunities, and access to birth control and legalized abortion. In 1970, she quit NOW to fight for the Equal Rights Amendment, and in 1975, was named Humanist of the Year. Of her, author Barbara Seaman wrote, "Betty Friedan is to the women's movement what Martin Luther King was to blacks."

In 1981, responding to critics who claimed feminism ignored the importance of relationships and families to most women, she penned *The Second Stage*, in which she called on men and women to work together to make the home and the workplace havens for both genders. Betty made another revolution with her 2006 book, *The Fountain of Age*, raising consciousness about society's stereotypes about aging decades after she had, as futurist Alvin Toffler so aptly put it, "pulled the trigger of history" with *The Feminine Mystique*. And she didn't stop there, but went on to advocate for better balance between work and family life with her book *Beyond Gender: The New Politics of Work and Family*, as well as finding time to pen a memoir, *Life So Far*. Betty passed away at home in 2006 due to a heart attack on her eighty-fifth birthday, but her life continues to inspire women the world over.

It's been a lot of fun making the revolution.

Betty Friedan

TONI MORRISON *the truest eye*

Toni Morrison comes from small-town, working-class Ohio, a state that fell "between" on the Civil War issue of slavery, a state with many stops along the underground railroad, and a state where many crosses burned "neither plantation nor ghetto." She has made this her canvas for her rich, original stories that dare tell uncomfortable truths. And for her daring, she won the Nobel Prize in Literature.

Born in 1931 as Chloe Anthony Wofford, Toni and her parents worked hard as sharecroppers in their adopted Northern home of Lorain, Ohio. She was keenly interested in language as a child and loved hearing ghost stories, songs, and thundering sermons at church. After high school, she attended Howard University and graduated at the age of twenty-two, following that with a master's program at Cornell. Her thesis paper examined the theme of suicide in the works of Virginia Woolf and William Faulkner. She began teaching at Howard and met and married a Jamaican architect, Harold Morrison, with whom she had two sons, Harold Ford and Slade. The marriage was short-lived, and Toni took the children and moved to Syracuse, and then later to New York City, where she was hired by Random House as senior editor. She worked on several major Black autobiographies of the time, including those of Black Power revolutionary Angela Davis and world champion boxer Muhammed Ali.

As a writer, Toni Morrison made an immediate mark upon America's literary landscape with *The Bluest Eye*, published in 1970, and *Sula*, published three years later. Her next book, *Song of Solomon*, won the National Book Critics' Circle Award in 1978. In 1983, she left Random House to devote herself full-time to writing and spent the next five years writing *Beloved*, the fantastical and tragic story of ex-slave Sethe and her children.

Her writing focuses on Black women who had previously been ignored. Her lyrical language combines with both realistic and mythic plot elements

to create a distinctive style all her own. In 1993, Morrison won the Nobel
Prize in Literature; she was the first Black American to do so. She said, "I
am outrageously happy. But what is most wonderful for me personally is to
know that the prize has been awarded to an African American. Winning as an
American is very special—but winning as a Black American is a knockout."

Had I loved the life that the state planned for me from the beginning, I would have lived and died in somebody else's kitchen.

Toni Morrison, in a speech to the International Literary Congress in New York

CHAPTER TWO
....

Ink in Their Veins
Theories of Relativity

Some women seem to have writing talent encoded in their DNA. This is especially true of several "literary dynasties" wherein several family members are extraordinarily gifted, each with a voice uniquely his or her own. How does this happen? Do the gods (and goddesses) look down from above and occasionally say, "Hmmm, let's endow this family with writing genius through the end of time"? Or can a special relationship with the Muses can be arranged and passed down from generation to generation?

Certainly, these creative kin have some strange magic in remarkable quantity. To wit, just two examples: the legacy of the Brontë lineage hasn't faded with time; new editions of books and films of *Jane Eyre* and *Wuthering Heights* are released every few years like clockwork. Stateside, their doppelgängers, the Grimké sisters, were stirring up hot controversy with virulent abolitionist texts that helped ignite the Civil War.

Bonded by blood and shelved side by side, the women profiled here are invariably very different from each other. But they all have one thing in common: a love of the written word.

> *It had been startling and disappointing to me to find out that story books had been written by people, that books were not natural wonders, coming up by themselves like grass.*
>
> Eudora Welty

THE BRONTËS *scribbling sisters*

The Brontë sisters were originally a troupe of five girls born in the early 1800s in a rural parsonage in Yorkshire, England. Mary Ann and Elizabeth died before they reached the age of ten, Emily and Anne lived to adulthood, and Charlotte outlived them all. Emily Brontë tends to be the most beloved in the family, but Anne and Emily had much in common. They also had many differences; their personalities could not have been more dissimilar. And all three aspired to be writers.

To make family dynamics even more complex, their father, Reverend Patrick Brontë, a failed writer himself, saw Emily as a genius, Charlotte as very talented, and Anne as not worthy of attention. The truth is, however, that the self-absorbed and somewhat silly patriarch had a staggering amount of talent under his roof. To have one daughter become a famous writer is amazing enough, but to have three is almost unimaginable.

The reverend proved more successful in theatrics, at least at home. In constant possession of a pistol, he shot through the open door if irritated and took a knife to one of his wife's silk dresses. When his wife died in 1821, he sent for his sister-in-law to care for the six children (there was one brother, Branwell). A few years later, all the girls except Anne were sent to boarding school, which turned out to be a horrible experience of physical deprivation; this is where the two oldest girls died. After their sisters' deaths, Charlotte and Emily were sent home.

Typically for the period, Reverend Brontë pinned his hope on his son, Branwell, an aspiring artist. Branwell was sent to university in London to pursue his dreams and failed miserably. Instead, he squandered his tuition and allowance on gin. When he had run through all of the money, he returned home, telling lies about having been robbed. The sisters ended up as teachers and governesses, but their passion was always writing.

In 1845, Charlotte discovered that Anne and Emily had been writing verse, as had she. She collected their poetry into one volume and published it herself, using the male pseudonyms—Currer (Charlotte), Ellis (Emily), and Acton (Anne) Bell—that they would retain throughout their careers. The book sold one copy. Not to be deterred, they all continued writing. Soon they were publishing to great acclaim.

Charlotte Brontë's *Jane Eyre* achieved spectacular success during her lifetime, and it has survived the test of time and been retold again and again in films. She also penned the well-received novels *Shirley* and *Villette*. Anne's *Agnes Gray* and *The Tenant of Wildfell Hall* are less known now but were critical and popular successes in their day.

But it is Emily who is considered by critics to be the literary genius of the family, based on her poems and her opus *Wuthering Heights*, which shone with a brilliance and sense of drama and mystery nearly unmatched in all of British literature. Family and friends marveled that sweet-natured Emily, always cleaning and ironing, was capable of the volcanic passions and drama she unleashed in her tale of love on the moors. Her Heathcliff is a brute, a primal presence as wild as the wind, a perfect foil for the spoiled, difficult Catherine. When it came out that the author was a woman, some critics of the day declared that *Wuthering Heights* must actually be the work of Branwell, on the grounds that no woman, particularly one who led such a sheltered existence, could have written such a passionate book.

Emily and Anne died young (at her brother's funeral, Emily caught the cold that would eventually kill her). Charlotte went on to be lionized as a literary giant and hobnobbed with the likes of William Makepeace Thackeray, Mrs. Gaskell, and Matthew Arnold. She married her father's curate in 1854 and died the following year.

> *I'll walk where my own nature would be leading;*
> *It vexes me to choose another guide.*
>
> Emily Brontë

ALICE JAMES *sibling rivalry*

Baby sister to brainy overachievers William and Henry James, Alice James, born in 1848, was also a writer of intensity and introspection. But she suffered greatly as a product of the Victorian Age: her brothers were the recipients of all the glory, and Alice was relegated to the house. Given the times, despite her great familial connections, Alice had little chance of publication and gradually receded into the shadows of the brothers' gargantuan reputations as geniuses in philosophy and fiction.

Alice was sick her whole adult life. Sadly, it seems that her frustrations about career and gender contributed to her illness and neurasthenia. She had her first spells at sixteen and was prescribed a regimen of treatments involving "blistering baths," electricity treatments, and sulfuric, ether, and motor therapy sessions. These medical advancements didn't seem to help so much as harm her, and she was depressed and suicidal by the age of thirty. Her father, a Christian mystic preacher and ambitious intellectual, magnanimously gave her "permission" to die, which lessened her interest in that option. The more sensitive sibling, novelist Henry James, noted that "in our family group, girls seem scarcely to have had a chance" and that his sister's "tragic health was, in a manner, the only solution for her of the practical problems of life." Alice and her longtime companion Katherine Peabody were the models for Henry James's novel about a pair of suffragist lovers in *The Bostonians*.

Despite her ill health, she did manage to keep a diary. Published after her death, it is now regarded as a seminal text in nineteenth-century feminist studies and a window into the world of invalidism. Nearly forgotten until the mid-1980s, Alice James has recently come to the attention of critics: a volume of her letters and an in-depth biography recognize her as a "silenced" voice of her era and tell a tragic tale of a woman trapped in a time in which the role of wife was the only real choice for women. Her long period of decay and isolation led her to view her eventual death from breast cancer as a respite from a torturous existence that offered no option to exercise her talent or will.

> *A written monologue by that most interesting being, myself,*
> *may have its yet to be discovered consolations. I shall at least*
> *have it all my own way, and it may bring relief as an outlet*
> *to that geyser of emotions, sensations, speculations, and*
> *reflections which ferments perpetually....*
>
> From *The Diary of Alice James*

AMY LOWELL *"maker of fine poems"*

Sometimes, a strong woman following her own distinct destiny becomes better known for her strength of personality and the celebrity surrounding it than for her actual accomplishments. Amy Lowell is just such a person.

Born in 1874 at the tail end of the Gilded Age, she came from a family of accomplished intellectuals and writers; she was cousin to the legendary New England poets James Russell Lowell and Robert Lowell and nearly every other male running MIT or Harvard. As a girl, she agonized over her weight, and despite desperate and severe diets, she couldn't surmount that personal issue. Her fears about her ability to fit in led to "nervous prostrations," but her love of the written word kept her going. "I am ugly, fat, conspicuous & dull," she wrote in her diary at the age of fifteen. "I should like best of anything to be literary."

Though she was in her own right a skilled critic and a fine poet, her recognition came in large part for her eccentricities—in particular, wearing tailored men's suits, smoking cigars, and keeping a pack of dogs. Her original approach to both her appearance and her personal habits certainly extended to her writing, and after her first traditionally lyric book of poetry in 1912, *A Dome of Many-Colored Glass*, she began working in the pioneering modernist and imagist style brought to international attention by Ezra Pound, H. D., and T. S. Eliot.

Indeed, Amy Lowell cited H. D. as a major influence on her open verse and cadence, what she referred to as "polymorphic prose." She also had a fascination with Asian art, poetry, and aesthetics, and in 1921 published *Fir-Flower Tablets*, a group of original poems combined with avant-garde translations of Chinese poetry in collaboration with Florence Ayscough. A powerfully insightful literary critic, she also lectured, compiled anthologies of poetry by H. D. and others, and completed an immense biography of the great English poet John Keats.

Part of her legacy as a writer includes a group of love poems called *The Letter and Madonna of the Evening Flowers*, inspired by her lover and companion Ada Dwyer Russell. After her parents' deaths, Amy invited Ada to live with her in their baronial mansion in a manner that caused several to compare them to the Paris-bound duo Gertrude Stein and Alice B. Toklas.

Indeed, they had the same relational dynamic, with former actress Russell playing Toklas's role as cook, nurse, and companion. Ada was no mere muse, however; the two worked together and sparked each other's creativity. Amy even talked about hanging up a shingle outside her family mansion, Sevenels, saying, "Lowell & Russell, Makers of Fine Poems."

Amy Lowell also pursued her poetic vision by traveling to meet others and sought out Ezra Pound, Henry James, D.H. Lawrence, H. D., Robert Frost, and John Gould Fletcher, with whom she forged lasting friendships. The success of her imagist masterpieces *Can Grande's Castle* and *Pictures of the Floating World* prompted Ezra Pound, ostensibly the founder of that movement, to start calling the radical new style "Amygism." In 1925, she wrote *What O'Clock*, which won a Pulitzer Prize for poetry after her death that year from a cerebral hemorrhage.

> Little cramped words scrawling all over the paper
> Like draggled fly's legs
> What can you tell me of the flaring moon?
> Through the oak leaves?
>
> Amy Lowell, from "The Letter"

MARY SHELLEY *Gothic greatness*

Nearly everyone in Mary Shelley's life was a writer. Her mother, Mary Wollstonecraft, was one of the first feminist writers and thinkers; her father, William Godwin, wrote philosophical theory. Their home in England was a regular gathering place for the radical elite; Charles Lamb and Samuel Coleridge were among their regular visitors. Politically, her parents were revolutionaries who disapproved of marriage, but still went through with the legalities to legitimize Mary upon her birth in 1797. Mary Wollstonecraft died eleven days after the baby was born, and Godwin fell apart, neglecting his daughter terribly, perhaps even blaming her for his beloved wife's death. He later remarried and let relatives, nannies, and his new wife take whatever care of Mary they chose. Mary recalled learning to write by tracing her mother's name on her gravestone at her father's urging.

At seventeen, Mary met the married playboy poet Percy Bysshe Shelley and ran away with him to Europe, returning after a few weeks to London as he was drowning in debt. By 1816, the couple had a more secure financial footing and headed for the continent again, this time to Switzerland's Lake Geneva, to a party with Shelley's friend Lord Byron. A bout of ghost stories told around the fire as a distraction from an unusually cold summer inspired nineteen-year-old Mary to pick up a pen. Written in one year, *Frankenstein* is now hailed as the first Gothic novel as well as a seminal work of science fiction.

In 1818, *Frankenstein* was published, and Mary and Percy Shelley returned to London and married after the death of his wife. What proved to be a watershed year for the pair because of the publication of her book was an extremely difficult one; Mary's half-sister Fanny and Percy Shelley's wife both committed suicide. Their marriage was met with extreme disapproval, and the newlyweds fled to Italy to escape the controversy. Mary had three children; all but one, a son, died. Mother and son survived husband and father when in 1822, an exiled Shelley and fellow rebel poets drowned in the Bay of Spezia in Italy.

His young widow and surviving son were left behind, virtually destitute. Mary managed to scratch out a living to support her father and two-year-old child, but she was an outcast from society. Mary wrote other romances, including *The Lost Man*, *Lodore*, and *Valperga*, but none reached the level of success or acclaim of her first. She idolized her late husband and memorialized him in her fiction, in addition to editing the first volume of his poetry in 1839. Mary Shelley died in 1851 of a brain tumor. Now, more than 150 years after her death, the book she wrote at the age of nineteen continues to inform, inspire, and amaze.

> *My imagination, unbidden, possessed and guided me.*
>
> Mary Shelley, from *Frankenstein*

MARY WOLLSTONECRAFT *feminist firecracker*

Though her life was troubled and turbulent, Mary has gone down in history as a major contributor to feminist literature. Her works, *Thoughts on the Education of Daughters* (1787) and *A Vindication of the Rights of Woman* (1793), are lucid and forward-thinking and are touchstones in gender studies. Born in 1759, Wollstonecraft worked for a London publisher, James Johnson, which bolstered her independence, but she left for Paris in order to see the French Revolution for herself. As a cover, she passed herself off as the daughter of American captain Gilbert Imlay, with whom she became involved, producing a daughter, Fanny. The affair broke up, and a brokenhearted Mary tried unsuccessfully to kill herself; ironically, her daughter Fanny would later succeed at suicide. She went back to London and her old publishing job in 1795. James Johnson had become involved with an extremist political group comprised of Thomas Paine, William Wordsworth, William Godwin, Thomas Holcraft, and William Blake. Mary and Godwin fell in love, and she became pregnant with her daughter Mary, who later attained enduring fame under her married name, Mary Shelley.

MODERN DUOS

At the turn of the twentieth century, Erica Jong's daughter Molly has taken up her pen and shows no fear of flying, while siblings Eliza and Susan Minot are authoring critically acclaimed novels and nonfiction. To their mutual enjoyment, they are witnessing the shock of readers and listeners who marvel at how "different" they are, as people and as writers.

DOROTHY WORDSWORTH *"wild lights in her eyes"*

Beloved poet William Wordsworth was one of his sister's biggest admirers and she his "dearest friend" during his life. She was the only girl of the five children born to the Dorsetshire family. When their mother passed away in 1778, when Dorothy was seven, relatives raised her away from her four brothers.

But despite being raised apart, William and Dorothy were extremely close. William, two years older than his sister, inherited some money of his own when he turned twenty-six and bought an English country cottage just for the two of them. William's destiny as a poet was already unfolding. Dorothy, to aid her brother and amuse him, began to keep a series of journals that not only reveal the lives of important literary figures but also have a purity and merit all their own. The portraits of their daily existence alone are priceless, but her machinations to inspire and "preserve" her brother as a poet are also remarkable. Today scholars pore over the journals for their wealth of information about the poet.

When William met and married Mary Hutchinson, at first Dorothy felt betrayed and abandoned. Eventually, her loyalty and love won out, and she pitched in to care for his children, for whom she wrote her own poetry, including "Peaceful Is Our Valley." The valley in which they lived, rhapsodized over by brother William, was peaceful indeed, an idyllic place visited often by friends William Hazlitt, Robert Southey, Charles Lamb, Thomas De Quincey, Samuel Coleridge, and Robinson. De Quincey penned reminiscences about his visits to the cottage, where he was shocked by what he perceived as Dorothy stepping outside a proper feminine role: "The exclusive character of her reading, and the utter want of pretension, and of all that looks like bluestockingisms."

Later writers, including Virginia Woolf, puzzled over her life. Was she stifled by the towering talent of her brother and held back by her gender? A closer look at her diaries and the beautifully sculpted entries there reveal one thing certainly: she was a happy person and one with nature and her own nature. While her brother sometimes labored over his works, under pressure to produce for the eyes of the world, she was free to allow her impressions to flow freely. However, not all was to remain rosy forever; she spent the last twenty-five years of her life struggling with both physical and mental illness.

> *The Sea perfectly calm blue, streaked with deeper colour by the clouds, and tongues or points of sand, on our return a gloomy red. The sun goes down. The crescent moon, Jupiter and Venus.*
>
> Dorothy Wordsworth

NALO HOPKINSON *fabulous fabulist of Caribbean culture*

Nalo Hopkinson, born in Jamaica in 1960, is a Canadian speculative fiction author and editor who has also been a professor of creative writing at UC Riverside since 2011; her teaching focuses on the fantasy, science fiction, and magic realism genres, and she is a member of a faculty research cluster in science fiction. Her writing draws on myth and folklore as well as Caribbean language, history, and storytelling traditions.

Her family moved around quite a bit; as a child, besides Jamaica and Canada, Nalo also lived in Trinidad, Guyana, and the United States. Her mother worked in libraries, and her father was a playwright, actor, and poet from Guyana who also taught both Latin and English. Literacy came early for her, despite learning disabilities that were only diagnosed when she was an adult; by age three, she could read, and at ten, she was reading Kurt Vonnegut and Homer's *Iliad*. From the beginning, she preferred fantastical fiction, including "everything from Caribbean folklore to Ursula K. Le Guin's science fiction and fantasy." Nalo had a firsthand experience of culture shock when her family moved from Guyana to Toronto, Canada, when she was sixteen, and she has stated she is "still not fully reconciled" to that shift. She lived in Toronto before attending Seton Hill University in Pennsylvania, where she earned an MA in the writing of popular fiction.

After working in various civil service positions dealing with the arts and in libraries, Hopkinson began to write speculative fiction in her early thirties; by the time she participated in the Clarion Science Fiction Writing Workshop at Michigan State University in 1995, she had already sold a couple of short stories. Two years later, her magical realism and folklore-inflected novel *Brown Girl in the Ring* won the Warner Aspect First Novel Contest; the prize included publication of the work by Warner Aspect. Her debut opus also won the Locus Award for Best First Novel. Her 2003 work *Skin Folk* garnered a World Fantasy Award and a Sunburst Award for Canadian Literature of the Fantastic, and 2004's *Salt Road* won a Gaylactic Spectrum Award for positive exploration of queer issues in speculative fiction. Her novel *The New Moon's Arms* drew both the Prix Aurora Award of Canada and a Sunburst Award, making Hopkinson the first author ever to receive the latter prize twice.

Despite this success, Hopkinson endured major financial difficulties when serious illness struck and she was unable to work for a lengthy period. She suffers from fibromyalgia and went through periods of acute anemia brought on by fibroids as well as serious vitamin D deficiency; due to these health challenges, she was unable to write or publish for a period of six years. She was even without housing of her own for a couple of years before beginning to teach at the University of California.

Hopkinson has written nine novels and about a dozen published short stories, as well as *House of Whispers* (2018), a graphic novel set in Neil Gaiman's *Sandman* universe that draws on Caribbean mythic, magical, and spiritual traditions. She has also edited a number of anthologies, including *Whispers from the Cotton Tree Root: Caribbean Fabulist Fiction* (2000); *Mojo: Conjure Stories* (2003); and *So Long Been Dreaming: Postcolonial Science Fiction & Fantasy* (2004). Besides folklore and Caribbean traditions, she incorporates feminist awareness and historical consciousness in her writing, often focusing on social issues and race, class, and sexuality. She draws inspiration from eclectic sources such as songs; her 2013 novel *Sister Mine* was inspired by Christina Rossetti's poem *Goblin Market*.

Professor Hopkinson says of herself that she loves "bopping around in the surf" and enjoys sewing, fabric design, and crafting objects in various media; she dreams of "one day living in a converted church, fire station, or library…or in a superadobe monolithic dome home."

JAMES TIPTREE, JR. *the writer who came in from the cold*

James Tiptree, Jr. was the main nom de plume of award-winning science fiction author Alice "Alli" Sheldon (1915–1987), née Bradley, who also wrote under a half-dozen other names. She was born in the Hyde Park district of Chicago to a lawyer/naturalist father and a prolific author mother. At age six, Alice ventured abroad to the Belgian Congo with her parents and naturalist Carl Akeley, a family friend. She visited Africa twice more as a child, in 1924–1925 (as part of a trip around the world) and in 1931. Mary Hastings Bradley, her mother, wrote books about their first two journeys, two of which Alice illustrated, the children's books *Alice in Jungleland* and *Alice in Elephantland*.

At nineteen, Alice eloped with a Princeton student she had met days earlier, William Davey, which ended her studies at Sarah Lawrence. She tried her hand at painting, but it didn't work out; in 1941, she divorced Davey and returned to Chicago, working at the *Chicago Sun* as their art critic. The next year, she joined the Women's Army Auxiliary Corps and later the Air Force, attaining the rank of major and working at the Pentagon as an aerial reconnaissance photograph interpreter. When World War II ended, she was transferred to a different unit; she ended up marrying her commanding officer, Colonel Huntington Sheldon. In 1946, the couple left the military, running a New Jersey chicken farm from 1948 to 1952. They were then asked to work for the CIA; she analyzed political shifts in Africa and continued her work with photographic intelligence, while he was director of current intelligence.

But Alice was not happy working at the CIA, and in 1955, she quit; she was having doubts about her marriage, so employing her intelligence skills, she "disappeared" for a time and went back to college, remaining apart from her husband for a year, although the reunited couple's marriage then continued for three decades. In 1959, she graduated from American University and went on to earn a PhD in experimental psychology from George Washington University in 1967. While completing her dissertation, she authored several of the type of science fiction stories she enjoyed reading. She felt that a masculine pseudonym would be useful as "camouflage" and became James Tiptree, Jr., having seen the name Tiptree on a marmalade jar label. She "was surprised to find that her stories were immediately accepted for publication and quickly became popular."

1973 was a banner year for Tiptree; in her pioneering, Hugo-winning cyberpunk novella *The Girl Who Was Plugged In*, set in a media-dominated future, a deformed homeless girl is enlisted to control the vacant body of a celebrity as a "remote" worker. This tale was ahead of its time in its portrayal of global corporations, product placement, and cultic devotion to celebrities. Tiptree also won a Nebula short story award for depicting alien psychology, making use of her academic background; "Love Is the Plan the Plan Is Death" is narrated from the point of view of an enormous alien arachnid.

In the mid-seventies, Tiptree wrote stories with a feminist twist: "The Women Men Don't See" (1973), in which a crashed airplane's passengers encounter temporarily stranded aliens, ends with the human women deciding to leave Earth with the aliens due to the limitations on women in Terran culture, which Tiptree clearly chafed at in her own life. 1976's *Houston, Houston, Do You Read?* told the tale of human male astronauts from the present day who travel in time to a future in which males have died out, where the astronauts must confront their sense of insignificance. *Houston* won a Nebula Award for best novella and tied for the 1977 Hugo Award.

"Tiptree" ended up being more than just an author name; it expressed an aspect of Alice Sheldon. But eventually she wanted to write from another dimension of herself and created "Raccoona Sheldon," another pseudonym for her other works. In a circumstance indicative of the level of sexism in publishing at the time, she had difficulties selling the Raccoona Sheldon stories until "Tiptree" wrote to publishers on "Raccoona's" behalf, describing Raccoona as an old friend and student of Tiptree's. The first Raccoona stories were often received as light in contrast to the short fiction authored under the Tiptree name, but a few Raccoona outings went much deeper, including 1977's Nebula-winning novelette *The Screwfly Solution*. It was a tale of men compelled by aliens to commit femicide to depopulate Earth for alien colonization and was eventually adapted as a made-for-TV film in Showtime's *Masters of Horror* series in 2006. It was also the last story Alice wrote before her identity was revealed.

Tiptree communicated a great deal with editors and other writers by post but kept her actual identity secret for years; however, Tiptree did mention "his" mother was from Chicago and an explorer. Upon publication of Mary Bradley's obituary in 1976, inquisitive Tiptree fans connected the dots; Alice Sheldon was revealed, overturning many suppositions by SF authors and others regarding "female writing" vs. "male writing." Many were convinced Tiptree was male due to such things as a seemingly "masculine" level of experience with the military and intelligence fields, including Harlan Ellison and Robert Silverberg. She made efforts at damage control by reaching out to longstanding contacts such as Ursula K. Le Guin, hoping to tell them before they heard. Numbers of them were supportive, including Le Guin, whose response was very positive, but the fallout of the revelation worsened the depression with which Alice had long struggled. Her confidence and her work suffered. Early one morning in 1987, she shot her sleeping eighty-four-year-old husband in the head, then turned the gun on herself; people close to the Sheldons, including his son by an earlier marriage, Peter, believe it was a suicide pact. SF authors Karen Joy Fowler and Pat Murphy later founded the James Tiptree, Jr. Award for F/SF literature that "expands or explores our understanding of gender."

Tiptree/Sheldon was complex in sexual orientation as well as gender identity; although she clearly had long-term connections with men, she stated, "I like some men a lot, but from the start, before I knew anything, it was always girls and women who lit me up." Of the army, she declared she had "felt she was among free women for the first time." One is left wondering what this brilliant author could have expressed in a more liberated time.

> *A male name seemed like good camouflage. I had the feeling*
> *that a man would slip by less observed. I've had too many*
> *experiences in my life of being the first woman in some*
> *damned occupation.*
>
> Alice Bradley Sheldon (known as James Tiptree, Jr.)

For many women writers, it took a masculine pen name to get published

Amandine Lucie Aurore Dupin, Baronne Dudevant: The famous French novelist George Sand

Mary Ann (or Marian) Evans: The great English Victorian novelist George Eliot

Anne Brontë, Charlotte Brontë, and Emily Brontë: The beloved Brontës, published under the names Acton, Currer, and Ellis Bell, respectively.

Marion Zimmer Bradley: Lee Chapman, John Dexter, and Morgan Ives were all noms de plume of Marion Zimmer Bradley, the bestselling author of *The Mists of Avalon*

Olive Schreiner: She used the name Ralph Iron to write her acclaimed *The Story of an African Farm*

Frances Miriam Berry: The first woman humorist in the United States, she used the name Frank to get published

Adele Florence Cory: As was eventually revealed, she used the pseudonym Lawrence Hope. According to *Womanlist* by Marjorie P.K. Weiser and Jean S. Arbeiter, Adele Florence Cory was "respectably married to a middle-aged British army officer in India, who wrote passionate poems in the 1890s. One described the doomed love of a married English lady for an Indian rajah in the Kashmir. When Hope's real identity was unmasked, all London was abuzz: was she telling the truth?"

MADELEINE L'ENGLE *the physics of love and a wrinkle in time*

Just over a century ago, Madeleine L'Engle was born in 1918 in New York City, the only child of two highly creative socialites: father Charles was a journalist who also wrote novels and plays, and mother Madeleine was a pianist. They often left young Madeleine in the care of an Irish Catholic immigrant housekeeper they called Mrs. O; L'Engle later recalled time with her as being full of "laughter and joy, the infallible signs of the presence of God."

When she wasn't with Mrs. O, she spent hours alone; as soon as she was able to hold a pencil, the imaginative Madeleine started writing. Having read all the books she had, she created her own stories and poetry. Her father's old manual typewriter was eventually passed along to her, which furthered her efforts as a novelist. But in 1930, Madeleine's life changed when her parents moved to Europe; she was deposited at Chatelard, an elite girls' boarding school in Switzerland. Besides missing her family terribly, she didn't fit in with the boarding school cliques and couldn't stand having no private space. She was forced to develop a "force field of silence" within which she "could go on writing my stories and my poems and dreaming my dreams," which in time helped her become a writer, she later said.

In 1933, the whole family moved back to the US. Madeleine was soon sent away to another boarding school in Charleston, South Carolina. Although making friends was still challenging, she was able to find a place for herself at Ashley Hall. She joined the drama club, both performing and trying her hand as a playwright, following in her father's footsteps. Her interest in various kinds of writing became a consuming passion. But her life was changed again when death touched her family, first taking her grandmother; then just before her eighteenth birthday, word came that her father was in the hospital, desperately ill with pneumonia. Young Madeleine traveled to Jacksonville to say farewell, but he had died by the time she arrived. Disconsolate, she pledged to herself in her journal that she had to succeed with her writing for her father's sake as well as her own. A faraway or absent father marked a number of her novels; this is seen in *A Wrinkle in Time*, in which Meg, the teenaged heroine, rescues her father and triumphs over evil by the power of love.

Madeleine went on to graduate from Smith College with a BA in English in 1941 and moved back to New York to begin her theater career. On tour and on Broadway, she stole time to write while waiting in the wings, making use of her internal cloak of silence. Her first novel, *The Small Rain* (1945), was hailed as "evidence of a fresh new talent" by the *New York Times*. Funds from sales of the novel kept the wolf from the door for some years, and *Ilsa*, her second novel, saw print in 1946. That same year, she met and married fellow actor Hugh Franklin; they moved to a quaint farmhouse in Goshen, Connecticut, which they named "Crosswicks" after her father's childhood home, and started a family. They bought the old Goshen general store, which she helped to run while also holding down full-time parenting duties and writing novels part-time. She later admitted that her force field of silence did fail in one set of circumstances: interruptions from crawling youngsters.

Nevertheless, she continued writing, and while a 1950s housewife, managed a wholly original creation: *A Wrinkle in Time* was both different from anything she'd ever written and distinct from anything by *any* author. This masterwork came after a time when she doubted herself both as a writer (since her works weren't selling) and as a homemaker, with fifties expectations of domestic perfection dogging her. During her crisis, a minister advised her to read religious tomes, but they only bored her; eventually, though, she found herself reinspired by physics. Reading Heisenberg, Einstein, and Planck, she found herself recalling her earliest memory: seeing the starry sky by the seashore one magically clear night as a tiny child. She found a mysticism within these contemplations of natural law and the beauty of creation, and in the writings that followed, repeatedly expressed this joining of scientific knowledge with the realm of the spiritual.

L'Engle's journals of the years previous to her breakthrough novel reflect its themes, from pondering her own shortcomings to the implications of relativity. She created a tale of the daughter of an unusual and creative family, with a father who had been torn from her and teachers who underestimated her, confronting an evil that controlled people by convincing them that not conforming was the problem. She eloquently expressed the interconnectedness of all things in her engaging work.

But editors didn't think there was a market for the hard-to-categorize novel, and it took two years before L'Engle found a publisher who'd take a chance on it, with dozens of rejection slips on the way there. She inwardly reflected, "I know [this] is a good book..... This is my psalm of praise to life, my stand for life against death." In 1962, it at last saw print; though well reviewed, conservative evangelicals claimed it promoted witchcraft and 'New Age' spirituality and tried to have it removed from school libraries and Christian bookstores. L'Engle was disappointed that her book and its four sequels were targeted as controversial, since evangelicals had no problem with the popular Narnia series. *A Wrinkle in Time* now holds the contrasting distinctions of being one of the most banned American novels, as well as selling over sixteen million copies (and counting) in more than forty languages and winning the prestigious 1963 Newbery Medal.

Its success changed her life; the family, now including three children, moved to an apartment in Manhattan's Upper West Side, keeping Crosswicks as a refuge for time away from the city. Madeleine volunteered as a church librarian, establishing a daily routine of work, worship, and writing accompanied by her Irish setters, and her husband Hugh returned to acting. She went on to write more than two dozen more books, as well as giving back to her community by on occasion giving free workshops on the writer's craft, at times with author friends, at the Episcopal cathedral where she did volunteer work. L'Engle joined the rarified list of writers who are not only recognized as literary rock stars while still alive, but live long enough to enjoy it. In the four decades that followed, she was able to watch as the series that began with *A Wrinkle in Time* inspired young people, particularly girls, and positively shifted the landscape for both novels with female protagonists and female writers of speculative fiction. During those years, her fan base mushroomed as she achieved further recognition: a National Book Award, the National Humanities Medal, no less than seventeen honorary doctorates, and much more, including a 2018 major motion picture film adaptation of *A Wrinkle in Time*.

In 1970, Hugh, who had acted in series including *Dark Shadows*, found career success when he was cast as Dr. Charles Tyler in the pilot of *All My Children*, where he continued for thirteen years. He was often buttonholed by autograph-seeking fans when in public, which amused his less-recognizable wife.

In later life, L'Engle traveled extensively, appearing at schools and colleges, literary festivals, religious conferences, retreats, particularly women's retreats, and doing children's book tours. She was a charismatic speaker who employed her theater background to good effect, even using props. Even after her husband's 1986 demise, she kept on with writing, speaking, and literary events as well as socializing with friends and family well beyond the milestone of turning eighty, until her death in 2007.

A book, too, can be a star, explosive material, capable of stirring up fresh life endlessly, a living fire to lighten the darkness, leading out into the expanding universe.

Madeleine L'Engle

CHAPTER THREE

....

Mystics and Madwomen
Subversive Piety

It's amazing that most of the women profiled in this chapter weren't burned at the stake! They are kindred of the "first ladies of literature" in spirit, if not in soul. They were writing at a time when it simply wasn't seemly for women to express independent thought, to reinterpret the Bible in their own ways, or really, to be writing at all. Most fascinating of all is the one recurring theme in many of their mystic revelations: the feminine face of God, or "God as mother." Despite decades and sometimes centuries separating these disparate mystics, their visions and revelations were similar in detail and description of a shining, goddess-like benevolent figure. Writing is a solitary venture, and these women have been the most solitary of all: anchorites imprisoned in monastic cells; spinsters in rooms of their own à la Emily Dickinson; pioneer wives stuck in remote parts of the rough-hewn New World; and faithfuls on pilgrimages through the most inhospitable of surroundings and circumstances. Their texts and tracts read like modern poetry—simple, spare, passionate, and beatific, in the original meaning as appropriated by the twentieth-century Beatniks.

Forward-thinking if nothing else, these women wielded their pens skillfully, unencumbered by fear of their fellow man. Saint Catherine of Siena's dictated writings and the letters she sent to prominent men of the day influenced the politics of the medieval church, while Hilda of Whitby mentored the greatest Old English poet, Caedmon. At age fifteen, neo-Gnostic Jane Lead began having visions of Sophia, "the magical woman within the soul who would bring redemption to male and female spirits alike." Indian poet-singer Mirabai became a wandering *sadhu* for her devotion to Lord Krishna, composing verse of unmatched beauty that is still sung four hundred years later. These transcendental talents are, in some cases, only now finding a readership, thanks to students of women's literature and religious scholars. Superstar Sufi poet Rumi may have to make room for these ecstatic lyricists. After all, these women, too, were divinely inspired to write.

HILDA OF WHITBY *patron saint*

An Englishwoman born in 614 CE, Hilda spent most of her life teaching and creating a network of monasteries and abbeys across England. In 657, a patron gave her a piece of land in Whitby, Yorkshire, on which she established a monastery that would come to be an important breeding ground for the developing scholarship and literature of the age. Populated by both men and women who lived separately, Whitby attracted a wide group of intellectuals. Hilda herself taught the arts, medicine, grammar, music, and theology.

Old English historian the Venerable Bede writes about Hilda and her crucial role as advisor to kings, noblemen, and laypeople. But she also had a lasting effect on the world of letters. Whitby had a large library, and the scribes of the monastery produced the *Life of Pope Gregory I*, one of England's earliest works of literature. Bede also tells of how the infinitely wise Abbess Hilda discovered the poetic potential of Caedmon, a lay brother who worked at the monastery, and encouraged him to write. As a result of her patronage, we have the earliest known examples of Christian poetry in Old English.

Originally a Celtic Christian, Hilda hosted the Synod of Whitby in 664, which was held to decide what direction Christianity would take. The synod voted to follow the Roman Catholic Church; independent though she was, Hilda went with the majority.

While most women were illiterate until relatively recently, the tenth-century Anglo-Saxon noblewoman Wynflaed actually willed her books upon her death to another woman, Æthelflaed.

SACRED SCRIBES THROUGHOUT THE AGES

In 1700 BCE, **Amat-Mamu** was an Assyrian priestess-scribe who for forty
years made her living in a cloister of 140 other such women. The clay tablets
on which they wrote have survived to this day. Three hundred years before she
and her sisterhood were recording the spiritual beliefs of the day, the priestess
Kubatum in Ur wrote and performed ritual enactments of holy erotic poetry
such as the sweet—literally—lines incorporated into the Bible's sexy *Song of
Solomon*: "Lion, let me give you my caresses…wash me with honey."

Marie de France was a French poet and the first women to write in a European
vernacular. Many scholars regard her as the greatest woman writer of the
medieval era because of her religious writing and short fiction, which preceded
Chaucer and Boccaccio. Her identity is enshrouded in mystery, perhaps for her
own protection. We hope that a modern scholar-sleuth will find this enigma a
potent lure and challenge and will make her works and her identity accessible
to us all.

J is believed to have been a tenth-century female Israelite of noble descent
who wrote several narratives that are embedded in the Old Testament, though
they were written six centuries before various scribes cobbled them together.
The women she wrote about—King David's lover Bathsheba, Rebecca, and
Tamar—come alive in her stories. While "J" the person remains a cipher, and a
very controversial one among biblical experts, her identity and authenticity have
recently been recognized by such a noteworthy as Harold Bloom, and a volume
of the J writings has been published.

Perpetua was an early Christian Carthaginian, citizen of the Holy Roman
Empire, and member of the Montanist sect, which espoused equality for
women. She converted her best friend, an African slave named Felicity, and
both were jailed for soliciting their faith. In prison, Perpetua began to have
visions and to write them down. Though facing death, she reaffirmed her faith
in court and was executed by a combination of wild beasts and gladiators in
a Roman circus. Her diary, a record of her trials and her unswerving faith,
survives her.

Elizabeth Cady Stanton, a most practical mystic, wrote *The Woman's Bible*, no small feat. This powerful text is both a testament to and a feminist critique of the male bias in the Judeo-Christian tradition; some sentiments were echoed in the "Declaration of Sentiments" printed for the Seneca Falls suffragette convention of July 19, 1848. "Resolved, That woman is man's equal—was intended to be so by the Creator, and the highest good of the race demands that she should be recognized as such."

> *I love inscriptions on flyleaves and notes in margins, I like the comradely sense of turning pages someone else turned, and reading passages some one long gone has called to my attention.*
>
> Helene Hanff, on the joys of secondhand books, from *84, Charing Cross Road*

HILDEGARD VON BINGEN the "Sibyl of the Rhine"

Although her canonization was twice undertaken in the fifteenth century, four hundred years after her death, no aspect of sainthood was ever realized for Hildegard von Bingen except for her inclusion in the Roman Martyrology. Hildegard began her life in Germany; the daughter of nobility, she discovered her calling at the age of three when she first started having visions. Throughout her life, she had frequent incidents of trances, fits, and frenzied states of godly joy.

At eight years of age, she entered the Benedictine Convent at Disibodenberg as an anchorite. As a religious devotion, anchorites were locked into tiny cells that they could never leave, receiving food through a small hole through which they also passed their wastes. Luckily for Hildegard, her cell was already occupied by a German anchoress named Jutta, who instructed her in the classics and certain sciences, notably botany. Hildegard lived that way for seven years, until word of her amazing brilliance and religious devotion had so spread that women who wished to study with her crowded her cell, and the order allowed her to leave her cell and become a nun. Hildegard had two confidantes: her anchorite teacher and her lifelong friend and biographer, a monk named Volmar. When

Jutta died, Hildegard was made abbess in 1147 and went on to found her own convent in Rupertsberg, near Bingen.

Hildegard kept her visions secret until a voice told her to reveal them. She accurately prophesied a major papal event that took place nearly two hundred years later—the schism of the Catholic Church in 1378. She recorded her illuminating messages received in trance in her mystic trilogy, composed of *Scivias*, covering the period from 1142 to 1151, translated as *Know Thy Ways*; from 1158 to 1163, *Liber vitae meritorium (The Book of the Lives of the Worthy)*; and from 1163 to 1173, *Liber divinorum operum (The Book of Divine Works)*. Bernard of Clairvaux, a highly regarded religious philosopher and scholar of the time, was deeply moved by Hildegard's work. With his imprimatur, Hildegard's reputation and influence expanded, leading her to play an important role in the affairs of Pope Eugenius III and the Holy Roman Emperor, Frederick Barbarossa. She also made four preaching tours, which was highly unusual for a woman.

A dynamic speaker and accomplished musician as well as a writer, Hildegard also invented a cryptic language and calligraphy. Her exquisite religious prayer and verse are heavily laced with an emphasis on the feminine divine. Yet her writing wasn't limited to mysticism; she also wrote scientific treatises on subjects ranging from geology to botany, physiology, cosmology, ethics, and pathology. Dubbed the "Sibyl of the Rhine," Hildegard von Bingen became in her lifetime a very famous woman. When she was elderly, she spoke of how she constantly saw a backdrop of radiance upon which her visions were projected. She called this "the shadow of living light."

In the last century, both her poetry and music are enjoying a wide revival, and she is a mainstay in spiritual anthologies.

Sophia! You of the whirling wings, circling encompassing energy of God—you quicken the world in your clasp.

Hildegard von Bingen, from *Antiphon for Divine Wisdom*

JULIAN OF NORWICH *the first Englishwoman of letters*

Julian was an anchoress in the Church of St. Julian in Norwich and was thought to have been undergoing a "rite of enclosure," a kind of burial service for the soul while in her solitary cell.

Julian became famous throughout England after she decided she had God's permission to share the details of her mystical experiences, a total of sixteen separate visions. Though she was keenly aware of her status as a woman, she felt no risk in recording these important messages from above. This remarkable series of events occurred two days after she turned thirty, in the year 1372. At the time, Julian was gravely ill, but instead of concentrating on her own misery, she began to feel pity and compassion for the suffering of Christ on the cross. Her condition progressively worsened, and she hovered near death, even receiving last rites. Immediately after the rites, she experienced a "sudden change" and started seeing images from another realm.

Julian's descriptions of these episodes, written in English, were published in a volume entitled *Revelations of Divine Love*. They tell of her visitations not just from Heavenly Hosts, but also from demons and Satan. She discussed God in terms of a maternal presence, in a section called "God the Mother."

Julian's *Revelations of Divine Love* was enormously popular reading and was copied repeatedly during her lifetime and after her death. She has never been officially beatified and is honored on the "casual" feast day of May 13. She is oft acknowledged as the first Englishwoman of letters.

As truly as God is our Father, so truly is God our Mother...and so Jesus is our true Mother in nature by our first creation, and he is our true Mother in grace by his taking our created nature.

Julian of Norwich, from *Revelations of Divine Love*

PASSIONATE PRIESTESS

Mechtild von Magdeburg, a nun from Germany, was installed by her wealthy, noble family in the convent of Helfta in Saxony, a prominent center for education and mysticism. Mechtild had been seeing visions from God since childhood, but had hidden the fact from everyone. In 1250, she began writing about them in *Das fließende* Licht der Gottheit (The Revelations of Mechtild). She wrote in a language of Swabian dialect, embedding prayers, hymns, and autobiographical information among short entries of her visions. Mechtild's book is a rarity in medieval German literature and came to be read all over Europe. A snippet: "Lord, you are my lover. My longing, my flowing stream, my sun, And I am your reflection."

CATHERINE OF SIENA *poet of prayer*

Catherine was the twenty-fourth of twenty-five children born to Jacopo Benincasa, a craftsman who made his living as a dyer of cloth in the city of Siena. At the tender age of six, Catherine knew she wanted to devote her life to God, but she didn't enter a convent as a novice until ten years later, in 1363. She became a nun in the Dominican order four years after that and began her lifelong work helping the sick and destitute. During the plague, she and her female followers tended victims and buried the dead.

Loved and respected for her devotion (she was eventually canonized) later in her life, she acted as a director to a circle of nuns as well as a spiritual minister to many people from her community. She was a mystic, given to visions, and a poet, creating prayerful verse celebrating her faith and the glory of God.

Catherine was also an activist at heart and participated in the politics of her time and place. She even went so far as to travel to Avignon to prevail upon the pope to return to the Vatican in Rome. She was always helping others and thinking of herself last, barely eating in her desire to purify her being and be closer to holiness. She flagellated herself three times a day, seeing her personal suffering as an offering in exchange for the good of the church, saying,

"O eternal God, accept the sacrifice of my life within this mystic body of holy Church."

Catherine never learned to write, but several of her fellow nuns wrote down her original verse, letters, and prayers. Those she uttered in solitude are lost to us forever. An ecstatic trance state often came over Catherine during her meditations, in which she would lie prostrate upon the ground. Other times, her words came in short bursts interchanged by lengthy silences. Often, she sang as she walked alone. Her health became very frail, probably due to starvation, and she died at the age of thirty-three, leaving a set of devotional works nearly unmatched in their innovative splendor.

There the soul dwells—like the fish in the sea and the sea in the fish.

Catherine of Siena

CATHERINE OF SIENA *This nun and devotional writer cared for the sick and dying during the plague*

Fifteenth-century nuns in St. Catherine's Convent in Nuremberg, Germany, loved books so much that in less than fifty years, they grew their library from forty-six books to over six hundred, mostly by hand-copying sermons, parts of the New Testament, tracts, and records of the saints' lives.

SAINT TERESA OF AVILA *pierced by God*

One of a dozen children of Spanish nobles, Teresa de Cepeda y Abumada was born to a life of privilege on March 28, 1515. Upon her mother's death when Teresa was thirteen, the girl was sent to live at a convent school. She was miserable there, and after she fell ill, her mind turned to thoughts of death and hell. Though she longed to leave the strict confines of the convent, the images of hell enabled her to keep from running away; "in servile fear" she "forced herself" to accept the nunnery.

For twenty years, she continued to battle with her will, her frail body, and the harshness of life in the cloister, aspiring to a life of devotion and spiritual growth with a Franciscan book as her only aid. Finally, she underwent a second conversion, and using "the eyes of the soul," began seeing visions with regularity. Her visions were colorful and like nothing she had ever seen before; she saw jewel-encrusted crucifixes and tiny, pretty angels, one of whom pierced her heart with a fiery, golden pin. When demons invaded her dreams, she merely threw holy water on them and they ran off. In one dream, she experienced "transverberation," a golden lance from God that pierced her heart over and over. She also began to hear the voice of God sharing his hopes for her destiny.

Teresa was encouraged by the voice to found a small convent among the "discalced," the unshod, sandal-wearing reform movement of the Carmelite order. The discalced felt the Carmelite order was too soft; they believed in "holy poverty," including begging for alms in order to survive. Teresa and her fellow sisters were determined to live this ascetic life, and in 1563 they moved into the small St. Joseph's convent, where they spearheaded the "barefoot" reformation, traveling under terrible conditions in a wooden cart to found seventeen more such religious communities.

She also wrote books, spiritual guides for followers of the movement. Her *Life* is still widely read and remains in print; *The Way of Perfection* and *The Interior Castle* were also met with an immediate readership of significant proportions. In *Uppity Women of the Renaissance*, Vicki León says that *The Interior Castle* was so well regarded that it "eventually won her the title of Doctor of the Church from the twentieth century's Pope Paul VI."

Teresa was referred to as a saint while still alive, but she ignored such approbation, and until her death in 1582, got on with the real business of life, scrubbing floors, begging for alms, and cooking for her sisters and converts, remarking that, "The Lord walks among the pots and pans."

> *All things are passing; God never changeth; patience endureth.*
>
> Teresa of Avila, from her *Breviary*

MIRABAI *Krishna's convert*

An Indian *bhakti* or saint-poet, Mirabai (1498–1565) is the best known of all the northern Indian poets of this style. A Rajput princess by birth, she was steeped in literature and music by tutors in the court of her grandfather, Rao Dudaji.

Renowned for her sanctity, Mirabai married the crown prince of the kingdom of Mewar, but her religious feelings caused her to reject a husband-wife relationship with her royal groom. Instead, she worshipped her Lord, the incarnation of Krishna called Giridhara, whose great works included lifting a mountain. Tradition has it that the crown prince's family tried to kill Mirabai twice, and that she rejected the family's deities and the proper widow's rite of immolating herself on her husband's funeral pyre upon his death.

If these legends hold any truth, they could easily explain why Mirabai began wandering, leaving behind all semblance of a normal life and devoting herself exclusively to worship of her Lord Giridhara. Toward the time of her death, she stayed at the temple compound of Ranachora at Dvarka. Her devotional hymns, prayers, and poems are still sung all over India and have recently found their way into printed form in English.

> Only those who have felt the knife can understand the wound.
> Only the jeweler knows the nature of the Jewel.
>
> Mirabai

JANE LEAD *Sophia's prophet*

Jane Lead is one of those wonderful early women writers who are ripe for rescue from obscurity. She was born in 1624 in Norfolk to the Ward family, and, in her own words, was brought up and educated "like other girls." Her difference emerged when she turned fifteen and a voice began instructing her during a Christmas celebration. This was her first mystical experience. Six years later, she married William Lead, an older, distant relative, and her religious devotions went on the back burner. The couple raised four daughters, and after her husband's death in 1670, when Jane was forty-six years old, her interests returned strongly to the study of mysticism and a state she called "Spiritual Virginity." Jane had a powerful vision of Sophia, meaning "wisdom," a female aspect of God.

Jane Lead pored over the writings of the German theologian Jacob Boehme, who was widely regarded as radical in his spiritual beliefs. Jane's convictions about the mystical way grew more fervent than ever, and she moved into the household of Dr. John Pordage, founder of an unorthodox religious sect. When Pordage passed away, Lead began to publish her own visions and beliefs with the help of a younger assistant, Dr. Francis Lee. Together they founded the Philadelphia Society, based on Boehme's doctrine.

Her writing and the intelligence shown therein were astonishing. In 1681, she wrote *The Heavenly Cloud Now Breaking*, followed by *The Enochian Walks with God* and the four-volume work *A Fountain of Gardens, Watered by the Rivers of Divine Pleasure*. In a way similar to the work of other well-known writer-mystics, her work is not deliberately feminist; it is deliberately religious, but it does contain imagery of a female presence in the soul, imbued with the power to renew and redeem both men and women.

> *This is the great Wonder to come forth, as Women Clothed with the Sun...with the Glove of this world under her feet...with a Crown beset with stars, plainly declaring that to her is given the Command and Power.*
>
> Jane Lead

MARY BAKER EDDY *true believer*

Mary Baker Eddy was a farm girl from Bow, New Hampshire. Born in 1821, she came from humble circumstances, belying the will and passion that would make her the author of one of the most widely read books in the world, *Christian Healing*, and the founder of Christian Science. She spent the first part of her life in poverty, and details about her life are obscured by carefully edited authorized biographies. We do know that she was keenly interested in spiritualism and wandered from one boarding house to another, seeking out those run by spiritualists. In the mythology propounded by Christian Science historians, these wanderings are likened to those of Christ. One difference worth noting, however, is that Mary Baker was receiving channeled information from the dead, while the Bible makes no mention that Jesus heard such ghostly voices.

She got married along the way and served as a medium on many occasions, holding active seances where long-dead loved ones appeared and her voice would change to sound like other voices. An affidavit by one Mrs. Richard Hazeltine described Mrs. Eddy's trances: "These communications [came] through her as a medium, from the spirit of one of the Apostles or of Jesus Christ." Mrs. Eddy soon began to practice healing and eventually went on to deny that she had ever had anything to do with spiritualism.

Her life story is a confusing series of illnesses and cures of herself and everyone in her acquaintance, seemingly. Her dedication to her beliefs was mightily compelling to others, and her theories include such ideas as the Copernican reversal of the roles of mind and matter, man being "the image and likeness of God" and therefore "not matter." Mrs. Eddy had, along with her other talents of mediumship, the ability to convince people and to lead them. She was nothing if not charismatic. She and her book have influenced, and perhaps even healed, many hundreds of people.

> *Change the mind, and the quality changes. Destroy the belief and tranquility disappears.*
>
> Mary Baker Eddy

EMILY DICKINSON *white witch of Amherst*

Emily Dickinson was one of the first female literary "superstars"—a rather unusual fate for a housebound recluse. Her brilliant, intense verse certainly created a legend for the poet, but her eccentricities added to the "glamour" in the original sense of the word, casting a spell that has lasted well over a century. Born in 1830 on December 10 in Amherst, Massachusetts, Emily Dickinson was the second child of a strict and sober lawyer, Edward Dickinson, and a sweet-natured and shy mother, also named Emily. Emily junior also had an older brother, Austin, and a younger sister, Lavinia. By all accounts, the family was happy and prosperous, pillars of the community. Emily also benefited from a good education at Amherst Academy and at Mount Holyoke Female Seminary, one of the first women's colleges in America, located, fortuitously for Emily, right outside Amherst.

It was during her last year at Mount Holyoke that Dickinson showed glimmerings of the qualities that made her so different from her contemporaries. Lavinia, Emily's sister, relayed an amusing story about Emily bluffing her way through a mathematics test: "When the [geometry] examination came and [she] had never studied it, she went to the blackboard and gave such a glib exposition of imaginary figures that the dazed teacher passed her with the highest mark." And a classmate reported a shocking instance when the principal of Mount Holyoke, Mary Lyons, asked "all those who wanted to be Christians to rise," Emily couldn't "honestly accede" and was the only one of all the women students present who "remained seated." This independence of will, mind, and imagination would inform her poetry and her life choices from that point on. She left school and returned home. (It is a topic of debate among her biographers as to whether evangelical pressure following this event caused Emily Dickinson to leave, and many believe that to be the reason, although Edward Dickinson also missed his elder daughter.) For the rest of her life, she rarely left the house and is now recognized to have been agoraphobic. She also fell victim to an eye disorder believed to have been exotropia, for which she was treated in Boston; this was nearly the only occasion upon which she would take a trip of any kind, except for a handful of journeys with her sisters to see their father, now a congressman living part of the time in Washington, DC.

Emily's journals indicate that she was aware that the "circumference" of her life was decreasing, after her lively girlhood of acting as hostess for her father's important parties and composing original verse for handmade greeting cards for her fellow students. As her daily existence narrowed, she began dressing only in white and seemingly embraced her new role as a mystical, poetic presence amid family and neighbors. She became such a hermit that she baked treats for the town's children and relatives and lowered them in a basket from her bedroom window, refusing to see or be seen by visitors. She only allowed the doctor to examine her as she walked past a half-open door, and wrote in a letter to her mentor, *Atlantic Monthly* editor Thomas Wentworth Higginson, "I do not cross my father's ground to any house in town." Emily was aware of her bizarre behavior and the effect it had, referring to herself when she did appear as "manifesting" like a ministering priestess with her token offerings of flowers, wine, and sweet cakes.

Since her death in 1886, many literary scholars have puzzled over what events might have driven her to become an invisible wraith, holed up with pen and paper. The most popular explanation is a failed romance with a mystery man, now believed to have been Reverend Charles Wadsworth, a married man she met in 1855 during one of her few outings in Philadelphia. Her letters include several fervent and openly erotic missives addressed to "Master" from "Daisy," an infantilized, victim-like "culprit" persona with a "smaller life" that she took on in these exchanges. No real agreement has ever come about as to the veracity of the "Master" letters, as they may have been an instance of what she stated to Higginson in discussing her poetry: "When I state myself, as the Representative of the Verse—it does not mean—me—but a supposed person."

Dickinson's and Higginson's literary relationship began when Emily read his article, "A Letter to a Young Contributor," in his magazine and wrote, submitting her poems, asking if they were "alive" and if she could be his "scholar." Higginson did indeed find her poetry to be living, perhaps overly so, and suggested she tone down her whimsical language and meter. But he was intrigued enough to travel to Amherst in 1870. She made an exception to her general rule and agreed to meet him in person.

Dickinson, despite her lack of exposure to the world at large, had her ambitions. She read deeply the writings of women writers from whom she drew inspiration—in particular, George Eliot and Elizabeth Barrett Browning, going so far as to display their images—and kept up with new writers with whom she identified; the Brontë sisters' explosively passionate novels were special favorites of hers. Dickinson also studied the Bible and the new Transcendentalism, upon which she based her own female- and nature-centered theology, describing the hills of Amherst as "strong Madonnas" and herself, the Poet, as "The Wayward Nun—beneath the Hill—Whose Service is to You."

Five years before Emily Dickinson passed away, a young woman, Mabel Loomis Todd, wrote a letter to her family of "the character of Amherst…a lady whom the people call the 'Myth;' she has not been outside of her own house in fifteen years.… She dresses wholly in white, and her mind is said to be perfectly wonderful." The poet had indeed captured Todd's imagination. Four years after her passing, in 1890, Todd published a volume of Emily Dickinson's poetry, a selection of 1,776 divine and abstruse poems that Emily had sewn into little booklets and tucked into a bureau.

Readers still thrill to the force of Dickinson's writing and her capacity to evoke the delicate beauty of a bee or a berry with the same scope and breadth of vision with which she addressed the big issues of God and the cosmos and sweeping emotions. The "little housekeeping person," as she described herself, was in fact one of the greatest poets of all time.

Rearrange a "Wife's" affection!
When they dislocate my Brain!
Amputate my freckled Bosom!
Make me bearded like a man!

Emily Dickinson, from poem 1737

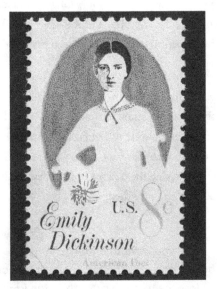

EMILY DICKINSON *agoraphobic, maybe; genius, definitely!*

MODERN MYSTICS OF THE POET'S MUSE

Warsan Shire *telling untold stories of those caught in conflict*

Warsan Shire is a British poet, editor, and activist. She was born in 1988 in Kenya to Somali parents but grew up in London, England. She has a bachelor's degree in creative writing and was named poet in residence in Queensland, Australia, in 2014. Shire is the author of the collections *Teaching My Mother How to Give Birth* (2011), *Her Blue Body* (2015), and *Our Men Do Not Belong to Us* (2015). Her poems have appeared in the anthologies *Salt Book of Younger Poets* (2011), *Long Journeys: African Migrants on the Road* (2013), and *Poems That Make Grown Women Cry* (2016), and in the musical performer Beyoncé's visual album *Lemonade* (2016). According to *New Yorker* reviewer Alexis Okeowo, her work "embodies the kind of shape-shifting, culture-juggling spirit lurking in most people who can't trace their ancestors to their country's founding fathers, or whose ancestors look nothing like those fathers. In that limbo, Shire conjures up a new language for belonging and displacement." Her poems tie together gender, sex, war, and the interplay of differing cultural beliefs. As a poet, she transforms the pain of exile and alienation.

Shire is the poetry editor of *Spook* magazine and has been a guest editor at *Young Sable LitMag*. She has read her work on three continents, and in 2013, she won Brunel University's inaugural African Poetry Prize. In 2014, she was named the first Young Poet Laureate of London, England; the next year, the editorial board of the *New York Times* quoted a passage from her eloquent poem "Home" in a piece asking the nations of the West to allow refugees more leeway in crossing borders and give them more aid:

> *you have to understand*
> *that no one puts their children in a boat*
> *unless the water is safer than the land*
>
> Warsan Shire, "Home"

Lang Leav *poignant* poems of love and loss

Novelist and poet Lang Leav was born in a Thai refugee camp as her family fled the Khmer Rouge regime. She grew up in the predominantly migrant town of Cabramatta, a suburb of Sydney, Australia. Leav is the winner of a Churchill Fellowship, a Qantas Spirit of Youth Award, and a Goodreads Reader's Choice Award. According to Publisher's Weekly, her first poetic volume, *Love & Misadventure* (2013), presaged the poetry renaissance that has been in the ascendant in the publishing world. Her later books, including her first novel, *Sad Girls*, are international bestsellers as well. With a combined social media following of 2 million, her messages of love, loss, and female empowerment continue to resonate with her many readers. Leav currently lives in New Zealand with her partner, fellow author Michael Faudet.

Amanda Lovelace *changing pain to self-worth with poetic alchemy*

Having grown up a word-devourer and an avid lover of fairy tales, it came naturally to Amanda Lovelace to begin writing books of her own. She flipped the fairy-tale script with her 2016 poetry collection *The Princess Saves Herself in This One*; the collection is a part of Lovelace's Women are some kind of magic series. She also incorporated the #MeToo movement into the series with the publication of *The Witch Doesn't Burn in This One*. The lifelong poetess and storyteller lives in New Jersey with her spouse and their ragdoll cats. She is a two-time winner of the Goodreads Choice Award for best poetry.

Nina Riggs *writing from the edge of mortality*

Poet, essayist, and memoirist Nina Riggs was only thirty-seven years old when she was first diagnosed with breast cancer—only in one small spot. But less than a year later, she received the terrifying news that her breast cancer was terminal. As it explores marriage, motherhood, friendship, and memory, Nina's writing asks: What makes a meaningful life when one has limited time? Her 2017 memoir *The Bright Hour* is about how to make the most of each day, even the ones when your body hurts. It's about the way literature, in particular the writings of Nina's direct ancestor, Ralph Waldo Emerson, and of her other muse, Montaigne, can bring solace and even be a form of prayer.

Madisen Kuhn *inward-looking inspiration*

Madisen Kuhn is a twenty-three-year-old poet (as of this writing) from Charlottesville, Virginia, whose poetry explores the topics of identity, belonging, sexuality, and mental illness. In 2015, after gaining a following on Tumblr and Instagram, she self-published *Eighteen Years*, her first collection of poetry. Her second collection, *Please Don't Go Before I Get Better*, was published in 2018 by Gallery Books. Her third volume of poems, *Almost Home*, published in 2019.

Clementine von Radics *redefining romance*

Clementine von Radics is a poet, editor, essayist, and publisher. Von Radics' work centers on the queer femme experience and how it relates to romance and the body, particularly as it involves dealing with sickness and/or disability. Von Radics' confessional and conversational style has drawn a wide audience to poetry collections including *Mouthful of Forevers*, *Dream Girl*, and *As Often As Miracles*. *Mouthful of Forevers* made it onto multiple bestseller lists and was a Goodreads Choice Award Finalist for Best Poetry Book of 2015. Clementine's second collection, *Dream Girl*, was released later that year by Where Are You Press. In total, Von Radics has sold over 100,000 books worldwide.

Clementine served as a founding collective member of Slamlandia, Portland's first and only scored slam, as well as the Slam Master at the Portland Poetry Slam, Portland's oldest and longest-running spoken-word event. Clementine was the winner of the nation-wide PSI sponsored video slam in 2016 and competed at the Individual National Poetry Slam and the Women of the World Poetry Slam. Clementine's poems from these and other events have been viewed over a million times on YouTube. Von Radics' poem "For Teenage Girls" has been featured on Huffington Post, Upworthy, and Everyday Feminism, and has since been adapted into an illustrated book. Von Radics' third collection, *In A Dream You Saw a Way to Survive*, was released in 2019.

Claudia Rankine *confronting the injustice of racism*

Claudia Rankine, born in Kingston, Jamaica, earned a bachelor's degree at Williams College and an MFA at Columbia University. She has published several collections of poetry, beginning with *Nothing in Nature is Private* (1994), which won the Cleveland State Poetry Prize, followed by *Don't Let Me Be Lonely: An American Lyric* (2004). In 2014, *Citizen: An American Lyric* won the National Book Critics Circle Award in Poetry, the PEN Center USA Poetry Award, and the Forward poetry prize.

Her work crosses genres; as critic Calvin Bedient observed, "Hers is an art neither of epiphany nor story…. Rankine's style is the sanity, but just barely, of the insanity; the grace, but just barely, of the grotesqueness." Her poems also appear in the anthologies *Great American Prose Poems: From Poe to the*

Present (2003), *Best American Poetry* (2001), and *The Garden Thrives: Twentieth Century African-American Poetry* (1996). Her play "Detour/South Bronx" premiered in 2009 at the Foundry Theater in New York. Rankine also coedited *American Women Poets in the 21st Century: Where Lyric Meets Language* (2002), *American Poets in the 21st Century: The New Poetics* (2007), and *The Racial Imaginary: Writers on Race in the Life of the Mind* (2014). Rankine has received fellowships from the MacArthur Foundation, the Academy of American Poets, the National Endowment for the Arts, the Lannan Foundation, and the Guggenheim Foundation. She was elected a chancellor of the Academy of American Poets in 2013, and in 2014, she won a Lannan Literary Award. She has taught at Barnard College, Case Western Reserve University, Pomona College, and the University of Houston.

Rupi Kaur *lyrical lines about love and life*

Rupi Kaur is a bestselling Canadian poet as well as the illustrator of two collections of poetry. Born in the state of Punjab in India, she was raised in Canada from age four; she speaks and reads Punjabi as well as English but writes only in English. She started to draw at the age of five when her mother handed her a paintbrush and told her to draw her heart out. Kaur has said that she sees her life as an exploration of that artistic journey. After completing a degree in rhetoric studies, she published her first collection of poems, 2014's *milk and honey*. The internationally acclaimed collection sold over a million copies and graced the *New York Times* bestseller list for over a year. Her second collection, *the sun and her flowers*, was published in 2017; throughout these collected works, she explores themes including love, loss, trauma, healing, migration, revolution, and the feminine. Her works have popularized Instapoetry, a new social-media driven genre of short and easily accessible poetry.

> *it is a blessing*
> *to be the color of Earth*
> *do you know how often*
> *flowers confuse me for home*
>
> rupi kaur

CHARLOTTE PERKINS GILMAN *her land is your land*

Niece of Catherine Beecher and Harriet Beecher Stowe, Charlotte Perkins Gilman also felt, in her own words, "the Beecher urge to social service, the Beecher wit and gift of words." Born in 1860, Charlotte attended the Rhode Island School of Design and worked after graduation as a commercial artist.

Exposed to the "domestic feminism" of the Beechers, the extremely sensitive and imaginative young woman had resolved to avoid her mother's fate of penniless desertion by her father and assiduously avoided marriage. But after two years of relentless wooing by artist Charles W. Stetson, Charlotte reluctantly agreed to marry. After she bore her daughter Katherine, she had the nervous breakdown that inspired her famous short story "The Yellow Wallpaper" and subsequent nonfiction accounts of her struggle with manic-depressive episodes. She wrote "The Yellow Wallpaper" for humanistic reasons: "It was not intended to drive people crazy," she said, "but to save people from being driven crazy, and it worked." Attributing her emotional problems in part to women's status in marriage, she divorced her husband and moved to California with her daughter; later, when Walter remarried, she sent Katherine to live with her father and stepmother, a move that was considered incredibly scandalous.

Although she suffered weakness and "extreme distress, shame, discouragement, and misery" her whole life, Charlotte's accomplishments are more than those of most healthy folks. A social reformer who wrote in order to push for equality for women, she lectured, founded the Women's Peace Party with Jane Addams in World War I, and wrote her best-known book, *Women and Economics*, in only seventeen days. At one point, she undertook a well-publicized debate in the *New York Times* with Anna Howard Shaw, defending her contention that women are not "rewarded in proportion to their work" as "unpaid servant(s), merely a comfort and a luxury agreeable to have if a man can afford it." Gilman was unbelievably forward-thinking for her time, even going so far as to devise architectural plans for houses without kitchens to end women's slavery to the stove so that they could take up professional occupations.

She wrote five more books pushing for economic change for women, a critically acclaimed autobiography, three utopian novels, and countless articles, stories, and poetry before her death by suicide after a long struggle with cancer in 1935.

With the passing of time, Charlotte Perkins Gilman is usually remembered only for "The Yellow Wallpaper" and for her feminist utopian novel *Herland*, in which three American men enter Herland, an all-female society that reproduces through parthenogenesis, the development of an unfertilized egg.

> *I knew it was normal and right in general, and held that a woman should be able to have marriage and motherhood, and do her work in the world, also.*
>
> Charlotte Perkins Gilman

SIMONE WEIL *the saint of all outsiders*

Complicated and committed, Simone Weil wrote with genius, though the factory and field work she felt morally driven to do hurt and scarred her hands. She was born in Paris to a wealthy and loving Jewish family in 1909 and was educated in the finest schools in France.

A politically precocious child, at ten years old, she announced to her solidly bourgeois family that her allegiance lay with the Bolsheviks and began studying the party's publications. As a teen, she showed her talent for analytical thinking and wrote extensively, albeit critically, on Marxism. She described her resistance to capitalism as coming from a social consciousness that was informed by a deep understanding of the inherent elitism, imbalance of resources, and fundamental systemic flaws that lay "between those who have the machine at their disposal and those who are at the disposal of the machine."

At the Sorbonne, her university classmates regarded Weil as brilliant but eccentric. They nicknamed her "the Red Virgin" because of the open vow of permanent chastity she had made at puberty. She had also sworn to teach free classes to rail workers, farmers, and miners and did so as an undergraduate. In later life, Weil continued to be unswervingly dedicated to the welfare and conditions of these laborers, gave most of her tiny teaching salary to them, and participated in their strikes and issues. She also worked alongside them at times as a field hand or an unskilled industrial laborer.

At university, Weil majored in philosophy and was so academically gifted that she received the top certificate for "General Philosophy and Logic" after testing above classmate Simone de Beauvoir (who came in second) as well as above all the men in the class. In *Memoirs of a Dutiful Daughter*, de Beauvoir describes Weil in a gray coverall, pockets overflowing with manifestos, surrounded by a flock of hangers-on: "She intrigued me because of her great reputation for intelligence and her bizarre getup. Great famine had broken out in China, and I was told that when she heard the news she had wept: these tears compelled my respect much more than her gifts as a philosopher. I envied her having a heart that could beat right across the world. I managed to get near her one day. I don't know how the conversation got started; she declared in no uncertain tones that only one thing mattered in the world; the revolution which would feed all the starving people of the Earth. I retorted, no less peremptorily, that the problem was not to make men happy, but to find the reason for their existence. She looked me up and down: 'It is easy to see you've never been hungry,' she snapped."

Upon graduation from the Sorbonne, Simone Weil taught high school in Le Puy for one disastrous year. Shortly after she obtained the position, Weil organized a march with the unemployed of Le Puy. Her teaching style was nontraditional, and her students couldn't pass standard midterms, but they stood loyally behind their teacher when she refused to obey her forced resignation for political activism. She regarded her firing as an occasion of gratitude and greeted it as a compliment. Her later teaching stint at Roanne went much the same way, with the exception that Anne Reynaud-Guerithault, Weil's student, had the foresight to keep her class notes. Decades later, these lectures are basic texts in philosophy courses.

Weil walked away from teaching to work as an unskilled laborer doing piecework in a factory. She couldn't keep up and barely scraped by, unable to cover her rent and food and insisting on paying her middle-class parents for every meal. Weil continued to write and extensively read and study both

Eastern and Western traditions. She began to endure severe migraines and wrote about her spiritual yearnings.

In 1937, she traveled to Spain to aid the anarchists in the Spanish Civil War. A miserable marksman, she nevertheless was at the front lines wielding a gun; she barely missed being massacred along with her unit. She stumbled into the cooking pit and accidentally stepped in hot oil. In 1938, she began writing about her visions, a series of profound mystical experiences that moved her powerfully and were published as her spiritual autobiography.

Simone Weil and her family emigrated to America in 1942 to escape Hitler's regime, but she suffered enormous guilt and went to join the Free French resistance in England. Her religious and philosophical treatises on the subject of the true nature of freedom and man's responsibility to his fellow man were regarded as a threat to the Third Reich. Though she was Jewish, she felt a great affinity for Catholicism and came to see suffering as a way to unite with God. In a letter, Weil remarked, "Every time I think of the crucifixion of Christ I commit the sin of envy."

Her moral principles would not allow her to eat more than the rations allowed in France during the Nazi occupation. Malnourished, Weil fell seriously ill and contracted tuberculosis in England. Stubbornly, she maintained her self-imposed vow of deprivation and spent her last year writing some of her primary essays. On her deathbed, she wrote "The Need for Roots," in which she outlined a book she believed could serve as the foundation stone for Europe's renaissance of justice and liberty.

Simone Weil's *Waiting for God* has become one of the best-loved spiritual writings of our age. Upon her early death at age thirty-four (deemed by some to be suicide by starvation), Weil left behind a new basis for reason and some of the most exquisitely enigmatic religious thought written by anyone of any age or faith. Other great writers and thinkers fall all over themselves in praising her. Albert Camus named Simone Weil the only great spirit of our time. André Gide ordained her the saint of all outsiders. Flannery O'Connor called Weil a mystery that should keep us all humbled, and T.S. Eliot believed she held a kind of genius akin to that of the saints.

> *A work of art has an author and yet, when it is perfect, it has something which is essentially anonymous about it.*
>
> Simone Weil

ZELDA SAYRE FITZGERALD *an unrealized talent*

Zelda Fitzgerald went straight from the quiet streets of Montgomery, Alabama, to the front page of the *New York Times* style section. Alongside her equally glittering husband, F. Scott Fitzgerald, she was like a shooting star heralding the initiation of a new age between the two world wars by living the fantasy life dreamed of by millions. And like a shooting star, she shone brightly with spectacular, even breathtaking, appeal, and then burned out—literally. Zelda died at the age of forty-eight in a fire at a mental institution after a twenty-year battle with her inner demons.

Named by her mother after a Romani queen in a novel she had read, Zelda seemed destined for glamour from the beginning. Stories of her antics circulated through Montgomery for decades, like the time young Zelda got bored on a Saturday afternoon and called the fire department to alert them to a poor young girl trapped on a rooftop, then proceeded to climb up onto her roof, kick the ladder down, and wait in glee for rescue; or the April Fools' Day prank in which she convinced the entire senior class to take the day off. From the time she was born in 1900, she seemed always in a rush to get somewhere she could never quite reach.

Always referred to as a rare golden-haired beauty, much of her magnetic attraction came from the unpredictable strength of her intensity—the sense that she could, and would, do anything at any moment. After Zelda married Scott, whose first novel *This Side of Paradise* had debuted to much acclaim, they were off on a wild ride of transatlantic partying that would capture the imagination of the entire country. From the Riviera to New York, back to Paris, and on to Washington, they always stayed at the best hotels, surrounded by society's most glamorous people, living out images from Scott's novels.

Zelda became the glamorous "First Flapper" of the Jazz Age, an era her husband had named and described as "a new generation grown up to find all gods dead, all wars fought, all faiths in man shaken." Hidden behind the glittering front-page parade, however, was a writer talented in her own right (brilliant but undisciplined, according to her husband). More tragic were the buried seeds of mental illness that began to emerge as early as 1925 when she collapsed while in Paris, leading her to begin a series of prolonged treatments. In between the parties and the emotional breakdowns, she managed to write a novel called *Save Me the Waltz*, which critics believe demonstrated her great promise.

By 1930, the shooting star that was Zelda's life had sputtered into darkness. Her seclusion in a series of mental institutions was broken up by brief periods when she would return to her family, filled with her legendary passion for life. Sadly, it is believed that had she lived in the present day of medical miracles, her terrible bouts and sensitive emotional condition could have been treated with simple medication, and her literary prowess might have come to fruition.

> *It is very difficult to be two simple people at once, one who wants to have a law to itself and the other who wants to keep all the nice old things and be loved and safe and protected.*
>
> Zelda Fitzgerald

KATHLEEN RAINE *modern mystic*

Kathleen Raine chose the path of the visionary poet in the tradition of William Blake. Her aim was "to see a World in a Grain of Sand…. Hold Infinity in the palm of your hand," in Blake's words. She was deeply committed to this life choice and devoted enormous energy to her poetry and her essays in support of her sacred craft. She has garnered a place for herself in the pantheon of scholars of mystical poetry, with fourteen volumes of her criticism published, along with four volumes on William Blake alone and a definitive analysis of Golden Dawn idealist poet William Butler Yeats.

Born in London in 1908 and schooled at Girton College, Cambridge, Kathleen Raine undertook her master's studies in the field of natural science, using the wild landscape of her youth to inform her poetry, and received a degree in

1929. She was the youngest and only woman among the Cambridge Poets of the 1930s and began to include women's writing as one of her interests when she read Virginia Woolf's *A Room of One's Own*.

Like some of her Romantic predecessors, she had numerous loves and married several times. Unlike others, however, her brilliance was recognized in her lifetime; Raine received many awards for her poetry, her translations—the most memorable of Honoré de Balzac—and her critical work. Her verse was greatly admired by her peers; esteemed poet-critic G.S. Fraser described it as "the poems of a sibyl, perhaps of a rapt visionary, but not of a saint."

Awards notwithstanding, she was given to the occasional extreme. At one time, she refused to include any poems containing "mere human emotion." She explained this shocking and extremely limiting measure for her *Collected Poems* as a commitment to "the symbolic language of…poets of the 'Romantic' tradition." Her editor and publisher convinced her not to exclude some of her finest works from the ultimate volume of her verse, but her attempt to do so certainly illustrates her radical pledge to uphold her alliance to her mystical roots: "I began as a poet of spontaneous inspirations, drawing greatly on nature and fortified by my more precise biological studies…. I have much sympathy for the young generation now reacting against material culture….. I am too firmly rooted in the civilization of the past to speak their language."

> *This too is an experience of the soul. The dismembered world that once was the whole god whose broken fragments now lie dead. This passing of reality itself is real.*
>
> Kathleen Raine, from *Isis Wanderer*

ANNE SEXTON *sonnets of singular struggle*

Born in 1928, Anne Sexton was raised in Weston, Massachusetts. Her father was a successful businessman, and her childhood was materially comfortable. However, her relationship with her parents was problematic, perhaps even abusive. After attending a boarding school, she went to Garland Junior College, a "finishing school," for a year. At age nineteen, she married Alfred "Kayo" Sexton II. While he was serving in Korea, she became a fashion model. At age twenty-five, after the birth of her first daughter, Anne suffered from post-partum depression, which led to her first breakdown, and she was admitted to a neuropsychiatric institution. Other hospitalizations followed. She continued to struggle with depression all her life before committing suicide at age forty-six.

During her treatment, however, her therapist encouraged her to write about what she was feeling, thinking, and dreaming. The therapist was impressed with her work and encouraged her to pursue this creative avenue. In 1957, Sexton began to participate in writing groups in Boston; these eventually led to forming friendships and other close relationships with the poets Robert Lowell, Maxine Kumin, George Starbuck, and Sylvia Plath. Her poems about her psychiatric struggles were published in her first book, *To Bedlam and Part Way Back* (1960); James Dickey wrote that they described the experiences "of madness and near-madness, of the pathetic, well-meaning, necessarily tentative and perilous attempts at cure, and of the patient's slow coming back into the human associations and responsibilities which the old previous self still demands."

Sexton's work is generally categorized as confessional, together with that of poets like Plath, Lowell, John Berryman, and W. D. Snodgrass. In an interview with Patricia Marx, Sexton revealed, "...[E]veryone said, 'You can't write this way. It's too personal; it's confessional; you can't write this, Anne,' and everyone was discouraging me. But then I saw Snodgrass doing what I was doing, and it kind of gave me permission." Subsequent books included *All My Pretty Ones* (1962), the Pulitzer Prize winner *Live or Die* (1966), *Love Poems* (1969), and the 1969 play *Mercy Street*. Her least confessional and most feminist volume was *Transformations* (1972), in which she retold several Grimm's fairy tales. In an ironic twist, the last collection of her work published during her lifetime was entitled *The Death Notebooks* (1974). Posthumous volumes include *The Awful Rowing Toward God* (1975), *45 Mercy Street* (1976), and *Words for Dr. Y: Uncollected Poems with Three Stories* (1978).

Sexton's writings were extremely popular during her lifetime, and she received many accolades, including a Guggenheim Fellowship, grants from the Ford Foundation, and honorary degrees; she also held professorships at Boston

University and Colgate University. Despite this literary recognition, critiques of her work usually focused on its autobiographical aspects. For instance, Dickey wrote of her poetry, "Miss Sexton's work seems to me very little more than a kind of terribly serious and determinedly outspoken soap-opera." In contrast, Beverly Fields contended that Sexton's poetry is not as autobiographical as it seems; they are poems, not memoirs. Fields analyzed many of Sexton's poems, pointing out the recurrent symbolic themes and the poetic techniques that in her view made these works so impressive.

Erica Jong, one of Sexton's earliest champions, contended in her review of *The Death Notebooks* that Sexton's artistic impact as a poet had been seriously underestimated: "She is an important poet not only because of her courage in dealing with previously forbidden subjects, but because she can make the language sing. Of what does [her] artistry consist? Not just of her skill in writing traditional poems.... But by artistry, I mean something more subtle than the ability to write formal poems. I mean the artist's sense of where her inspiration lies....There are many poets of great talent who never take that talent anywhere....They write poems which any number of people might have written. When Anne Sexton is at the top of her form, she writes a poem which no one else could have written."

SYLVIA PLATH *eloquently unfiltered*

Sylvia Plath was one of the most distinguished and potent poets of the last century. Though she lived to be only thirty before taking her own life in 1963, she was by then already known as a literary force. In the years since, her works have touched untold numbers of readers with their wrenchingly expressive treatment of the dark side of the human experience: despair, morbid fixation on death, and turbulent storms of emotion. Plath's intensely autobiographical poems explore her own inner pain and the difficulties in her troubled relationships with her parents and with her husband, fellow poet Ted Hughes. On the *World Socialist* website, Margaret Rees said of her work, "Whether Plath wrote about nature or about the social restrictions on individuals, she stripped away the polite veneer. She let her writing express elemental forces and primeval fears. In doing so, she laid bare the contradictions that tore apart appearance and hinted at some of the tensions hovering just beneath the surface of the American way of life in the postwar period."

In the *New York Times Book Review*, former US poet laureate Robert Pinsky wrote, "Thrashing, hyperactive, perpetually accelerated, the poems of Sylvia Plath catch the feeling of a profligate, hurt imagination, throwing off images and phrases with the energy of a runaway horse or a machine with its throttle stuck wide open. All the violence in her work returns to that violence of imagination, a frenzied brilliance and conviction." In the *Dictionary of Literary Biography*, essayist Thomas McClanahan said of her, "At her most articulate, meditating on the nature of poetic inspiration, she is a controlled voice for cynicism, plainly delineating the boundaries of hope and reality. At her brutal best—and Plath is a brutal poet—she taps a source of power that transforms her poetic voice into a raving avenger of womanhood and innocence."

Sylvia Plath was the daughter of Boston college professor Otto Plath and Aurelia Plath, née Schober, who had been one of Otto Plath's students. Young Sylvia lived by the seaside for the first eight years of her life, but when her father died in 1940, financial straits forced Aurelia Plath to move to Wellesley, where she became a teacher of advanced secretarial studies at Boston University. Sylvia was highly successful as a student; she won academic awards, and her poems and stories found publication in magazines while she was still a teenager. She had written over fifty short stories in advance of beginning her studies at college, which commenced after she earned a scholarship to Smith College. While a student there, Sylvia won a *Mademoiselle* magazine fiction contest; the next summer, the magazine bestowed the plum of a guest editor position on her. But during her college years, depression began to beset her, and at age twenty, Plath attempted suicide by taking sleeping pills. She survived the attempt and was treated with electroconvulsive (a.k.a. "shock") therapy in the hospital; this experience provided grist for her sole published novel, *The Bell Jar*.

In a 1958 journal entry, Plath wrote, "It is as if my life were magically run by two electric currents: joyous positive and despairing negative—whichever is running at the moment dominates my life, floods it." This passage eloquently expresses the sensation of bipolar disorder (formerly known as manic depression), and in the decades of Plath's life, there was no effective treatment available to stabilize sufferers of this biochemical illness. She did, however, return to Smith College after her hospitalization to complete her degree, going on to study at Cambridge funded by a Fulbright grant. There she met poet Ted Hughes, and in 1956, they married.

In 1960, a volume of Plath's collected poetry titled *The Colossus* was published; both *The Bell Jar* and *The Colossus* were well received, but recognition could not save her marriage from ending in mid-1962 when she discovered her husband was having an affair. Sylvia Plath was left with two children under three years of age to look after all alone, and less than a year after the end of her marriage, she killed herself by putting her head in a gas oven, after carefully making certain the gas would not reach the room where her children were. She was under the care of a physician who was visiting her daily and had prescribed an antidepressant a few days previously, but most such medications require about three weeks to have much of an effect. Plath had written of the feeling of despair that she was experiencing as "owl's talons clutching my heart."

In the months after separating from her husband, Plath had been in a period of inspiration during which she wrote most of the poems which are the foundation of her reputation, including at least twenty-six of the poems published posthumously in the poetic volume *Ariel* (1965). Noted poet Robert Lowell said of these works in his preface to *Ariel* that they were poems that "play Russian roulette with six cartridges in the cylinder." She had felt that her poetry was a side pursuit and sought success in publishing stories and other prose works, but that proved elusive. She is known primarily for the brilliance of her poetry, which is seen in context with the work of her poetic contemporaries, W.D. Snodgrass and Robert Lowell. Many of her later works dealt with what one critic called the "domestic surreal"; Plath took the objects and events of everyday life and twisted the context to evoke a feeling of nightmare in expressing her inner experience. It is notable that she was close friends with fellow poet Anne Sexton, who followed Plath in suicide eleven years later. Sexton later said of their conversations, "We talked death with burned-up intensity, both of us drawn to it like moths to an electric lightbulb, sucking on it."

Winter Trees and *Crossing the Water* found publication in 1971 in the UK; they brought to light nine previously unseen poems that had been cut from the original version of the *Ariel* manuscript. Ten years later, *The Collected Poems*, which included poems written between 1955 and the end of her life, were published; paradoxically, her former husband, Ted Hughes, edited the volume and wrote its introduction. Her headstone has been repeatedly defaced by people outraged that "Hughes," her estranged husband's last name, appeared on it. There have been many attempts to chisel it off and leave only her name on the marker. Sylvia Plath was posthumously awarded the Pulitzer Prize. *Sylvia*, a biopic in which Gwyneth Paltrow played the title role, was released in 2003. She is remembered as a groundbreaking poet "whose final poems uncompromisingly charted female rage, ambivalence, and grief, in a voice with which many women identified," in the words of writer Honor Moore.

FLANNERY O'CONNOR *literature's odd bird*

Certainly one of the most original writers in any language is Flannery O'Connor, who was born in Georgia in 1925. Her stories are all powerfully crafted, and to the vast majority of her readers, incredibly weird. For example, Hazel Motes, backwoods protagonist of her first novel *Wise Blood*, was such an ardent Christian that he founded the Church of Jesus Christ without Christ and blinded himself so he could see.

Gifted with an extraordinary ear for language and an ability to evoke an almost tactile experience of the scenes she described, Flannery O'Connor was also the odd woman out. Uninterested for the most part in the civil rights movement of her time and a devout Roman Catholic in the heart of the fundamentalist South, she wrote stories that all—in one way or another—centered around the profoundly spiritual issue of redemption. But redemption was not a simple concept for her; it was a deeply individual evolution. And to the shock of many a good Christian, her work was populated with the bizarre, the grotesque, the maimed, and the seriously disturbed, which Flannery managed to imbue with a powerful, if twisted, sense of dignity. In a way, she was the true chronicler of the underside of Southern life, and she used her characters' physical, mental, and moral disabilities to mirror their spiritual struggles.

The most formative event of her childhood was the slow, agonizing death of her father when she was just twelve. He died of lupus—the same disease that would soon take over her own life. Literary acclaim came early. After graduating from the Georgia College for Women, she joined the Iowa Writers' Workshop, where she won the Rinehart-Iowa prize for the beginnings of *Wise Blood*. The award also gave the Holt-Rinehart publishing company an option on her novel. But when Flannery turned in the early portions of *Wise Blood* to the Holt editor assigned to her, he found the manuscript "bizarre" and sent a letter offering to work with her to "change the direction" of her work into a more conventional form. Then only twenty-three years old, she politely refused and pulled the book from Holt; the editor complained that she suffered from "hardening of the arteries of cooperative sense."

Flannery's vision and style were intensely personal, and though often criticized and generally misunderstood, she never wavered. She once reflected that "I have found…that my subject in fiction is the action of grace in territory held largely by the devil. I have also found that what I write is read by an audience which puts little stock either in grace or the devil."

After she was diagnosed with lupus in 1950 at the age of twenty-five, she moved in with her mother on a dairy farm in north Georgia. By this time, lupus was controllable with massive doses of steroids, but it was a debilitating and exhausting existence. Flannery's deep religious beliefs served her well. She graciously accepted her condition and focused all the energy she had on three hours of writing each morning and raising peacocks.

When she died in 1964 at age thirty-nine, she left behind a modest body of work, including the novels *Wise Blood* (1955) and *The Violent Bear It Away* (1960) as well as collections of stories, *A Good Man Is Hard to Find* (1955) and *Everything That Rises Must Converge* (1965, published posthumously). But the impact of her words was never measured in quantity. She died recognized throughout the world as one of the truly great contemporary American writers.

I divide people into two classes: the Irksome and the Non-Irksome without regard to sex. Yes, and there are the Medium Irksome and the Rare Irksome.

Flannery O'Connor

ELLEN GLASGOW *bad advice not taken*

Another woman writer who ignored all the advice she got from men was Ellen Glasgow. In her autobiography, *The Woman Within*, she tells of the "help" she once received: "In the end, as in the beginning, Mr. Collier (a noted figure on the American literary scene) gave me no encouragement. 'The best advice I can give you,' he said, with charming candor, 'is to stop writing, and go back to the South and have some babies…. The greatest woman is not the woman who has written the finest book, but the woman who has had the finest babies.' " Fortunately, Ellen Glasgow, born in 1873 in Richmond, Virginia, and deaf by the time she was twenty, ignored Collier's advice. Instead she became a prolific writer, winning the Pulitzer Prize in 1942 for her novel *In This Our Life*.

MARY OLIVER *wild & precious poet of the heart*

In 2007, the *New York Times* described Mary Oliver as the country's bestselling poet. Her work has won numerous awards, including the Pulitzer Prize, the National Book Award, and a Lannan Literary Award for lifetime achievement. In commentary on *Dream Work* (1986) in *The Nation*, reviewer Alicia Ostriker described Oliver as one of America's finest poets, writing that Oliver was as "visionary as Emerson." Born in 1935, Mary Oliver was raised in Maple Hills Heights, outside Cleveland, Ohio. As a child, she used the nearby woods as a retreat from a difficult home, and there she would write poems. Though she attended both The Ohio State University and Vassar College, she did not receive a degree from either institution. As a young poet, Oliver was deeply influenced by Edna St. Vincent Millay; she even briefly lived in Millay's home and helped Norma Millay organize her sister's papers. After meeting her eventual life partner, Molly Malone Cook, the couple moved to Provincetown,

Massachusetts, where the surrounding Cape Cod landscape found its way into her work. Known for its clarity and expressive reliance on imagery involving the natural world, Oliver's poetry is grounded in a sense of place and in the nature tradition of the Romantic movement.

Critics took notice of her early on, and 1983's *American Primitive*, her fifth book, won a Pulitzer Prize. *Dream Work* (1986) continued her quest to "understand both the wonder and pain of nature," according to *LA Times* book reviewer Holly Prado. Striker of *The Nation* declared Oliver "among the few American poets who can describe and transmit ecstasy while retaining a practical awareness of the world as one of predators and prey." She started to transition to more personal realms in 1992's *New and Selected Poems*, which won the National Book Award. Writing in the *LA Times Book Review*, critic Susan Salter Reynolds noted that Oliver's early poems were nearly always oriented toward nature and seldom examined the self. In contrast, Oliver presents her own voice constantly in her later works. Nonetheless, Oliver continued to celebrate the natural world in her works *Winter Hours: Prose, Prose Poems, and Poems* (1999), *Why I Wake Early* (2004), *New and Selected Poems, Volume 2* (2004), and *Swan: Poems and Prose Poems* (2010). Oliver has been compared by literary critics to other great American lyric poets and celebrators of nature such as Marianne Moore, Elizabeth Bishop, Edna St. Vincent Millay, and Walt Whitman.

A prolific writer, Oliver published a new book every year or two. Her main themes continued to be the intersection between the human and the natural world. The books she wrote late in life include *A Thousand Mornings* (2012), *Dog Songs* (2013), *Blue Horses* (2014), *Felicity* (2015), *Upstream: Selected Essays* (2016), and *Devotions: The Selected Poems of Mary Oliver* (2017). She held a chair at Bennington College until 2001. Besides the Pulitzer Prize and National Book Award, Oliver also received fellowships from the Guggenheim Foundation and the National Endowment for the Arts; she was a winner of the American Academy of Arts & Letters Award, the Poetry Society of America's Shelley Memorial Prize, and the Alice Fay di Castagnola Award.

Mary Oliver lived in Provincetown, Massachusetts, and Hobe Sound, Florida, until her passing at age eighty-three in early 2019.

JOY HARJO *"I sang...a song to call the deer"*

Joy Harjo is a poet, author, activist, and musician who was born in 1951 in
Tulsa, Oklahoma; she is a member of the Mvskoke (Muscogee/Creek) Nation
and was named Poet Laureate of the United States, the first Native American
ever to hold the position, in the summer of 2019. Young Joy went to high
school at a BIA (Bureau of Indian Affairs) boarding school. She then began her
post-secondary studies at the Institute of American Indian Arts, then went on to
earn a BA from the University of New Mexico and an MFA from the University
of Iowa Writers' Workshop Creative Writing Program. She draws on First
Nations storytelling and oral history traditions and incorporates feminist and
social justice movements in her poetry; indigenous myths, symbols, values, and
ethics are also found in her writing. Her work is connected to the natural world.
It is also frequently autobiographical and focuses on survival and the limitations
of language. Her poems resonate with a sense of place, including not only the
Southwest and Southeast regions but Hawaii and Alaska as well. Her 1989
prose poetry collection *Secrets from the Center of the World* paired color photos
of Southwestern landscapes with Harjo's poems. Within her poetry, prayer-
chants and images of animals communicate spiritual experiences.

She published her first book of poetry, *The Last Song*, in 1975. Her seven
books of poetry have won her many awards and fellowships, including the
New Mexico Governor's Award for Excellence in the Arts, the William Carlos
Williams Award from the Poetry Society of America, the Ruth Lilly Prize in
Poetry, and the Lifetime Achievement Award from the Native Writers Circle of
the Americas.

Besides writing poetry, Harjo is a noted teacher, singer, and saxophonist. For
many years, she performed with her band, Poetic Justice; currently, she tours
with the group Arrow Dynamics. She is a songwriter who has released four
albums: *Native Joy for Real*; *She Had Some Horses*, also the name of one of her
most well-known poems; *Winding Through the Milky Way*; and *Red Dreams, A
Trail Beyond Tears*. In 2009, Harjo won a Native American Music Award for
Best Female Artist of the Year. Since then, she has been performing her one-
woman show, *Wings of Night Sky, Wings of Morning Light*; she is currently at
work on a musical play, *We Were There When Jazz Was Invented*. She has taught

creative writing at the University of Illinois at Urbana-Champaign and the University of New Mexico and is currently Professor and Chair of Excellence in Creative Writing at the University of Tennessee at Knoxville.

Her recent books include a book for children and young adults, *For a Girl Becoming* (2009), a prose and essay collection entitled *Soul Talk, Song Language* (2011), and a volume of poetry, 2015's *Conflict Resolution for Holy Beings*. C. Renee Field said of her, "To read the poetry of Joy Harjo is to hear the voice of the Earth, to see the landscape of time and timelessness, and, most important, to get a glimpse of people who struggle to understand, to know themselves, and to survive."

KIM ADDONIZIO *street poems, city dreams, and more*

Kim Addonizio was born in 1954 in Washington, DC, the daughter of former tennis champion Pauline Betz and sports writer Bob Addie. After briefly attending and dropping out of both Georgetown and American University, she moved to San Francisco, where she earned both her BA and MA at San Francisco State University. She has remained in the Bay Area, where she raised daughter Aya Cash with partner Eugene Cash, a Buddhist teacher, and currently lives in Oakland. Addonizio has received many awards for her work; these include fellowships from the Guggenheim Foundation and the National Endowment for the Arts, a Pushcart Prize, a John Ciardi Lifetime Achievement Award, and the San Francisco Commonwealth Club Poetry Medal. Her poetry is known for its grit, sharp-edged wit, and streetwise sense of narrative.

She produced two early volumes of poetry: 1994's *The Philosopher's Club* and the verse novel *Jimmy & Rita* in 1997, which introduced her unflinching approach to writing about life, death, drugs, and love. In 1997, Addonizio cowrote *The Poet's Companion: A Guide to the Pleasures of Writing Poetry* with Dorianne Laux, a text focused on the process and craft of writing poetry. A *Library Journal* reviewer said of *The Poet's Companion* that it was "head and shoulders above" most other writing textbooks. In 2009, she published another poetry guide called *Ordinary Genius: A Guide for the Poet Within*, which details Addonizio's insights into the craft and creative process of writing, including writing exercises and Addonizio's own writing experiences—along with sample rejection slips!

Addonizio published a third poetry collection in 2000, *Tell Me*, which was nominated for a National Book Award. *Tell Me* was followed by 2004's *What Is This Thing Called Love* and 2009's *Lucifer at the Starlite*, in which she continued to deliver an insightful and incisive view of humanity and city life. She also released two short story collections, 1999's *In the Box Called Pleasure* and *The Palace of Illusions* in 2015. In 2016, both her poetic volume *Mortal Trash* and her memoir *Bukowski in a Sundress: Confessions from a Writing Life* were published. Interestingly, she has also coedited the 2002 anthology *Dorothy Parker's Elbow: Tattoos on Writers, Writers on Tattoos*. Besides poetry, short stories, and her nonfiction works, Addonizio has also found time to write novels, including *Little Beauties* (2005) and *My Dreams Out in the Street* (2007), which returned to her verse novel characters Jimmy and Rita, scraping by in San Francisco. Writer Andre Dubus III said of *My Dreams Out in the Street*, "Kim Addonizio writes like Lucinda Williams sings, with hard-earned grit and grace about the heart's longing for love and redemption, the kind that can only come in the darkest dark when survival no longer even seems likely."

> *Writing is an ongoing fascination and challenge, as well as being the only form of spirituality I can consistently practice. I started as a poet and will always return to poetry—both reading and writing it—for that sense of deep discovery and communion I find there. There are only two useful rules I can think of for aspiring writers: learn your craft, and persist. The rest, as Henry James said, is the madness of art.*
>
> Kim Addonizio, interviewed in *Contemporary Authors*

CHAPTER FOUR

....

Banned, Blacklisted, and Arrested
Daring Dissidents

Writers turned radicals and renegades, the women featured here were not just inspired; they were inflamed by their own activist muses. This is an especially gutsy group, both brilliant and brave, whose incendiary books got them in the hottest water, outcasts who paid the price and were (usually posthumously) embraced as leaders. Here we have the lesbian novelists who chose jail over the closet, political idealists whose unrelenting stance on behalf of their often just causes cost them their livelihood, and pioneering women who refused to be held back by gender, scandalizing society, and husbands alike.

Imagine the price Anna Akhmatova paid for her refusal to go along with the pressure of the Communist Party during the purges—left with no food, no heat, her husband executed, and her son jailed in the long, hard Russian winters. Never once did she give in, though, and her poetry was crystallized by hardship and grief into diamondlike perfection. Consider the shock of novelist Radclyffe Hall, once lauded and awarded for her writing, then put on trial for her gender-bending opus. Consider how it must have felt to go from critical darling to unpublishable pariah. Ponder the pressure to rat out and cave in that playwright Lillian Hellman and the Algonquin Roundtable along with Dorothy Parker endured during the McCarthy scare, only to find themselves blacklisted out of a living.

Though their books were banned and their reputations blackened, these viragos rose like so many phoenixes from the ashes of their burned books and have regained all that was lost to them, though usually not during their own lifetimes. Nadine Gordimer, the anti-apartheid novelist, has been one of the exceptions—she received a Nobel Prize and witnessed a sea change in her native South African government, which pivoted from trying to oust and exile her to prizing her as their greatest writer. Stalwart warriors of the written word, it is to these women that we as readers and writers owe the most gratitude.

> *Poetry ennobles the heart and eyes, and unveils the meaning of all things upon which the heart and eyes dwell. It discovers the secret rays of the universe, and restores us to forgotten paradise.*
>
> Dame Edith Sitwell

SAPPHO *the literato of Lesbos*

Lyric poet Sappho is universally regarded as the greatest ancient poet. She came to be known as the "tenth muse." Although scholars can't agree whether Homer even existed, Sappho's work was recorded and preserved by other writers. An unfortunate destruction of a volume of all her work—nine books of lyric poetry and one of elegiac verse—occurred in the early Middle Ages, engendering a search for her writing that continues even now. The Catholic Church deemed her work to be far too erotic and obscene, so they burned the volume containing her complete body of work, thus erasing what could only be some of the finest poetry in all of herstory.

Known for her powerful phrasing and intensity of feeling, erotic and otherwise, Sappho's poetry is immediate and accessible to the reader. Upon reading Sappho, you can feel that you know her, her ecstatic highs as well as the depth of her pain and longings.

Sappho is believed to have been married to a wealthy man from the island of Andros, and she had one daughter. She taught at a small college for girls who were devotees of music and poetry, and, it is thought, of Aphrodite. One haiku-like fragment reports that she "taught poetry to Hero, a girl athlete from the island of Gyra." She was banished to Sicily for some time, but the majority of her life was lived on the island of Lesbos. Much of her work, her most lustful in fact, is written to other women, whom she exalts for their beauty, often achieving a poetic frenzy of desire. She also writes for her brother Charaxus and makes the occasional reference to the political arena of the ancient world she inhabited.

Legend has it she flung herself to her death in the sea after being rejected by the beautiful youth Phaon. This event, real or not, has been the subject of several subsequent works, ranging from a section of Ovid's *Heroides* to plays by John Lyly in 1584 and by Percy MacKaye in 1907.

To Atthis

Though in Sardis now,
she thinks of us constantly
and of the life we shared.
She saw you as a goddess
and above all your dancing gave her deep joy.
Now she shines among Lydian women like
the rose fingered moon
rising after sundown, erasing all
stars around her, and pouring light equally
across the salt sea
and over densely flowered fields
lucent under dew. Her light spreads
on roses and tender thyme
and the blooming honey-lotus
Often while she wanders she remembers you,
gentle Atthis,
and desire eats away at her heart
for us to come.

Sappho

SAPPHO *The tenth muse*

MADAME ANNE LOUISE GERMAINE DE STAËL
Napoleonic nemesis

You know you have really been banned when the self-appointed ruler of the world exiles you! Germaine de Staël was a noblewoman of French-Swiss descent who took full advantage of the educational opportunities her upbringing afforded her. Her father was Jacques Necker, a banker and general manager of the finances of the French monarchy who was a minister in the court of Louis XVI. Her mother was Suzanne Curchod, who prior to her marriage to De Necker was engaged to Edward Gibbon, author of the epic history *The Decline and Fall of the Roman Empire*. The Neckers were very freethinking for their day, hosting salons and encouraging their daughter, born in 1766—ten years before the revolution in America—to read and write and to form her own opinions. Germaine certainly made good on that and became the foremost female intellectual of the Romantic period.

In 1786, she married the Baron de Staël-Holstein, ambassador of Sweden. Their marriage was tumultuous, and she took many lovers, most notably the Romantic poet August Schlegel and Benjamin Constant, a writer with liberation politics who became her longtime companion. In Paris, Madame de

Staël convened a salon, a hotbed of politics and culture. She invited in new and established writers, artists, and thinkers alike.

Her praise of the German State prompted Napoleon to banish her from France. She picked up her life and moved to an estate she maintained in Switzerland at Coppet on Lake Geneva, where she assembled another equally dazzling group of cerebral companions, including Jean-Jacques Rousseau, Lord Byron, and Percy Bysshe Shelley.

As a writer, de Staël greatly influenced the Europe of the day with her cardinal work *On Germany*, as well as a nonfiction sociological study of literature, her novels *Corinne of Italy* and *Delphine*, and her memoir, *Ten Years of Exile*, published in 1818.

Corinne is her best-loved work, a daring story of an affair between a brilliant Italian woman and an English noble that explores themes of purity, free love, the place of domesticity, Italian art, architecture, geography, politics, and woman as genius as seen through the Romantic lens. Even today, Madame de Staël has not quite escaped her banned status. At this writing, there is no English translation of *Corinne* in print, and prior to the most recent one, there had been no new translation of the novel in nearly a hundred years, despite de Staël's status as one of the preeminent women of letters of all time.

> *Wit consists in knowing the resemblance of things which differ and the difference of things which are alike.*
>
> Madame de Staël

MADAME DE STAËL *Liberated even before France*

HARRIET BEECHER STOWE *civil warrior*

Most schoolchildren are taught that Harriet Beecher Stowe was an extremely creative young woman who, almost accidentally, wrote a book that tore America apart. The truth is that *Uncle Tom's Cabin* was written with precisely the intent to publicize the cruelty of slavery and to galvanize people to act. It came as no surprise when her book was banned in the South as subversive. (It still makes lists of banned books today.)

Extremely bright even as a child, Harriet was keenly interested in improving the lot of humanity. Born in 1811, she grew up in a large family as one of nine children. Her father was a Calvinist minister; her mother died when she was five. She was very attached to her older sister, Catherine, who founded the Hartford Female Seminary. The year 1832 found the Beecher family leaving their longtime home of Litchfield, Connecticut, and moving to Cincinnati, right across the Ohio River from Kentucky. From this vantage point so much closer to the South, Harriet had much greater exposure to slavery. A young, idealistic student of theology, Harriet was horrified. Her brothers became involved in the antislavery movement and were extremely vocal about their feelings. Harriet, for her part, aided a runaway slave.

In 1836, Harriet met Calvin Stowe, one of the professors of religion at her father's seminary and married him, eventually bearing him six children. Around this time, she discovered her love of writing, contributing articles to numerous religious magazines and papers. She also began working on her first novel, *The Mayflower: Sketches and Scenes and Characters among the Descendants of the Puritans*.

In 1850, the Fugitive Slave Acts passed Congress. It was this event that moved Harriet to write *Uncle Tom's Cabin*. She couldn't abide the inhumanity of slaves being hunted down and forcibly returned to their former owners after struggling so hard for the freedom that was their birthright. Horror stories of the torture of runaway slaves galvanized the sensitive Harriet to action, and she wrote the book with the full intention of sending out a cry against the whippings, maimings, and hangings of slaves.

Uncle Tom's Cabin or Life Among the Lowly was first run as a series of installments in *The National Era*, an abolitionist newspaper. Upon publication in book form in 1852, Stowe's work was very well received. The entire printing of five thousand copies sold out in two days, and three million copies of the book were sold around the world before the advent of the Civil War! Harriet had outstripped her wildest dreams and had truly fired the first shot in what was to become the war between the States. She also received critical acclaim from such literary luminaries as Henry Wadsworth Longfellow and Leo Tolstoy, who declared *Uncle Tom's Cabin* the "highest moral art." Abraham Lincoln himself called Harriet "the little lady who made this big war."

Harriet's strategy was to show the extremes of slavery, culminating in the savage beating of the gentle old slave, Tom. The world was captivated by Stowe's dramatic story. Reviled in the South, Stowe met all her pro-slavery detractors with dignity, even going so far as to publish a critical *Key to Uncle Tom's Cabin* and writing a second novel about the plight of slaves, *Dred: A Tale of the Great Dismal Swamp*.

Basking in her fame, she and her husband traveled in Europe, where she was lauded everywhere she went. In the 1860s, she wrote a series of books on her husband's recollections of his childhood in New England. These are considered to be some of the first of what came to be called "local color writing" in New England.

> *I won't be any properer than I have a mind to be.*
>
> Harriet Beecher Stowe

HARRIET BEECHER STOWE *The "little lady who made this big war," according to Abe Lincoln*

ANGELINA EMILY AND SARAH MOORE GRIMKÉ *forces to be reckoned with*

The Grimké sisters were raised in the South in the early 1800s like Scarlett and her sisters in *Gone with the Wind*, but unlike the fictional characters, the sisters grew up hating slavery. The privileged duo, two of twelve children, had all the Southern advantages of private tutors and training in the arts at their palatial Charleston, South Carolina, home and were brought up to be good high-church Episcopalians. But they first showed their abolitionist spunk when Sarah was twelve; she was caught teaching a slave to read and write, a criminal offense. Because Angelina supported her, they were both punished.

Soon, they left the South. Sarah moved to Philadelphia in 1821 and converted to Quakerism because of its antislavery beliefs. Angelina followed eight years later.

A fervent abolitionist writer, Angelina had a nose for publicity and got her passionate condemnation of slavery published in William Lloyd Garrison's magazine, the *Liberator*. She followed this up with a pamphlet entitled, "An Appeal to the Christian Women of the South," which tried to appeal to women's consciences in opposing slavery: "But, perhaps you will be ready to query, why appeal to women on this subject? We do not make the law which perpetuates slavery. No legislative power is vested in us; we can do nothing to overthrow the system, even if we wished to do so. To this I reply, I know you do not make the laws, but I also know that you are the wives and mothers, the sisters and daughters of those who do; and if you really suppose you can do nothing to overthrow slavery, you are greatly mistaken…. 1st. You can read on the subject. 2nd. You can pray over this subject. 3rd. You can speak on this subject. 4th. You can act on this subject."

Her appeal created a storm of controversy. In her hometown of Charleston, the postmaster burned all copies and put out a warning that Angelina had better never return to the South. At that point, sister Sarah took up the charge and attacked the religious defense of slavery in her "Epistle to the Clergy of the Southern States."

The fearless siblings took their abolitionist act on the road, speaking to mixed crowds of men and women. This raised the hackles of so-called "proper" society—ladies were not supposed to appear in public with men who were not their husbands, and women were not supposed to lecture or preach—and those who disapproved returned fire with a printed attack from the Massachusetts clergy that was preached to every available congregation in 1837. In it, the clergy condemned women reformers and preachers, issuing a caution regarding any female who "assumed the place and tone of man as public reformer…. Her character becomes unnatural."

The irrepressible duo fired back in grand style with letters in the *Spectator* and in Sarah's book, published in 1838, *Letters on the Equality of the Sexes and the Condition of Women*. This was a brilliant manifesto declaring woman as absolutely and naturally endowed with equal rights, and that the only "unnatural" behaviors being performed in American society were those of men suppressing women. Later, Angelina became the first woman in America to speak to a legislature when she presented her antislavery petition, signed by 20,000 women, to the Massachusetts state legislative body.

The duo fought against slavery and for women's rights their whole lives. They even caught the eye of Henry David Thoreau, who described them as "two elderly gray-headed ladies, the former in extreme Bloomer costume, which was what you might call remarkable."

> I ask for no favors for my sex. I surrender no claim to equality. All I ask our brethren is, that they will take their feet from off our necks and permit us to stand upright on the ground which God designed us to occupy.
>
> Sarah Grimké

BOOKS ABOUT BOOKSTORES

Women who love books open bookstores, and write about it in fiction and nonfiction:

Bookstore: The Life and Times of Jeanette Watson and Books & Co by Lynne Tillman

Shakespeare and Company by Sylvia Beach

The Bookshop by Penelope Fitzgerald

84, Charing Cross Road by Helene Hanff

RADCLYFFE HALL *soldier of fortune*

Preferring tweeds to tulle, pioneering lesbian novelist Radclyffe Hall spent her life trying to find herself, but ironically, she has nearly been lost to modern readers. One can only hope that a biographer as accomplished as Diane Middlebrook will rescue her, alongside Billy Tipton, from the dustbin of history. What we do know about Hall from Lady Una Troubridge, her lover for more than a quarter-century, is that she was born in 1886 in Bournemouth, Hampshire, and had a wretched childhood. Abandoned by her father by age three and ignored by a mother preoccupied with a romance, Marguerite Radclyffe Hall began her life with a sense that she didn't matter. This was greatly reinforced when Mrs. Hall remarried an Italian singing instructor who matched both mother and father in his cruel inattention to the growing girl.

By her teens, Radclyffe was alternately calling herself Peter or John and had one relatively unsuccessful year at King's College, during which she struggled with her sexuality. At the age viewed as adulthood by most, twenty-one, Radclyffe inherited an immense trust fund and tried to forge a new life with her only familial tie, her mother's mother, with whom she moved to Kensington. Hall's grandmother had been the only source of affection up to that point. The relationship seems to have set a pattern for her future, as her first serious romance was with a woman twenty-three years her senior. The older woman, Mabel Veronica Batten, was a music patron with a secure position in society. She mentored Radclyffe and urged her to give up sports and take up more acceptable pursuits such as books and horses. Mabel Batten provided Hall with the education and nurturing she had missed in her childhood and molded her into an intellectual seeker and writer. Batten died in 1916, and Una Troubridge's friendship during Hall's grief led to love; they remained partners, living together until Hall's death in 1943.

Hall dressed as a man in beautifully cut custom tweed suits and short clipped hair, which was shocking to some gentlefolk. A serious writer, Hall published several books of poetry and two novels before winning public attention in 1926, when she won the Femina–Vie Heureuse Prize and the James Tait Black Memorial Book Prize for *Adam's Breed*, a novel of religious awakening.

Her writerly accomplishments didn't garner her nearly the attention—nay, commotion—she stirred up with her 1928 novel *The Well of Loneliness*. The book depicted a troubled but full and uncloseted pursuit of happiness. With an introduction written by no less an authority than psychologist Havelock Ellis, Hall told the story of a girl named Stephen Gordon whose father wanted a son, not the daughter born to him. Stephen is a lively protagonist, pursuing other women lustily and working with the London Ambulance Column during World War I. Stephen professes to be a man inside a woman's body trying to deal with the difficulties of the congenital invert in this portrayal of the lesbian as a biological blight.

Though it's problematic for the more psychoanalyzed and feminism-aware reader of today, *The Well of Loneliness* was extremely radical for 1928. It exploded like one of the WWI shells that wounded Stephen's ambulance passengers. The scandal following Hall's new book concluded with a trial and the book's prohibition. Several notables such as Virginia Woolf and Vera Brittain rushed to her defense, but English courts banned the book. Just like the subjugation of sapphists, both the character Stephen Gordon and her creator, Radclyffe Hall, were squelched. Radclyffe Hall followed her banned opus with several religious fictions, but the prosecution caused her to limit the scope of her subject matter, and, sadly, she was largely ignored from then on.

> *The coming of war had completely altered the complexion of her life, at all events for three years.*
>
> Radclyffe Hall, from *Miss Ogilvy Finds Herself*

ANNA AKHMATOVA *brilliance unbowed*

A poet and writer of the highest personal and literary standards, during her lifetime, Anna Akhmatova was denied her deserved international reputation as one of Russia's greatest writers. Of noble birth, Anna Gorenko was born in Odessa, Ukraine, in 1889. In an indication of the independent nature that became her hallmark, she changed her name when she was seventeen. She went on to study law at university, but always wrote poetry. During this time, she met Nikolai Gumilev, a poet and literary critic with whom she shared a love of literature. They married in 1910 and together threw themselves into Acmeism, a literary school dedicated to clear and tightly constructed verse in reaction to the ruling style of the day, Russia's popular symbolism. Gumilev, a romantic figure with distant dreams, took off for Africa, leaving his new bride on her own for great stretches of time. Focused on her poetry, Anna had her first book, *Evening*, published to high praise in 1911. A striking Tartar beauty, Akhmatova developed a great following and read to doting crowds at an underground cabaret, the Stray Dog café. That same year, she gave birth to son Lev. Domesticity was not Anna's destiny, however, and Gumilev's mother, who despised Anna, took Lev from her.

While the couple explored their craft, chaos surrounded their home in St. Petersburg. Toward the end of the nineteenth century, Russia's tsars had been under attack politically, and parties formed illegally in opposition to the royal rulers. One such party was the Social Democratic Party, a faction of which was led by Vladimir Lenin. Lenin's sect, the Bolsheviks, were fairly radical in their fervor to effect the overthrow of the tsar, seemingly by any means.

Anna's second book, *Rosary*, debuted in 1913 to even greater fervor, so much so that the book inspired a parlor game in which each person took turns quoting a verse until the entire book was finished.

Anna's success caused strife at home; her husband was quite jealous, and they both began relationships outside the marriage. The two writers eventually divorced, and Anna married Voldemar Shileiko, but she and her first husband maintained a friendship. Anna suffered a severe shock when the Bolsheviks executed her first husband in 1921 over a trumped-up charge of a plot to overthrow the government. Anna's book *Anno Domini* came out the following year. She in turn suffered at the Bolsheviks' hands and became something of a pariah.

This was a time of great hardship when Anna's household rarely had enough to eat or fuel for heat. Most of their friends left Russia during this terrible time of persecution. By 1924, in the wake of Lenin's death, Stalin took power and wreaked even greater terror upon the Russian people. During his "purges," millions of people were killed and imprisoned, including any writer who didn't bow to the dictates of the new regime. Anna's son Lev was arrested in 1933 and 1935, and her writings were banned from 1925 to 1940. She turned to literary criticism and translation and Pushkin scholarship. During the 1930s, she courageously composed an epic poem, "Requiem," in honor of Stalin's victims, which went unpublished in Russia until 1987. In 1940, an anthology of her poetry, *From Six Books*, was published, only to be withdrawn a month later.

During Germany's siege of the Soviet Union in 1941, Anna urged the women of Leningrad, formerly St. Petersburg, to be brave during this war. Astoundingly, the government, aware of her status as a beloved and respected figure in Russian culture, had asked her to do this even though they forbade the publication of her writing.

The postwar period found Anna briefly enjoying popularity once again, but Andrei Zhadanov, Secretary of the Central Committee, soon removed her from the Writer's Union and decreed a ban on her writing, destroying a book of her poems and decrying her as "half nun, half harlot." Expulsion also lost Anna her ration card and any means of access to food and supplies, forcing her to ask for support from friends until the end of her life. in 1949, Lev Gumilev was arrested again and imprisoned for seven years, until Nikita Khrushchev took leadership of the party, denounced Stalin, and released prisoners.

Anna's poetry was published in the late 1950s with heavy-handed censorship. Now a legend to the youth of Russia for her staunch idealism and enduring dedication to poetry, budding Russian literati including Joseph Brodsky sought her out as a connection to pre-Communist Russia. A great admirer of the great lady of letters from the "Silver Age" of Russian poetry who had survived the devastation of the Communist holocaust, Brodsky named Anna Akhmatova "the muse of keening" for her elegies for the dead and for a dying culture.

*We thought: we're poor, we have nothing, but when
we started losing one after the other
So each day became remembrance day.*

Anna Akhmatova, from *In Memoriam, July 19, 1914*

ҚАЗАҚСТАН
KAZAKHSTAN 60

Анна Ахматова (1889-1966)

Ақын, жазушы

ANNA AKHMATOVA *Persecuted and starved by
Stalin, she refused to stop writing*

KATE CHOPIN *dangerous deb*

Nineteenth-century ladies were not encouraged to write frankly about sex.
Anyone who did most certainly found herself in the center of a hot scandal.
Kate Chopin's *The Awakening*, fiercely brave for the time and hugely
controversial, was an open and honest examination of her own sexuality and
coming of age. Published in 1899, *The Awakening* was attacked as an essentially
vulgar story; libraries banned the book immediately, even in her hometown
of St. Louis. Chopin was refused publication of her collection of short stories
shortly thereafter and experienced a sense of failure after the storm of bad
press and the rejection of her book. She died in 1904, having been paid only
a pittance in royalties, and her brave book fell into the shadows until it was
rediscovered by feminist scholars in the 1960s.

Kate Chopin came from a privileged St. Louis background as the daughter
of a French Creole aristocrat mother and a hardworking, very successful Irish
immigrant father. Born in 1850 and raised as a strict Catholic, Kate had a
primly proper Victorian upbringing and emerged as a debutante and belle of

the great river town. Her successful debut in St. Louis society led to a happy marriage to a wealthy New Orleans Creole cotton trader, Oscar Chopin, who bought a plantation in Cloutierville. The couple had several children, and Kate was in all ways a dutiful and devoted wife and mother who always kept journals and diaries.

The loss of her husband to swamp fever in 1883 devastated Kate Chopin. During her mourning period, she went beyond her self-described "scribbles" and started writing seriously. The bereaved family returned to St. Louis and set about creating a new life. Critics received Kate's stories as charming portraits of "genteel Creole life." (But the same set of reviewers who lauded the storyteller turned savage when Chopin presented *The Awakening*.)

After settling back in her hometown, Kate Chopin was befriended by her family physician, Dr. Frederick Kohlbenheyer. A voracious reader who eschewed religion, he directed Kate to read Aldous Huxley, Charles Darwin, Gustave Flaubert, Sarah Orne Jewett, Emile Zola, and Mary Wilkins Freeman.

One recommended writer particularly struck a chord with Kate: Guy de Maupassant. The Frenchman's espousal of liberty and his disregard for literary convention greatly inspired her. This pursuit of freedom came across clearly in *The Awakening*'s central female character, Edna Pontellier. This is obvious in Edna's choice about her way of life and demand for equality in the boudoir: "I give myself where I please."

The critics who preferred corsets laced up tightly and women kept in their place dashed Kate Chopin's daring. Their burial of her book for more than fifty years was an enormous loss to American readers. Shortly after its "rediscovery" in the 1960s, the novel was hailed as a classic and a feminist breakthrough. Scholars poring over the body of Chopin's work have gone on to identify the elegant subversiveness in her early stories. There has been speculation that the shame and discredit over her novel caused her illness and death, but the blow she struck for women's erotic liberation still reverberates nearly a century later.

> *When she abandoned herself a little whispered word escaped her slightly parted lips. She said it over and over under her breath; free, free, free!*
>
> Kate Chopin, from "The Going Away of Liza"

Throughout history, reading was often seen as corrupting to women. Many men believed that women should not be taught to read unless "they wish to be nun," as the nobleman Philippe de Novare wrote in the fifteenth century, "since they might otherwise, coming of age, write or receive amorous missives."

MERIDEL LE SUEUR *prairie populist*

Perhaps it was Meridel Le Sueur's birth at the turn of the twentieth century that marked her for a forward-thinking life filled with dreams of a better tomorrow. A native of Murray, Iowa, in America's heartland, Meridel and her stepfather (Mama and Papa were long gone) made their way south, living in Kansas, Oklahoma, and Texas. Her childhood was fairly unusual; her stepfather was a virulent Socialist, and the women he exposed Meridel to were fellow radicals. Her lifelong idealism was ingrained at an early age, and she lived a much freer life than most women of her day. As prolific as she was opinionated, Le Sueur was taught to work for the common political cause and learned the best way she could help spread the word was by writing about it. Ultimately, she came to make her living mostly as a journalist and biographer, receiving positive notice for her short stories, poetry, and novels as well.

Le Sueur's life and work were one and the same. She lived in an anarchist commune for a time with none other than the fiery radical Emma Goldman. She and her like-minded associates were strenuously advocating for a redistribution of wealth to American laborers and the poor. As a journalist, Le Sueur was firmly entrenched in the leftmost political viewpoint; her bibliography includes the *Anvil, Daily Worker, Dial, New Masses, Pagany, Partisan Review*, and *Scribner's*. Her nomadic childhood made for a sense of adventure, and she also acted in early Hollywood and did a stint as director of the Little Theater in Sacramento, California.

Le Sueur never gave up her writing, though, and turned to recording the stories of plain folk in her social history, *North Star Country*. This endeavor attracted much attention for its use of the common parlance and its faithful ear to source material. She married a labor organizer, Harry Rice, and raised a family. In 1928, Le Sueur had the first of two daughters, and she began to think of her daughter's life ahead of her. Her early stories of America's ordinary townspeople and farmers evolved into studies of working class and pioneer women and the solidarity between them.

The McCarthy era was not good to Meridel; she was blacklisted as a Communist sympathizer. The blacklisting led to critical neglect of her writing even though she was just hitting her stride with her prizewinning prairie populist papers. She wrote several books that went unpublished due to her damning blacklisted status until near the end of her life.

Though she labored in obscurity, Meridel Le Sueur continued the bright positivism that marked her politics and her passions. Throughout her life, she believed a better world was inevitable and that this wonderful new future would soon be "birthed." Her book *Ancient Rites of Ripening*, written at the age of eighty-two, bespeaks her anticipation of society's rehabilitation through the influence of women. In her later years, she also wrote books for children with an emphasis on nature and values, including *Sparrow Hawk* and the story of Abe Lincoln's mother, *Nancy Hank of Wilderness Road*. Ever the diligent dreamer, Meridel Le Sueur sang the song of the unsung.

> *Old men and tramps lie on the grass all day. It is hard to get work. Many people beside Karl are out of work. People are hungry just as I am hungry. People are ready to flower and they cannot.*
>
> Meridel Le Sueur, from *Annunciation*

DAWN POWELL *angel on toast*

Dawn Powell, contemporary of Theodore Dreiser, Ernest Hemingway, and John Dos Passos, could drink them under the table and hold her own in hard living as well as in the prodigious output of novels. Her life and work have certainly taken plot twists even she might have been hard pressed to dream up, from toast of the town to scattered bag of bones.

An Ohio girl who escaped to Greenwich Village as a permanent visitor, Powell looked at Manhattan and its citizens with a comic's eye. An original voice whose titles alone—*The Wicked Pavilion, The Locusts Have No King, Angels on Toast*—evince a creativity and cheek, Powell wrote fifteen slightly shocking books which quickly slid out of print, and after her death in 1965, were held hostage by a literary executrix who refused all queries until threatened with legal action.

Powell's life didn't fit the cookie-cutter mold of flag-waving World War II. A friend of Dorothy Parker, she was an inveterate writer of juicy letters and essays such as her "drinking tour" of New York City. Her open marriage to an impoverished alcoholic poet, her scarily silent savant son, and her predilection for bar fights made the satirist risqué reading.

Though not the best candidate for white-glove publicity, the critically regarded Powell did appeal to a small number of select sophisticates. Ernest Hemingway named her "his favorite living writer," and Gore Vidal campaigned to have her acknowledged as America's greatest comic writer.

Low sales aside, however, Dawn Powell watched her brilliant career go up in smoke and suffered intolerable indignities even after her death. She willed her body to science only to have her corpse thrown into a field by a day crew of convicts, her remains mixed in with a jumble of paupers, prostitutes, and orphans.

While most '40s readers might not have been ready for Dawn Powell's send-ups of New York society, a new generation is primed for her wicked and wise pen. Discovered by literary champion Tim Page, a Pulitzer Prize-winning critic for the *Washington Post*, Powell's novels are finally seeing the light of day. Page, who describes her as having "a dark, mordant attitude toward that world [that] rankled," happened upon Dawn while reading Edmund Wilson's decades-old essay declaring Powell the equal of Evelyn Waugh and Muriel Spark. For a few thousand dollars, Page bought her entire literary estate and donated it to Columbia, and he is shepherding her blacklisted backlist back into print.

I give them their heads. They furnish their own nooses.

Dawn Powell, speaking about her characters

LENORE KANDEL *word alchemist*

Bold and beautiful, Lenore Kandel's poetry attempts to bridge the chasm between the sacred and the sexual, between religion and the eroticism of the body. Replete with tantric symbolism, her works reflect Buddhist influence as well as a celebration of the corporeal.

Born in New York City in 1932, Lenore moved with her family that same year to Los Angeles when her father, the novelist Aben Kandel, got a movie deal for his novel, *City in Conquest*. A minor classic, the film starred Jimmy Cagney.

By the age of twelve, Lenore had decided to become a Buddhist and started writing. She spent the next fifteen years going to school and voraciously reading "everything I could get my hands on, particularly about world religions." In 1959, she began sitting zazen in New York and had three short collections of her poetry published. In 1960, she moved to San Francisco and met Beat poet Lew Welch at East-West House, a co-op started by Gary Snyder and other Zen students.

Welch was on the scene in the early part of the San Francisco Renaissance, the collection of poetry schools pulled together by Robert Duncan in his efforts to create a poetry community after the fall of Black Mountain College in North Carolina. Lew was intertwined with the Beat and the Black Mountain College scenes, but refused to align with any one school of poetry. He was friends with Jack Kerouac, Lawrence Ferlinghetti, and fellow Buddhist scholar Gary Snyder.

Lenore recalls how she ended up in San Francisco, living at the East-West House and studying with Shunryu Suzuki Roshi. "I'd been meaning to come to San Francisco, and I decided to come here for a weekend and I stayed. I met Lew and all the people in that whole trip, and when Jack came into town, we all went to Big Sur."

An omnivorous reader, Lenore was very familiar with Jack Kerouac's work and was especially fond of *On the Road*. His poetic style piqued her interest, and she found him to be inspiring to her own work. He too was impressed by her intensity and intellect as well as her physical stature. It would be in Jack's *Big Sur* that he would immortalize Lenore as "a big Rumanian monster beauty of some kind I mean with big purple eyes and very tall and big (but Mae West big), but also intelligent, well read, writes poetry, is a Zen student, knows everything." She was tall, indeed taller and larger than Lew, yet she carried a distinctly female aura, and was described by Carolyn Cassady in *Off the Road* as a "Fertility Goddess."

Like many of the other Beats, her work provoked controversy. *The Love Book*, her most notorious collection of what she calls "holy erotica," sent shock waves throughout the San Francisco Bay Area when it was published in 1965. After police raids on the Psychedelic Shop and City Lights bookstore in San Francisco, the chapbook was deemed pornographic and obscene. When challenged in court, Lenore defended it as a "twenty-three-year search for an appropriate way to worship" and an attempt to "express her belief that sexual acts between loving persons are religious acts."

Although Lenore has been incapacitated since 1970 from a motorcycle accident with her then-husband, Hell's Angel William Fritsch, she still reads voraciously on all subjects, including religion, and writes daily. "It's important to be a speaker of truth, especially if you put your words out there, they gotta be true."

Kenneth Rexroth once praised the fluidity and striking austerity of her words, which he saw as delineating the sharp paradoxes of the body and soul. Disregarding convention, she delves into the essence of being, writing provocative poems that intend to stir the heart as well as the mind. The strong Buddhist influence in her work molds emotions into stanzas, giving shape to the ineffable. Lenore Kandel is a true word alchemist.

> *we have all been brothers, hermaphroditic as oysters*
> *bestowing our pearls carelessly*
> *no one yet had invented ownership*
> *nor guilt nor time*
>
> Lenore Kandel, from "Enlightenment Poem"

DORIS LESSING *observant eye & fearless fighter against racism and war*

Doris Lessing was a British-Rhodesian (Zimbabwean) novelist, essayist, and playwright who won the 2007 Nobel Prize in Literature, with the Swedish Academy particularly recognizing her epic work in writing about "the female experience" with "skepticism, fire, and visionary power." Lessing, for her part, when previously under attack as "unfeminine" for having expressed female anger and aggression, responded, "Apparently what many women were thinking, feeling, [and] experiencing came as a surprise." She explored the politics of race as well as gender in her writing and examined the role of the family and the individual in society in new ways.

Doris May Lessing (née Tayler) was born in 1919 in Persia, now known as Iran, to British parents; her father, who had lost a leg during military service in World War I, had met her mother, a nurse, at the hospital where he recuperated from the amputation. Her family moved to the south of Africa, and Doris grew up on her parents' farm in Southern Rhodesia (now Zimbabwe). Her mother was very strict and eventually sent her to a convent school, then an all-girl high school, from which Doris, age thirteen, soon dropped out, ending her formal education. But she read, and then read some more: Kipling, Stevenson, Scott, and Dickens; then Tolstoy, Dostoevsky, Stendhal, and D.H. Lawrence. To free herself from her hidebound mother's sphere of influence, she left home at fifteen, taking a job as a nursemaid and reading further in sociology and politics. She also began to write and sold two stories to South African magazines that year. In 1937, she moved to Salisbury (now Harare), where she worked as a telephone operator for a year. Then at nineteen, she married and had two children; but feeling trapped, she left her new family in 1943. Doris joined a local leftist reading club, a group of people "who read everything, and who did not think it remarkable to read." She was drawn to Gottfried Lessing, one of its central members; they soon married, and in 1946, had one child.

When her second marriage ended in 1949, Lessing was done with colonial Africa. She moved to London with her young son; her first novel, *The Grass is Singing*, was published there in 1950. The novel established Lessing's reputation: it explores the shallowness, complacency, and contradictions of white colonialist society in Southern Africa. Her Children of Violence novel series (1952–1969) was majorly influenced by her involvement with communism and rejection of the wifely domestic role; like many of her fiction works, the five novels were influenced by her own life experiences to the point of being semiautobiographical. She was banned from South Africa and Rhodesia in 1956 due to her frank writing about the dispossession of Black Africans by white settlers and her anti-apartheid activist work. She also actively campaigned against nuclear arms.

In 1962, she broke new ground with *The Golden Notebook*; according to Natasha Walter of *The Independent*, it "rip[ped] off the masks that women were accustomed to wearing, and…show[ed] up the dangers and difficulties that many women encounter if they try to live a free life in a man's world." The protagonist, Anna, eventually goes through a nervous breakdown. Only through disintegrating is she is able to come to a new and more authentic wholeness. Lessing returned to the theme of pressures to socially conform in her next two novels, *Briefing for a Descent into Hell* (1971), an amnesia story, and *The Summer Before the Dark* (1973); Kate, its heroine, comes to a degree of enlightenment through another breakdown process. In the late 1970s and early 1980s, she further explored the role of the family and the individual in society in her five-volume Canopus in Argos series of "space fiction." The fourth of these speculative fiction works was adapted as an opera by noted composer Philip Glass, with Lessing writing the libretto. They later collaborated again on a 1997 opera adaptation of the second Canopus in Argos novel.

She returned to realistic fiction with *Diary of a Good Neighbour* (1983) and *If the Old Could…* (1984); but in a twist, submitted them for publication under the name Jane Somers. After numbers of rejections, they were printed, but only in small runs that did not receive much reviewer attention. Naturally, when their true authorship was revealed, the books were reissued and much more warmly received. In 1985's *The Good Terrorist*, Lessing returned to politics with the story of a group of political activists who set up a squat in London. 1988's *The Fifth Child* carried on her themes of alienation and the dangers of a closed social group.

In 1995, she received an honorary degree from Harvard, and that year, she visited her daughter and grandchildren in South Africa, the first time she had been there in four decades; in an ironic twist, she was acclaimed there as a writer on the very topics for which she had been banished in 1956. She also collaborated with Charlie Allard on an early SF graphic novel, 1995's *Playing the Game*. Her autobiography was published in two parts: *Under My Skin* (1994), followed by *Walking in the Shade: Volume II of My Autobiography 1949–1962* (1997). In 2007, Doris Lessing was awarded the Nobel Prize for Literature. The entire lecture she gave to the Swedish Academy when accepting the prize was published under the title *On Not Winning the Nobel Prize* (2008). She also produced a book of essays based on her life experiences and the novel *Alfred and Emily* (2008), which explored the lives of her parents. She lived to be ninety-four, publishing more than fifty novels in total.

> There [was] a whole generation of women, and it was as if their lives came to a stop when they had children. Most of them got pretty neurotic—because, I think, of the contrast between what they were taught at school they were capable of being and what actually happened to them.
>
> Doris Lessing

NOBEL LADIES

From 1901 to 1999, only nine women received this most prestigious award for literature:

Selma Ottilia Lovisa Lagerlöf (1909), "in appreciation of the lofty idealism, vivid imagination, and spiritual perception that characterize her writings."

Grazia Deledda (1926), "for her idealistically inspired writings which with plastic clarity picture the life on her native island and with depth and sympathy deal with human problems in general."

Sigrid Undset (1928), "principally for her powerful descriptions of Northern life during the Middle Ages."

Pearl Buck (1938), "for her rich and truly epic descriptions of peasant life in China and her biographical masterpieces."

Gabriela Mistral (1945), "for her lyric poetry which, inspired by powerful emotions, has made her name a symbol of the idealistic aspirations of the entire Latin American world."

Nelly Sachs (1966; shared), "for her outstanding lyrical and dramatic writing, which interprets Israel's destiny with touching strength."

Nadine Gordimer (1991), "who through her magnificent epic writing, has—in the words of Alfred Nobel—been of very great benefit to humanity."

Toni Morrison (1993), "who in novels characterized by visionary force and poetic import gives life to an essential aspect of American reality."

Wislawa Szymborska (1996), "for poetry that with ironic precision allows the historical and biological context to come to light in fragments of human reality."

NADINE GORDIMER *the alienist*

South African Nadine Gordimer's unstinting literary resistance and refusal to back down is a testimony to bravery. She dared to face powerful opposition to her writing about government-sanctioned racial oppression, repressive policies that normalized daily beatings, jailings, and murder. Three of her books were banned, but she never stopped exercising her right as an artist to openly state her condemnation of apartheid. Beloved by anyone who had read her fiction and hated by anyone who feared the polemic potential of her writing, this defiant woman helped create the post-apartheid future she envisioned in her novels.

She was born in 1923 in the East Rand town of Spring, the daughter of a Latvian jeweler father, who had been drawn to the diamond mining money in the southern Traansvaal tip of Africa, and a hypochondriac British mother. Nadine was frequently kept home from convent school by her housebound mother, and at age nine, felt the urge to pick up a pen. By the time she was fifteen, *Forum* magazine had published a story by the gifted girl.

Through her father's business she came to learn of the terrible conditions in the diamond mines. The mines, which were managed by whites who sent Black South Africans into the hot and dangerous shafts, quickly taught the sensitive and observant Nadine about the stratified society ordained by the white Afrikaners in power. The sense of injustice that informed her sensibility as a young woman only developed with time as the incongruity of colonial cruelty increased in a country straining toward modernity.

Gordimer claims as a major influence Georg Lukacs, a Hungarian philosopher and essayist whose writings at the turn of the century and beyond helped shape European realism. Gordimer's first book, *The Lying Days*, was published in 1953 and traced the impact of Europeans in South Africa. From this historical beginning, her short stories and novels amplified her complaint against acculturated segregation and a caste system enforced upon the people native to Africa. Reviewer Maxwell Geismar declared her fiction "a luminous symbol of at least one white person's understanding of the black man's burden."

The novels that have emerged as a legacy for this outcast writer include *The Conservationist*, *July's People*, and *Burger's Daughter*. Readers praise Gordimer's painterly quality of rich detail, full characterization, and symbolic setting, though a few object to the mechanics of her narratives, judging it as unfashionable to see a story through to completion. A few critics even carp at her attention to race and lack thereof to feminism, but her own insistence is to speak to the issues of humankind, inclusive of race and gender.

Decried by whites in her home country, Nadine Gordimer continued to live in Johannesburg despite pressure to leave. For a time, recognition of her skill as a writer and the validity of her message only came from abroad. The *New Yorker* published her often, and she taught in American universities during the politically restive '60s and '70s. After the Soweto uprising in South Africa, her powerful novel *Burger's Daughter* was banned for its potential to inflame insurrectionists. In response, Gordimer focused with greater intent on her political opposition to apartheid and cofounded the Congress of South African Writers. She went on to work in documentary films along with her son, Hugo Cassirer, and published nonfiction about subjects specific to South Africa. She refused the Orange Award because of its restriction to women, but joined the exclusive ennead of Nobel-winning women in 1991. The academy had previously passed her over a number of times, and she herself stated, "I had been a possible candidate for so long I had given up hope." Gordimer said upon accepting the prize that as a young writer, she feared that the isolation of apartheid separated her from "the world of ideas," but eventually came to realize that "what we had to do to find the world was to enter our own world fully first. We had to enter through the tragedy of our own particular place."

At great personal risk and in spite of the constant threat of ostracism, this woman's pen marked the dividing line between white and Black South Africa and the ways of life on either side. With unmatched lucidity, she examined the rituals of persecution and life under the fist. Her Nobel Prize for Literature was a tribute to her singular courage and life's work of telling the truth through fiction.

> *Perhaps more than the work of any other writer, the novels of Nadine Gordimer have given imaginative and moral shape to the recent history of South Africa.*
>
> Jay Dillemuth, *The Norton Anthology of English Literature*

NADINE GORDIMER *For a time, this anti-apartheid novelist was popular everywhere in the world but her native South Africa*

> *I was gravely warned by some of my female acquaintances that no woman could expect to be regarded as a lady after she had written a book.*
>
> Lydia M. Child

MAYA ANGELOU *how the caged bird sings*

"You're going to be famous," Billie Holiday told Maya Angelou in 1958, "but it won't be for singing." Billie was prophetic. Mute as a child, Maya Angelou went on to become one of the most powerful voices in American society. Who can ever forget the powerful, precise voice that dominated the 1993 inauguration of President Bill Clinton as she recited "On the Pulse of Morning"?

Her journey from silence to worldwide acclaim is an amazing one, told by her in five autobiographical volumes: *I Know Why the Caged Bird Sings*; *Gather Together in My Name*; *Singin' and Swingin' and Getting' Merry Like Christmas*; *The Heart of a Woman*; and *All God's Children Need Traveling Shoes*. But it is precisely one of these volumes, *Caged Bird*, that has garnered her the dubious distinction of being one of the most banned writers in the United States. The powerful depiction of her childhood rape has caused schools and libraries across the country to deem it "inappropriate."

Maya Angelou was born Marguerite Johnson in St. Louis in 1928. At age three, she was sent to live with her paternal grandmother in Stamps, Arkansas, a town so segregated that many Black children, she claimed, "didn't, really, absolutely know what whites looked like."

" 'Thou shall not be dirty' and 'Thou shall not be impudent' were the two commandments of Grandmother Henderson upon which hung our total salvation," she remembers in *I Know Why the Caged Bird Sings*. "Each night in the bitterest winter we were forced to wash faces, arms, necks, legs and feet before going to bed. She used to add, with a smirk that unprofane people can't control when venturing into profanity, 'and wash as far as possible, then wash possible.' "

When Maya Angelou was seven, while on a visit to her mother, she was raped by her mother's boyfriend. She reported this to her mother, and the man was tried and sent to jail, which confused and upset the young girl. When he was killed in prison for being a child molester, she felt responsible and spent the next five years in total silence.

With the help of her grandmother and another woman, Bertha Flowers, who introduced her to literature, Maya slowly came out of herself, graduating at the top of her eighth-grade class, and moved to San Francisco to live in her mother's boarding house. She went to school, took dance and drama lessons, and in her spare time, became the first African American streetcar conductor in

San Francisco. An unplanned pregnancy made her a mother at age sixteen, and she later had a short-lived marriage with Tosh Angelos; still later, she adapted his surname and took the nickname her brother used for her as her first name.

Working at a variety of odd jobs, she eventually began to make a living as a singer and dancer. In 1954, she toured Europe and Africa with a State Department-sponsored production of *Porgy and Bess*. Upon returning to the United States, she created a revue, Cabaret for Freedom, as a benefit for Martin Luther King, Jr.'s Southern Christian Leadership Conference (SCLC). Later, at King's request, she served as the northern coordinator for the SCLC.

In 1961, she and her son left the United States with her lover, Vusumzi Make, a South African freedom fighter, to live in Cairo, where she tried to become the editor of the *Arab Observer*. The Egyptians wouldn't consider a woman in such a position, and her lover was equally outraged. She left him and moved to Ghana, where she lived for five years, working as an editor and writer for various newspapers and teaching at the University of Ghana. She loved the people of Ghana. "Their skins were the colors of my childhood cravings: peanut butter, licorice, chocolate, caramel. There was the laughter of home, quick and without artifice," she wrote in *All God's Children Need Traveling Shoes*. But she never felt completely accepted and returned to the United States in 1966.

She began writing books at the urging of James Baldwin, who had heard her tell her childhood stories and encouraged her to write them down. (Another story has it that it was a chance meeting with cartoonist Jules Feiffer that was the impetus.) But the multitalented dynamo continued to act in both plays and films and began to write poetry and plays as well. In 1972, she became the first African American woman to have a screenplay produced, the Björkman film *Georgia, Georgia*, and she won an Emmy nomination for her performance in *Roots*. When *I Know Why the Caged Bird Sings* was made into a TV movie, Maya wrote the script and the music. She also wrote and produced a ten-part TV series on African traditions in American life. She has received many honorary degrees, serves on the board of trustees of the American Film Institute, and is Reynolds Professor of American Studies at Wake Forest University in Winston-Salem, North Carolina.

Her autobiographies have been criticized for not being completely factual, to which she once replied, "There's a world of difference between truth and facts. Facts can obscure the truth. You can tell so many facts that you fill the stage but haven't gotten one iota of truth." Despite *I Know Why the Caged Bird Sings* having been one of the most banned books in America, she is deeply respected throughout the country for her amazing capacity not merely to survive, but to triumph.

The ability to control one's own destiny...comes from constant hard work and courage.

Maya Angelou

MAYA ANGELOU *One of the most often banned writers in America for her completely honest autobiography*

JUDY BLUME LEADS WITH FIVE

Books written by women that have been challenged, burned, or banned in the United States in recent years include:

The Clan of the Cave Bear by Jean Auel

The Color Purple by Alice Walker

Diary of a Young Girl by Anne Frank

Flowers in the Attic by V.C. Andrews

Forever by Judy Blume

Harriet the Spy by Louise Fitzhugh

I Know Why the Caged Bird Sings by Maya Angelou

Iggie's House by Judy Blume

It's Okay If You Don't Love Me by Norma Klein

Love Is One of the Choices by Norma Klein

Ordinary People by Judith Guest

Silas Marner by George Eliot

Are You There, God? It's Me, Margaret by Judy Blume

Uncle Tom's Cabin by Harriet Beecher Stowe

The Handmaid's Tale by Margaret Atwood

Changing Bodies, Changing Lives by Ruth Bell

A Wrinkle in Time by Madeleine L'Engle

Beloved by Toni Morrison

The Joy Luck Club by Amy Tan

Little House in the Big Woods by Laura Ingalls Wilder

Bridge to Terabithia by Katherine Paterson

Blubber by Judy Blume

Heather Has Two Mommies by Lesléa Newman

The Headless Cupid by Zilpha Keatley Snyder

The Great Gilly Hopkins by Katherine Paterson

On My Honor by Marion Dane Bauer

My House by Nikki Giovanni

Tiger Eyes by Judy Blume

My Friend Flicka by Mary O'Hara

While the Judy Blume works listed above are not her only titles to have encountered such efforts at censorship—*Then Again, Maybe I Won't* and *Superfudge* have also been banned—the Blume books on this list put her on the list of most challenged authors, as the five titles above have been banned no less than 237 times in total.

Literature is my Utopia. Here, I am not disenfranchised. No barrier of the sense shuts me from the sweet, gracious discourse of my book friends. They talk to me without embarrassment or awkwardness.

Helen Keller

CHAPTER FIVE
....

Prolific Pens
Indefatigable Ink

There are those women who, once they have begun writing, cannot be stopped. These writers have drawn upon oceans of ink and forests of paper to create entire libraries of their own. They are an especially amazing breed because, as any of them can tell you, writing is probably one of the loneliest professions—necessitating a good relationship with yourself and full access to the recesses of your imagination. Most of these women have chosen a singular genre, a specific field they till again and again, reaping new characters, crimes more heinous than ever, or still steeper heights of passion.

These women have legions of readers and rabid fan bases ever eager for the next book and the next book and the next book after that. Dame Barbara Cartland penned more than a thousand original works, earning her the title of the "Queen of Romance." As destiny would have it, life imitated art when she was dubbed a dame by the royals themselves and, by marriage twice over, came to be related to Princess Diana, whose life and tragic death could have come from the pages of an especially riveting Cartland page-turner.

America's Danielle Steel is her colonial cousin in spirit. She has written so many bestsellers that she, too, has led a life as close to that of a princess as is possible in the provinces. She has a stately fifty-five-room mansion with its own ballroom in San Francisco, equipped with a thirty-foot hedge for privacy from the paparazzi. Her apartment in Paris was previously owned by none other than his purple musical majesty, Prince. She bears the additional distinction of being the bestselling living author of all time, as well as the fourth bestselling author *ever*.

And then there's the sisterhood of crime—Agatha Christie, Dorothy Sayers, and Sue Grafton, whose skillful sleuths have become as beloved as the writers themselves, inspiring countless television shows, miniseries, and feature films. Who can forget Angela Lansbury as Miss Marple personified, dominating Sunday night television for years?

What drives an author to write one book after another? Maybe there is a clue in the unforgettable question asked by Sayers' character Harriet Vane, in her novel *Gaudy Night*: "Do you find it easy to get drunk on words?"

CHRISTINA GEORGINA ROSSETTI *poetic pre-Raphaelite*

Well-loved poet Christina Rossetti was born to the arts. Her father, a poet in exile from his home in Italy for his politics, moved to England and taught at King's College. Her two brothers were the equally gifted pre-Raphaelite painter Dante Gabriel Rossetti and William Michael Rossetti, a poet and editor of a widely known periodical of the day. Christina's older sister Maria, a writer and scholar of the Italian poet Dante, joined an Anglican order and dedicated her life to serving the needy.

Shyly beautiful and alleged to be hot-tempered, Christina was used repeatedly as a model for the Virgin in the memorable paintings of her brother. Her sharp wit was appreciated by the friends her brother Dante Gabriel would invite to their home—Edmund Gusset, William Shields, Sir Edward Coley Burne-Jones, Coventry Patmore, William Morris, Richard Garnett, and Walter Watts-Dunton, as well as writers, political thinkers, and all manner of creative, intelligent people who gathered to exchange views, artistic and otherwise.

Christina pursued poetry passionately. Influenced by John Keats, she wrote prodigiously from a young age. By age seventeen, her first collection had been published. She wrote more than 1,100 poems, many resonant with a religious fervor, while both she and her mother worked at a day school to help support the family.

One of the most widely read women writers of her day, achieving both acclaim and respect, Christina fell in love with her brother's friend, the artist James Collinson, when she was thirty. But she ultimately turned away from the relationship because of a difference in religious doctrines. Deeply spiritual, she had ascetic tendencies, abandoning the game of chess because she was "too eager to win." She wouldn't attend plays (sinful), prayed several times a day, and fasted and confessed regularly. She memorized the Bible and could quote it at length. Ten years after spurning Collinson, Christina gained the affections of her father's student, Charles Bagot Cayley. Once again, his faith didn't garner her approval, and she refused her last chance for love and marriage.

At the age of forty-one, she fell ill with Graves' disease. Christina kept to herself after that, always writing, until she died from cancer in 1894 at the age of sixty-four. When she was on her deathbed, her brother was shocked when she screamed out, "My heart then rose a rebel against light." She died as her brother had portrayed her, a virgin, her passions poured out on the page.

> *Pain is not pleasure*
> *If we know*
> *It heaps up treasure—*
> *Even so!*
> *Turn, transfigured Pain,*
> *Sweetheart, turn again,*
> *For fair thou art as moonrise after rain.*

> *Christina Rossetti*

EDITH WHARTON *"historic ravager"*

I wonder what Edith Wharton, Henry James, and Jane Austen would think if they realized that, long after the span of their own lifetimes, their works rule Hollywood as favorite novels-turned-movies? Henry James, mentor to Edith Wharton, would probably not be surprised at their dominion over the current fascination with social mores. James couldn't seem to reach high enough heights with his hyperbolic praise for Wharton, calling her "the whirling princess, the great and glorious pendulum, the gyrator, the devil-dancer, the golden eagle, the Fire Bird, the Shining One, the angel of desolation or of devastation, the historic ravager."

Born in 1862 in New York to a wealthy family, Edith Newbold Jones was from the privileged background she described in her novels. She summered in Newport, Rhode Island, and lived abroad in Italy, Germany, and France, riding out the depression that immediately followed the Civil War and affected her family's fortunes.

She was homeschooled by a governess and prepared for her debut into society at the age of seventeen. Unlike many of her fellow debs, however, Edith Newbold Jones was already writing. The teenager took her craft very seriously, at sweet sixteen producing a volume of poetry that her parents had printed despite their misgivings about her pursuit of writing as a career. She also read insatiably, devouring the books in her father's library; otherwise, she claimed, her "mind would have starved at the age when the mental muscles are most in need of feeding.... I was enthralled by words.... Wherever I went they sang to me like the birds in an enchanted forest."

In 1885, she married Edward "Teddy" Robbins Wharton, the son of an elite Boston family. Teddy was thirteen years her senior, and they quickly created a life reflecting their genteel parentage. Sadly, Edith's husband was not her intellectual match and had few interests in that direction; he was more interested in having children, which rapidly became a major issue in their marriage. They remained childless and kept up a façade of compatibility to the world.

Meanwhile, Edith struggled to write on a level in accordance with her own ambitions, finally getting her inspiration and footing after a voyage through the Greek Isles. She then wrote and published a series of very well-received articles for *Scribner's*, *Harper's*, and *Century*, even collaborating with a Boston architect, Ogden Codman, Jr., on a book entitled *The Decoration of Houses* in 1897. Despite these efforts, she fell into a severe depression she called her "paralyzing melancholy" and had to get a "rest cure" for nervous illnesses.

In 1899, two collections of her short stories were published, coinciding with the end of her nervous condition and depression. After this, she consigned herself over to writing completely and published a book a year for the remainder of her life. In 1905, with *The House of Mirth*, she achieved the height of her power and range as a writer. Subsequent novels, such as *The Reef*, *The Custom of the Country*, and *The Age of Innocence*, caused comparisons to her friend and counselor, as a "female Henry James." She was clearly on her own track, while also making a study of symbolists such as Joseph Conrad and the modern musical compositions of Igor Stravinsky.

Edith Wharton began an affair with a member of her literary circle, James' protégé Morton Fullerton. While the Whartons' marriage crumbled around them, Edith and Teddy sold their stately Lenox home, "The Mount," and moved to France. Teddy suffered a nervous breakdown and checked into a Swiss sanatorium; he divorced Edith in 1913. She remained in Europe, making a home for herself in France.

Edith Wharton found the life of a divorcée to be revelatory. She could travel, entertain, write, and have friendships with men without any interference. She also got involved in public and political affairs, and among her significant charity works, founded shelters for refugees during World War I.

In 1930, Edith Wharton was elected to the National Institute of Arts and Letters, and four years later, to the American Academy of Arts and Letters. She lived to the age of seventy-five, at which time she had a fatal stroke. During her life of letters, she contributed enormously to the novel form. Her subtlety and sophistication continue to bring her books to many readers, far beyond the bounds of the new elite of Hollywood.

> *The books ARE in bad shape, and as some are interesting it's a pity. I told Miss Hatchard they were suffering from dampness and lack of air.... I'm so fond of old books that I'd rather see them made into bonfire than left to moulder away like these.*
>
> **Edith Wharton, from *Summer***

EDITH WHARTON *Henry James called her "the angel of desolation or of devastation"*

BELOVED BOOKS ON WRITING BY WOMEN WHO LOVE BOOKS TOO MUCH

Escaping into the Open by Elizabeth Berg

Writing the Natural Way by Gabriele Lusser Rico

The Writing Life by Annie Dillard (who also deserves mention for her great book *Living by Fiction*)

Writing Down the Bones by Natalie Goldberg

Becoming a Writer by Dorothea Brande

Bird by Bird by Anne Lamott

If You Want to Write by Brenda Ueland

One Continuous Mistake by Gail Sher

MARGARET MEAD *no stopping her*

Margaret Mead still stirs controversy in some circles for her pioneering work in social anthropology. Like Rachel Carson, she wrote a scientific study that crossed over into the general population and became a bestseller. For this, she received derision from the academic community. But that didn't bother this free spirit, who was one of the first women to earn a PhD in anthropology.

Margaret was fortunate to be born in 1901 into a family of academics who disregarded convention and put learning and involvement in the world ahead of society's rules. The firstborn of five children, Margaret was the child of Edward Mead, a professor who taught finance and economics at the University of Pennsylvania, and Emily Fogg Mead, a teacher, sociologist, and ardent feminist and suffragist. Margaret was homeschooled by her very able grandmother, a former teacher and school principal.

Margaret's apple didn't fall too far from the tree when she started The Minority, an anti-fraternity at DePauw University, where she was attending. Bored, she transferred to Barnard College, where the academic standards were more in accordance with her needs. Originally an English major, in her senior year Margaret attended a class given by anthropologist Franz Boas, a virulent opponent of the school of racial determinism. She also met Ruth Benedict, then Boas' assistant, who encouraged Margaret to join her at Columbia under Boas' instruction. Margaret agreed and went on to graduate school after marriage to a seminary student, Luther Cressman. Soon after, true to her heritage as a freethinking Mead, Margaret went against her mentor Boas' urgings that she do fieldwork with America's First Nations peoples, a pet project of his; instead she followed the beat of her own drum, setting off for Polynesia to explore island cultures. She reasoned that the islanders were better subjects because they had been less exposed to outside cultures and were therefore less assimilated than Native Americans.

She was absolutely right. She wrote her field studies after living with and working alongside the Samoans for three years. The date was 1926. Divorcing Luther, she married Reo Fortune, and in 1928 published *Coming of Age in Samoa*, a groundbreaking work that shocked some circles with its frank and completely objective report of, among other things, sexual rituals and practices among the Samoans. Nearly overnight, Margaret was a superstar, which was fairly rare for anthropologists and even rarer for twenty-seven-year-old female anthropologists!

After a stint at the American Museum of Natural History, Margaret headed to New Guinea. Her resulting book, *Growing Up in New Guinea*, was another huge hit in both academic and popular circles. While in New Guinea, Margaret met and fell in love with fellow anthropologist Gregory Bateson; after her second divorce, she and Gregory married, and she gave birth to a daughter, Mary Catherine Bateson. Margaret and Gregory worked together in New Guinea, but ultimately Gregory claimed she was stifling his creativity, and they divorced in 1943.

Margaret Mead spent the rest of her life working full tilt in anthropology. She was astonishingly prolific, publishing forty-four books and more than a thousand articles and monographs, as well as working as a curator at the American Museum of Natural History between trips into the field. She also sought to support the work of young anthropologists. At the core of all her work was an analysis of childhood development (she was the first anthropologist ever to study child-rearing practices) and gender roles, overturning many timeworn assumptions about personality and place in society for both sexes. Again and again, her studies demonstrated that there is nothing natural or universal about particular "masculine" or "feminine" roles; rather, they are culturally determined.

In her later years, she wrote a wonderful autobiography, *Blackberry Winter*, that contains her reflections on her childhood as well as on the fieldwork methods she developed. Through her prodigious output, average people came to read about and reflect on the lives of those they had previously considered "strange."

I have spent most of my life studying the lives of other peoples, faraway peoples, so that Americans might better understand themselves.

Margaret Mead

MARGARET MEAD *To some of her fellow academics,* Coming of Age in Samoa *was a sexy shocker!*

IRIS MURDOCH *fiction's philosopher*

Jean Iris Murdoch was born in Dublin in 1919. By the time of her death in 1998, she was regarded as one of the finest writers in the English language. Unlike many of her peers, she was able to cross genres and wrote philosophy and literary criticism in addition to the novels for which she became adored.

She was part of a writer's clique with fellow upstarts William Golding, author of *Lord of the Flies,* and Kingsley Amis, who authored *Lucky Jim.* Iris' first effort was *Under the Net.* She and her cohorts' books were all published in 1954, a banner year for new British fiction. The trio took their writing very seriously, as Iris explains in several essays in which she defines their work as an important new "liberal" school of fiction following in the heritage of the "best fiction makers," such as Jane Austen, George Eliot, and Leo Tolstoy's "absurd irreducible uniqueness of people and of their relations with each other." Murdoch argued very effectively that the darlings of the day, Imagists T.S. Eliot and Ezra Pound, confined characters and readers in a dry, feelingless vacuum. Murdoch, on the other hand, believed life as lived by real people to be much less tidy and much more filled with emotions, and that it was vitally important that this freedom be allowed experientially through fiction, written for a "community of free beings."

Although Jean-Paul Sartre and Murdoch might seem strange bedfellows at first, she drew much philosophic and creative inspiration from his existentialism and his avowed dedication to the cause of freedom. In London, she studied economics, and at Somerville College in Oxford, did her graduate work in classical humanities, which included studying the "great" Greek and Latin philosophers. She met Sartre in Belgium during World War II, when she was a young woman working in England's civil service. In 1947, she won a scholarship to attend Cambridge, where she met another major figure in twentieth-century philosophy, Ludwig Wittgenstein, whose beliefs were to become undercurrents in *Under the Net*, particularly his now-famous dictum from Tractatus, "Whereof we can not speak, thereof we must remain silent."

Another core Murdoch tenet in both her philosophical and fiction writing is respect for other people's differences, especially in love relationships. She claimed her novels' *raison d'être* was drawn from Sartre's "breath-taking argument" for the novel. In 1953, she wrote a tract, *Sartre: Romantic Rationalist*, one of several nonfiction works that also included *The Sovereignty of Good* and *The Fire and the Sun: Why Plato Banished the Artists*, wherein she delineated her keen interest in "goodness" outside religious restrictions, a doctrine she explained late in life as "mysticism" without the presence of God.

Murdoch found such beliefs to be fertile ground for her more than two dozen novels and countless essays; indeed, her aim was to place art over philosophy, in the belief that it is art that expresses ultimate truth. She lived a peaceful life with her husband, critic John Bayley, in a small country village in England. Bayley, who shared her interests and philosophies, has written a lovely memoir of their last years together, when she began her decline due to Alzheimer's disease, telling how he chose to care for her himself instead of installing her in a nursing home.

Now, after her death, Iris Murdoch, the friend, the wife, the philosopher, and the novelist, continues to be cherished for her uniqueness and for the gifts she so freely shared.

> *Art is about the pilgrimage from appearance to reality.*
>
> Iris Murdoch

DOROTHY L. SAYERS *mystery maven*

Born in 1893, Dorothy Sayers is one of England's most revered writers, particularly for her twelve detective novels. But she also wrote twenty works of poetry, critical essays, and plays in addition to her popular fiction, and penned forty-four short stories as well.

Educated at Oxford, where she earned honors in medieval studies and was one of the first women ever to earn a degree, she taught for several years and then gained work as a reader for publisher Basil Blackwell. Her first publication was a volume of her poetry published during this period. Sayers changed jobs in the 1920s and went to work for an advertising agency. She also made another important shift in hobbies by joining the Detection Club. This enterprise, which included fellow member G.K. Chesterton, was dedicated to raising the reputation and quality of detective fiction.

Dorothy Sayers was most effective at improving the genre by her own efforts, and for the next twenty years became the top writer of detective fiction. Her first novel was *Whose Body?*, released in 1923; eight years later, she was making a good living solely from her witty, sophisticated novels.

Her recurring character is Lord Peter Wimsey, an aristocrat who did sleuthing as a pastime. Clearly a favorite of both Sayers and her readers, Lord Wimsey is present in all but one of her detective novels. Another recurring character is Harriet Vane, a woman sleuth based on the author herself, who provided equal opportunity for both genders in the genre that became her domain. After writing *Busman's Honeymoon* in 1937, she turned to composing religious scripts for radio, as well as essays on a multitude of topics such as theology and—what else?—murder mysteries.

Dorothy Sayers' *Five Red Herrings* is regarded as one of the classics of its kind, and her oeuvre continues to sell briskly more than fifty years after her death in 1957.

> *Allow me to inform you that I never at any time either sought or desired an Oxford fellowship.... Neither was I "forced" into either the publishing or advertising profession.... Nor do I quite understand why earning one's living should be represented as a hardship. 'Intellectual frustration' be blowed! ... It was all very good fun while it lasted.*
>
> Dorothy L. Sayers, in a 1955 letter to the *Church Times*, which had erroneously described her as a wannabe Oxford don

SUE GRAFTON *W is for writer*

What is mystery writer Sue Grafton going to do when she finishes with the alphabet? Born in Louisville, Kentucky, on April 24, 1940, she lived there through her time as a student at the local university, where she studied literature. Before she found her fortune in writing detective fiction, she worked as a cashier, an admissions clerk, and a medical secretary. While struggling to support herself and three children, Grafton wrote seven novels, mostly unpublished, before she came up with her winning formula in 1982 with *A Is for Alibi*. Her twenty-five alphabetical novels (she's finished Y as of this writing) are now published in twenty-eight countries and twenty-six languages, creating reader bases in such places as Bulgaria, Estonia, and India. She has reframed the alphabet for devotees of her spunky female detective character, Kinsey Millhone, with *B is for Burglar, C is for Corpse, D is for Deadbeat, E is for Evidence*, and so on. Fans worry about "life after Z."

> *So there I was barreling down the highway in search of employment and not at all fussy about what kind I'd take.*
>
> Sue Grafton

BARBARA CARTLAND *the world's best-known romance writer*

Barbara Cartland's status as a preeminent "prolific pen" is doubtless: she wrote 623 books and sold more than 650 million copies of her novels worldwide in many languages. Even *The Guinness Book of World Records* named her as the world's top-selling author! Upon her passing on May 20, 2000, she remained the twentieth century's best-known writer of romance.

Born on July 9, 1901, this British writer went on to dominate popular fiction throughout the century. She began her writing career with a gossip column in the *Daily Express* newspaper, an ironic choice for a woman who would become the relative of one of the most gossiped-about women in the history of the world, Princess Diana. By 1925, Cartland had moved to full fiction with her debut novel, *Jigsaw*, and had been presented at court. From this beginning, she released new novels at a furious pace, with such titles as *The Ruthless Rake, The Penniless Peer*, and *The Cruel Count*, as well as several volumes of autobiography and other nonfiction works, such as *The Etiquette Book*; *Love, Life, and Sex*; *Look Lovely, Be Lovely*; and *Barbara Cartland's Book of Beauty and Health*, for which she received strong criticism due to a very old-fashioned and rather antifeminist view of women as the "inferior" gender.

This dissatisfaction passed quickly, though, and Barbara retained her crown as the world-renowned queen of romance novels. In 1950, she moved to Camfield Place, the house built by Beatrix Potter's grandfather, where Potter wrote *The Tale of Peter Rabbit*. Many movies have been based on Cartland's beloved books, including *A Hazard of Hearts, A Duel of Hearts, The Flame Is Love, The Ghost of Monte Carlo*, and *The Lady and the Highwayman*, and her position at the top of the heap is in no danger. No other writer has written so much for so many as Dame Barbara Cartland.

BARBARA CARTLAND *Princess Diana's aunt by marriage, this hardworking author of 623 books never rested on her laurels*

TAKING ROMANCE SERIOUSLY

Romance readers love their books—romance books generate approximately one billion dollars in sales yearly. And romance writers are passionate about their genre.

Founded in 1980 in Houston, Texas, by thirty-seven authors frustrated with writing conferences that seemed to ignore romance writers, the Romance Writers of America has grown into the largest national genre writers' association in the world. According to their website, the organization "provides networking and support to individuals seriously pursuing a career in romance fiction," and its eight thousand-member organization is now "considered 'The Voice of Romance.' " In 1999, RWA had more than 120 chapters throughout the world. Each summer it hosts a national conference with more than a hundred workshops and gives annual awards. To find out more, contact them via their website: www.rwa.org

MARGARET ATWOOD *oracle of Ottawa*

On at least one occasion, prodigious writer Margaret Atwood has mentioned the comic book fantasies she read as a child in Ottawa as her primary influences, but she seems much more closely aligned with the Victorians she studied in her postgraduate work at Harvard. Born in Ottawa in 1939, she traveled with her entomologist father into remote areas of northern Canada and the bush of Québec. Educated at the University of Toronto, Radcliffe, and Harvard, she knew she wanted a career in writing by the age of sixteen and started actively working toward her dream two years later as a student at the University of Toronto's Victoria College. By nineteen, she began to publish her poetry as well as articles in Victoria's literary journal, *Acta Victoriana*.

Atwood's writing often delves into the mythic, retelling Homer's *Ulysses*, for example, from the vantage point of the women who were seduced and left behind. Her novels, including *The Edible Woman, Surfacing, Lady Oracle, Life Before Man, The Handmaid's Tale*, and *Alias Grace*, give voice to the silenced. The natural world is another major theme for Atwood, as are her unique twists on the psychological. Her published work includes nine novels, four children's books, twenty-three volumes of poetry, and four works of scholarship. She also is the editor of five anthologies. A film based on *The Handmaid's Tale* was released in 1990, and her dystopian tale of women confined to a permanent underclass has now been adapted as a famed Hulu miniseries. *The Testaments*, a sequel to *The Handmaid's Tale* set fifteen years later, was published in 2019. Her novel *Alias Grace* has been released as a Canadian miniseries to great acclaim, earning a 99 percent approval rating on the Rotten Tomatoes review site. In 2016, Atwood collaborated with illustrator Johnnie Christmas to create *Angel Catbird*, a graphic novel about a scientist who, in a way similar to the Hulk and Spiderman before him, is accidentally fused in a mutation-meld with the powers and some of the body parts of an avian and a feline.

In addition to being prolific, she is also among the most awarded writers, having received more than a hundred prizes for her excellent poetry and fiction. Moreover, she is claimed by her country of origin, Canada, as having helped to establish an identity for Canadian literature. Her work in the 1970s for Anansi Press very directly aided this cause. *Survival*, which she wrote in 1972, was an attempt at "a map" for charting Canada's writers, followed by *The Oxford Book of Canadian Verse* in 1982. Her sense of place is often a theme in her fiction and poems.

Although she does not call herself a "feminist writer," Atwood said in an interview with Penguin Books that the question that drove her while writing *The Handmaid's Tale* was, "If you were going to shove women back into the home and deprive them of all of these gains that they thought they had made, how would you do it?" (She has also stated that sales of that 1990 work jumped following the 2016 election in the United States.) Strong women rising against all odds appear again and again in her work, underlining her heroine's final words in *Surfacing*: "This above all, to refuse to be a victim."

> *I'm not a very good gardener, for the same reason I wouldn't make a very good poisoner: both activities benefit from advance planning.*
>
> Margaret Atwood, from *Various Gardens*

MARGARET ATWOOD *Canada's mythic naturalist and novelist*

ATWOOD ONLINE

Those who wish to pursue their interest in Margaret Atwood's work have a variety of web sources to choose from. She herself has an official page where you can read interviews, see her answers to frequently asked questions, and even get a list of her favorite quotes at: margaretatwood.ca

DANIELLE STEEL *solid gold Steel*

America's sweetheart Danielle Steel is one of the hardest working women in the book business. She has a unique approach, differing from other prolific writers who claim to focus on one project at a time; she works on up to five books at a time, juggling storylines, writing one while editing others. Add her movie scripts and adaptations from her fiction and you have a virtuoso at work, and a very successful one. Make no mistake, however; her books are not "cranked out"; her research process alone usually takes at least three years. Once she has fully studied her subjects in preparation for diving into a book, she can spend up to eighteen to twenty hours nonstop at her 1946 Olympia typewriter.

Steel hails from New York and was sent to France for her education. Upon graduation, she worked in the public relations and advertising industries. She left these to craft a career as a writer and clearly found the work for which she was best suited. She also married and raised nine children. Never considered particularly feminist, Steel creates female protagonists in her romance novels who are powerful women, often driven career women, who juggle work, life, and love. *Palomino*, published in 1981, is centered around a woman rancher who founds a center for handicapped children; *Kaleidoscope* is the story of an orphan girl who survives a series of foster homes and recovers from rape to track down her sisters and reunite her family.

The statistics about Danielle Steel's career are staggering: 650 million copies of books in print, over fifty *New York Times* bestselling novels, and a series of Max and Martha illustrated books for children to help them deal with difficult issues such as death, new babies, divorce, moving, new schools, and other real-life problems. She has written a volume of love poems, and her 1998 book about the death of her son Nicholas Traina, *His Bright Light*, shot to the top of the *New York Times* bestselling nonfiction list upon its release. At this point, twenty-eight of her books have been adapted for films, and one, *Jewels*, garnered two Golden Globe nominations. She is listed in *The Guinness Book of World Records* for the amazing run of one of her titles on the *Times* bestseller list for 381 weeks straight. Since that accomplishment, another Steel title has beaten her own record with 390 consecutive weeks.

Danielle Steel doesn't rest on either her many laurels or her beauty, wealth, fame, and unstoppable talent. She also works diligently on behalf of various charities—she serves as the National Chairperson for the American Library Association, on the National Committee for the Prevention of Child Abuse, and as spokesperson for the American Humane Association.

Not content with a posh Parisian pied-á-terre, a view of the Golden Gate Bridge, and her undisputed status as the bestselling living author, Danielle Steel realizes her readers are her most important resource and has made herself accessible to them via email through her publisher, Random House. While she is often compared to the fictional heroines of her own invention, her life is undoubtedly much quieter. But if she does have anything in common with them, it is her strength of will and her inimitable style. There is only *one* Danielle Steel.

> *I believe in dreams, not just the kind we have at night. I think that if we hang onto them, they come true.*
>
> Danielle Steel

JOYCE CAROL OATES *her heart laid bare*

Seemingly, Joyce Carol Oates can turn her hand to any subject and inject it with her trademark layered depth. She is well on her way to becoming one of the world's most abundant artists, having authored, as of this writing, forty-one novels and novellas, twenty-five collections of short stories, eight volumes of poetry, and nine collections of essays (including one on boxing), and has edited thirteen prestigious anthologies, most notably the *Norton Anthology of Contemporary Fiction*.

While she crosses barriers of time frequently in her novels, from postmodern urban settings to the Victorian era and back again, and works in genres ranging from Gothic to realism, she does have one overriding theme: violence. From prostitutes to primordial goddess figures (her novel *Blonde*, based on the life of Marilyn Monroe, was published to raves in March 2000), her writing fascinates as much as it shocks. She has received a fair amount of criticism for the disturbance in her fiction, but she explains it thusly: "The more violent the murders in *Macbeth*, the more relief one can feel at *not* having to perform them. Great art is cathartic; it is always moral."

She was born in Lockport, New York, to an Irish Catholic family of modest means. Joyce's intelligence saw her to the head of most classes, and she graduated Phi Beta Kappa from Syracuse University before doing her master's work in English literature at the University of Wisconsin. Her writing talent was noted early—she won the *Mademoiselle* fiction contest while still in college.

A reportedly excellent teacher, she has taught at several schools, most recently at Princeton, with her husband, academic Raymond Smith, while maintaining her grueling writing schedule. Her body of work averages a novel every two years, beginning in 1963. At certain times, she has published a book a year. As of this writing, her new work '*Night. Sleep. Death. The Stars*' is expected in 2020.

When asked how she manages to produce such critically acclaimed works so quickly, she told the *New York Times*, "I have always lived a very conventional life of moderation, absolutely regular hours, nothing exotic, no need, even, to organize my time." When labeled a workaholic by a reporter, she retorted, "I am not conscious of working especially hard, or of 'working' at all. Writing and teaching have always been, for me, so richly rewarding that I don't think of them as work in the usual sense of the word."

To read widely and to be open and curious about other people, to look and listen hard, not to be discouraged by rejections— we've all had them many times—and revise your work.

Joyce Carol Oates' advice to other writers

CHAPTER SIX
....

Speculative Sorceresses of Science Fiction
Word-Weavers of Wonder

Speculative fiction is a family of genres encompassing science fiction, fantasy, and magic realism. It is a field where women are only now really beginning to gain parity with their literary brethren—which is deeply ironic, considering that it was a woman who wrote the very first science fiction novel! Mary Shelley is acknowledged by many as the mother of the SF genre for her groundbreaking novel *Frankenstein, or The Young Prometheus*, which first saw print back in 1818; and as early as the seventeenth century, Margaret Lucas Cavendish, Duchess of Newcastle-upon-Tyne, published the utopian romance *The Description of a New World, Called the Blazing World*. (See Chapter Two for more on Mary Shelley's life and how she produced her pioneering work, written when she was still in her late teens!) And as we fly further into the new millennium, fully half a dozen women (most of whom are profiled in the pages of this chapter) have been recognized as Grand Masters of F & SF by the Science Fiction & Fantasy Writers of America.

In between, there have been some pretty thin times for female speculative fiction writers. Publisher statistics from 2013 say that male authors of high fantasy and science fiction in English still outnumber female authors by approximately two to one, although in subgenres like paranormal romance, urban fantasy, and young adult fantasy (thinking of all those vampire and werewolf tales here, among others), women writers are definitely now in the majority. But why, you might ask, is speculative fiction so important? The answer lies in the way that articulated visions can become reality—from technology (hello, cell phones!) to changes in society and culture, many evolutions in the human experience were first imagined by science fiction and fantasy writers. Speculative fiction is a lens through which we can see what *might* be, and it also allows us to try on strange new worlds where the restrictive notions of gender roles still so common here on our home planet just don't apply!

So buckle up and get ready to take a journey into the lives and minds of some of the most imaginative women ever to set pen to paper on Terra!

URSULA K. LE GUIN *pioneering grande dame of science fiction & fantasy*

Ursula Kroeber Le Guin (1929–2018) was the distinguished and well-loved author of twenty-one novels, nearly a dozen volumes of short stories, four essay collections, a dozen children's books, six volumes of poetry, and four translated works. She grew up in Berkeley, California, the daughter of anthropology professor Alfred Kroeber and Theodora Kroeber, writer of the noted biography *Ishi in Two Worlds*, an account of the life of the last survivor of the Yahi tribe of California Indians. The Kroeber family had a large book collection, and the household was visited by a goodly number of interesting academics such as Robert Oppenheimer. Le Guin later modeled the protagonist of her award-winning novel *The Dispossessed*, a physicist named Shevek, on Oppenheimer. She enjoyed reading fantasy and hearing the Native American stories her anthropologist father would tell, as well as exploring Norse and other mythic traditions.

At nine, Ursula wrote her first story; two years later, she made her first short story submission to *Astounding Science Fiction*, but it was rejected, and she did not try submitting any of her writing for publication for the next decade. She had an interest in biology but was limited in her ability to pursue the sciences due to difficulty with math. She attended Radcliffe, graduating Phi Beta Kappa in 1951 with a BA in Renaissance French and Italian literature, and went on to earn an MA in French from Columbia in 1952. Ursula won a Fulbright grant to study in France from 1953 to 1954; on her voyage there aboard the *Queen Mary*, she met Charles Le Guin, a graduate student also on a Fulbright grant to further his studies of history, and they married in Paris in 1953. She later said that the marriage spelled "the end of the doctorate" for her.

As they settled in together, Ursula Le Guin helped support their young family by teaching French and working as a secretary while Charles worked toward his PhD, first at Georgia's Emory University and then at the University of Idaho, until 1957, when their first child, Elizabeth, was born. Caroline followed in 1959, and that year, they moved to Portland, where Charles had secured a history instructor position at Portland State University. A son, Theodore, was born in 1964. Portland ended up being the couple's permanent home, but for a couple of sojourns Ursula made to London when she received further Fulbright research grants in 1968 and 1975.

Le Guin began her writing career in earnest between the births of her first and second children, but as the primary caregiving parent, the time she was able to devote to her writing was limited, especially while her three children were small. Besides writing, she also did editorial work and taught college courses at institutions of higher learning including Tulane, Bennington College, and Stanford. Her first few novels were deemed inaccessible by publishers, so she turned her attention to writing within the science fiction genre, as she knew there was a market for SF works and presumably had tired of receiving rejection slips. Indeed, she started selling; at first, she made sales of short stories to SF magazines like *Fantastic Science Fiction* and *Amazing Stories*. Some of these early stories introduced fictional universes which she fleshed out later in the Earthsea series and the Hainish trilogy, which began with *Rocannon's World*.

Rocannon's World, her first full-length novel to see print, was published by Ace Books in 1966 as a double volume along with its sequel, *Planet of Exile*; this work gained her enough recognition that the third volume in the trilogy, *City of Illusions*, was published as a stand-alone volume the following year. Critics began to notice Le Guin, and there were several reviews in science fiction magazines. The Hainish trilogy deals with themes often found in Le Guin's works, including the inner journey of self-discovery undertaken by a protagonist which is mirrored in an actual physical journey, the challenges of understanding between two or more cultures, and the quest to uncover one's authentic self and understand one's identity.

But real understanding of Le Guin's capabilities with the written word had not yet unfolded; when she sold her short story "Nine Lives" to *Playboy* magazine in 1968, she was asked if they could run it using her initials only rather than her first name. She agreed to this stipulation, and the story ran under the byline of "U. K. Le Guin." Later, she wrote that it was the sole time she had encountered gender prejudice from a publisher or editor, along with the realization that "it seemed so silly, so grotesque, that I failed to see that it was also important." When the story appeared again in later printings, it ran under her full name.

The tide turned later that same year when *A Wizard of Earthsea*, arguably her best-known novel, was released. She had never intended to write a novel aimed at young adults, but when an editor at Parnassus Press who realized that demographic might offer major potential for success requested that she give it a go, she wrote a coming-of-age story that was very well received both in the US and the UK. Although written initially for teenagers, *A Wizard of Earthsea* is now considered a fantasy classic and is beloved by many readers far past their teens; millions of copies have been sold all over the world. It is very possible that without the college for wizards on Roke Island so vividly imagined by Le Guin, Hogwarts would never have been dreamed up by J.K. Rowling.

Her next novel put Le Guin solidly on the map of science fiction and fantasy greats; 1969's *The Left Hand of Darkness*, a book set in her Hainish universe, "stunned the science fiction critics" and went on to win both of the top two prizes in those speculative fiction genres. Le Guin was the first woman ever to win either a Hugo or a Nebula award, which was especially fitting considering that it was her first book dealing with feminist issues. The story takes place on a planet where humans are able to change sex in a nonsurgical manner, opening up all kinds of questions about gender and sexuality and what is innate to a person. Le Guin then continued the *Earthsea* trilogy with *The Tombs of Atuan* (1971) and *The Farthest Shore* (1972), which carried readers on a journey through magic, mortality, and the borderline between life and death.

Critic Harold Bloom has described *A Wizard of Earthsea* and *The Left Hand of Darkness* as Le Guin's masterpieces. In 1973, she won another Hugo Award for her novel *The Word for World Is Forest*, which dealt with the effects of military-backed Terran colonialism on the indigenous inhabitants of the fictional planet Athshe; these concepts were particularly vivid given that the Vietnam War was then still raging with horrifying impacts on Vietnamese civilians. With *The Dispossessed* (1974), Le Guin returned to the Hainish universe in a tale of people working to create an idealistically utopian society, which included anarchist concepts. Her writing had begun to include more of her political ideas and feelings, as reflected in these last two novels.

In 1983, Oakland's distinguished Mills College engaged Le Guin to give a commencement speech; she put her own stamp on it, titling it "A Left-Handed Commencement Address." *American Rhetoric* included the address among its top hundred speeches of the twentieth century; it was later published in *Dancing at the Edge of the World*, a collection of Le Guin's nonfiction work.

Le Guin wrote for a total of nearly sixty years of her life before its peaceful end at home at age eighty-eight; in total, she won eight Hugo Awards, six Nebulas, twenty-four Locus Awards, the PEN/Malamud, and a multitude of other prizes. The US Library of Congress recognized her in 2000 as a Living Legend in their "Writers and Artists" category. Upon granting her the Margaret Edwards Award in 2004, the American Library Association panel declared that she had "inspired four generations of young adults to read beautifully constructed language, visit fantasy worlds that inform them about their own lives, and think about their ideas that are neither easy nor inconsequential." Vanishingly few American authors have produced such a quantity and array of different types of works with such consistently stellar quality. *The New York Times* called her "the greatest living science fiction writer" in 2016, and Bloom summed her up as a "visionary who set herself against all brutality, discrimination, and exploitation."

C.L. MOORE *pioneering mastery of noir and interplanetary romance*

Catherine Lucille Moore (1911–1987) was among the first female authors in the science fiction and fantasy genres, and her work paved the way for the many women writers of speculative fiction who followed. She was the first woman ever to be nominated as a Grand Master by the Science Fiction Writers of America, though she did not accept due to health difficulties late in life. She first attained recognition writing as the gender-neutral "C.L. Moore," though, interestingly, she did not employ this nom de plume to conceal the fact that she was a woman but rather because she didn't want her employers at the Fletcher Trust financial institution to find out she was moonlighting as a writer.

As a child, she was often in ill health and spent countless hours taking in the literature of the fantastic. Her first three stories to see print ran in *The Vagabond*, a student magazine at Indiana University, in 1930–1931; they were works of short fantasy fiction that appeared under the name "Catherine Moore." As the 1930s rolled on, she sold a number of short stories to *Weird Tales*; one of her two early series featured one of the first female protagonists in the sword-and-sorcery subgenre, Jirel of Joiry. Her Jirel of Joiry tale "The Black God's Kiss" was the cover story for an issue of *Weird Tales* in 1934, with an illustration of the heroine and a huge ebony statue. In 1936, Moore received a fan letter from a fellow science fiction writer; due to her pseudonym, he was under the impression that she was male. She met Henry Kuttner and went on to write a story with him featuring both Jirel of Joiry and another of her series characters, Northwest Smith, entitled "Quest of the Starstone" (1937). In 1940, they married, and many further collaborations ensued, with some credited to their actual names and some under one of seventeen joint pseudonyms, such as Laurence O'Donnell, but most often their stories appeared under Lewis Padgett, a name created by combining their mothers' maiden names.

Moore had already achieved fame before she started to work with Kuttner; this recognition came with her first professional-level story in *Weird Tales*, 1933's "Shambleau," a tale of a psychic *femme fatale* vampire set on a 'planetary romance' version of Mars. A gradual consensus has emerged that Moore was in fact the stronger writer of the two. She did continue to create solo works, and many of her short stories ran in *Astounding Science Fiction* through the 1940s; one of these, the 1944 novella *No Woman Born*, went on to be reprinted in no less than ten different anthologies, including *The Best of C.L. Moore* (1975). The novella tells the story of a badly burned dancer who is given a robot body and becomes a cyborg. But most of the couple's writing during this time was in creative partnership; it is said either of them could pick up any story where the other had left off. They successfully combined her emphasis on the emotions and senses, which had broken ground in the genre, with his more cerebral narrative style.

Their 1940s novels for *Startling Stories*, many of which were erroneously attributed to Kuttner alone, were early examples of the hybrid genre of science fantasy, neatly fusing her romanticism with his vigorous plotlines. Their collaborative F/SF works include the classics "Mimsy Were the Borogoves" (1943), adapted as the 2007 film *The Last Mimzy*, and 1946's "The Vintage Season," source of the story line for the 1992 film *Timescape*. They also wrote a couple of 1940s mystery novels writing as Lewis Padgett. In 1950, the couple both began studies at the University of Southern California. They continued to write mysteries but not many more science fiction stories, though Moore produced one solo novel, 1957's *Doomsday Morning*, a futuristic thriller. She retired from writing fiction upon Kuttner's death in 1958, though she continued to teach a writing course at USC, from which she earned a master's degree in English in 1963.

Moore worked as a television screenwriter for detective series and for Westerns including *Maverick* from 1958 to 1962, with her screenplays credited to "Catherine Kuttner," but left screenwriting in 1963, which was also the year of her second marriage to Thomas Reggie. Two decades later, after a long and gradual illness, she passed away at home in Hollywood at seventy-six years of age. She received the World Fantasy Award for life achievement in 1981 and was posthumously inducted into the Science Fiction Hall of Fame in 1998.

ANDRE NORTON *first woman in the Science Fiction Hall of Fame*

Andre Alice Norton (born Alice Mary Norton in 1912) was a prolific classic science fiction and fantasy author for over half a century, as well as a writer of contemporary and historical fiction and the editor of such anthologies as *Catfantastic*; she wrote many series as well as over sixty single novels and dozens of short stories. Her main nom de plume was Andre Norton, and she also wrote under the names Allen Weston and Andrew North. Norton was the first woman ever to win either an SFWA Grand Master Award or a Gandalf Award for achievement in the fantasy and science fiction genres, as well as the first woman to be inducted into the Science Fiction and Fantasy Hall of Fame. She has been called the Grande Dame of Science Fiction and Fantasy by media outlets such as *Time* magazine.

Norton wrote her first novel, a thriller called *Ralestone Luck*, while still in high school; it was eventually published as her second book in 1938. She had planned to study teaching, but the Depression forced her to go to work as a librarian instead. She continued working in libraries for nearly two decades, eventually spending a couple of years on staff at the Library of Congress. She legally adopted the pen name of Andre Norton in 1934 in order to sell more books in the fantasy market, which was then composed largely of boys. In the 1950s, she was a prolific novel writer, and many of these books were aimed at young readers. She worked at New York SF publisher Gnome Press from 1950 to 1958 as a reader; then, having already published twenty-one novels while working at day jobs, she turned to writing full-time.

Her stories often involve a rite of passage type experience involving challenges requiring lead characters to rapidly rise to the occasion and be resourceful. She pioneered the concept of traveling through alternate worlds in her 1956 work *The Crossroads of Time*, and, in 1978, she published the first novel based on the Dungeons & Dragons game, *Quag Keep*. She was the author of many popular series, such as Time Traders; Beast Master; Mark of the Cat; the Cycle of Oak, Yew, Ash, and Rowan; and the bestselling Witch World books.

Andre Norton died at her home in Tennessee in 2005; that year, an annual Andre Norton Award for outstanding science fiction or fantasy for young adults was established. She deeply influenced the entirety of the fantasy and science fiction genres, publishing over three hundred works over the span of seventy years, and inspired many popular authors such as C.J. Cherryh and Mercedes Lackey.

LEIGH BRACKETT *the queen of space opera*

Author Leigh Brackett mostly wrote science fiction but was also a screenwriter for both the large and small screen. She worked on scripts for such cinematic works as a 1946 film noir starring Bogart and Bacall titled *The Big Sleep* and 1959's *Rio Bravo*, as well as other John Wayne Westerns, and she contributed to the screenwriting process for *The Empire Strikes Back*. She was born in

Los Angeles in 1915; her father, himself an aspiring writer who worked as an accountant, died three years later of influenza during the pandemic that killed over 600,000 Americans and countless millions worldwide. Her mother and grandparents then raised her in Santa Monica. Young Leigh was a tomboy who enjoyed playing volleyball and reading Tarzan stories; she went on to attend a private school for girls. She did not attend college due to the family's financial situation.

At age twenty-four, she joined the Los Angeles Science Fiction Society, where she met such authors as Robert Heinlein, who published his very first story, "Life-Line," that same year, and Ray Bradbury, who at that point had yet to publish any of his works of speculative fiction. She soon started to attend Heinlein's Mañana Literary Society gatherings; it is likely that this social milieu was inspiring and supportive, and Brackett's first story, "Martian Quest," was published in *Astounding Science Fiction* in 1940. Her first science fiction novel, *Shadow Over Mars*, was originally serialized in 1944 in the magazine *Planet Stories*, but was not published in book form (as *The Nemesis from Terra*) until 1961. Though it was somewhat rough-edged, it marked the starting point of a new film noir-inflected style of science fiction.

Her first published book-length fiction, a detective mystery novel titled *No Good from a Corpse* (1944), was good enough that director Howard Hawks told his secretary to call in "this guy Brackett" to help William Faulkner on scriptwriting for Raymond Chandler's *The Big Sleep*, which is seen as one of the best detective movies ever made. Screenwriting became her main occupation until 1948, when she returned to speculative fiction. While working on *The Big Sleep*, she had no time to finish her novella *Lorelei of the Red Mist*, so she engaged Ray Bradbury to complete it, and it was published under both their names in *Planet Stories* in 1946.

On the last day of that year, she married Edmond Hamilton, a fellow space opera and mystery writer a decade older than she, who had been precociously intelligent enough to start college at age fourteen. They bought a house in rural Ohio and eventually a second home in California's high desert and worked side by side for a quarter-century, though they only rarely collaborated in a formal sense. From 1948 through 1951, Leigh wrote a series of longer SF stories such as her novel *Sea-Kings of Mars* (1949), creating evocative planetary settings. Also in 1949, she began to produce a series of stories featuring Eric John Stark as protagonist; though her character was from Earth, he was raised by semi-sentient aboriginal denizens of the planet Mercury. She wrote and sold three stories featuring Stark: "Queen of the Martian Catacombs," "Enchantress of Venus," and 1951's "Black Amazon of Mars" before turning her writing focus from plot-driven tales of high adventure to fiction with more attention to mood that contemplated such concepts as the passing of civilizations.

Brackett regularly sold short fiction to science fiction magazines through 1955, while at the same time producing a number of book-length works, including *The Starmen* (1952) and the post-nuclear holocaust novel *The Long Tomorrow* (1955). That year, however, *Planet Stories*, her most reliable buyer, ceased publication; her fittingly titled story *Last Call* graced its final issue. But later in 1955, both *Startling Stories* and *Thrilling Wonder Stories* folded, and with that, Brackett's magazine market for her short stories had evaporated. Though she did write some short stories in the years that followed (some of which saw print after evolving into full-length books), for the next decade or so she focused her efforts on writing for the more financially rewarding big screen and television markets.

In 1963–64, she revisited the Martian setting of her early adventure works in two short stories, "The Road to Sinharat" and the amusingly titled "Purple Priestess of the Mad Moon," which was at least somewhat of self-parody. After several years more, she returned to science fiction in the mid-seventies with her trilogy *The Book of Skaith*, which revived her Eric John Stark character of decades earlier but shifted the setting to Skaith, a fictional world outside Earth's solar system. Brackett never wrote any more tales set in our own solar system after the Mariner probes proved there was no life on Mars; instead, she invented her own faraway planets. Her narratives often involved clashes between planetary civilizations or tensions between colonizers and local sentient beings.

Leigh Brackett published twenty original novels spanning genres including SF, mysteries, crime, and Western, as well as more than fifty works of short fiction and sixteen screenplays for cinema and TV. She died in California after a battle with lung cancer in 1978, shortly after completing a first-draft script for *Star Wars: The Empire Strikes Back.*

On William Faulkner's handling of collaboration with her on The Big Sleep:

He greeted me courteously. He put the book down and said, "We will do alternate sections. You will do these chapters and I will do these chapters" and so on. But that's the way he wanted it done. He turned around and walked into his office and I never saw him again except to say good morning.

Leigh Brackett

JUDITH MERRIL 'the strongest woman in science fiction'

Judith Merril (1923–1997) was an American-born Canadian science fiction editor, critic, and anthologist who left her mark on the genre. Born Josephine Juliet Grossman to Jewish parents in Boston, she lost her father to suicide in 1929. Her mother, who had been a suffragette, moved the family to the Bronx borough of New York City when Judith was in her mid-teens. Judith took an interest in politics while still in high school, studying Marxism, as well as Zionism, which her mother espoused. Judith graduated from high school in 1939 at only sixteen; she soon experienced a shift in political values due to events of the time and became interested in Trotskyist thought. At a Trotskyite picnic the next summer, she met Dan Zissman, and four months later, they married. In 1942, they had one daughter, Merril Zissman, but the marriage ended in 1945.

During these years, Judith became involved with a New York science fiction group, the Futurians, and in 1946, science fiction author Frederik Pohl, whom she had met in the group, came to live with her. In this period, she changed her last name to Merril. She married Pohl in late 1948 when her divorce was finalized, and they had a daughter, Ann Pohl, in 1950. This second marriage was short-lived as well; they divorced in 1952. As these events unfolded, Judith concurrently worked on science fiction fanzines and began to write professionally in other genres in 1945. Her first SF short story, "That Only a Mother," a disturbing tale about nuclear radiation, was published in 1948 in *Astounding*. She followed it with her debut novel, *Shadow on the Hearth* (1950), an understated nuclear World War III story told from the viewpoint of a suburban housewife, which was later adapted for television under the title *Atomic Attack*.

Beginning in 1950, she edited anthologies of short science fiction, including the popular "Year's Best" anthology from 1956 to 1967; she was one of a short list of people who brought greater professionalism and literary standards to the field. In total, she edited more than two dozen anthologies and published twenty-six original short stories of her own. She collaborated with fellow SF writer and Futurian C.M. Kornbluth on two novels published under the name 'Cyril Judd,' *Outpost Mars* (1951) and *Gunner Cade* (1952). Her 1960 novel *The Tomorrow People* melded suspenseful psychological mystery with science fiction; after that year, she did not publish much more fiction. *Homecalling and Other Stories: The Complete Solo Fiction of Judith Merril* was posthumously published in 2005.

Merril moved to the Canadian city of Toronto in 1968 in reaction to the US government's suppression of citizen action against the Vietnam War; there she was one of the founding residents of the Rochdale College experiment in cooperative housing and education run by students themselves. She founded a wide-ranging collection of speculative fiction at the Toronto Public Library in 1970, donating the books and periodicals she had personally amassed to kick it off; later, in the 1990s, the library named the individually housed collection after her. In 1976, she became a citizen of Canada; she was active in its peace movement, and once, she even traveled to the seat of Parliament in Ottawa in witchy garb to cast a hex on them for having allowed the US to test cruise missiles in Canadian airspace.

In 1997, the Science Fiction and Fantasy Writers of America named her their Author Emeritus for the year, and she was posthumously inducted into the Science Fiction and Fantasy Hall of Fame. Her fragmentary autobiographical memoir, *Better to Have Loved: The Life of Judith Merril* (2002) was completed by her granddaughter Emily Pohl-Weary; in an ironic twist, it won a Hugo

Award for Best Related Book. Noted SF author J.G. Ballard once called Judith Merril "the strongest woman in a genre for the most part created by timid and weak men."

KATE WILHELM *antiwar author who transcended sexist science fiction*

Kate Wilhelm (1928–2018) wrote more than three dozen novels, as well as a great deal of short fiction, split between the science fiction and mystery/suspense genres. She won both the Hugo and Locus Awards for her SF novel *Where Late the Sweet Bird Sang*, and won both of these again for her nonfiction work *Storyteller: Writing Lessons and More from 27 Years of the Clarion Writers' Workshop*. Her science fiction novel *Juniper Time* won the Prix Apollo of France. She also won three Nebula Awards for short science fiction and actually took a part in designing the physical Nebula Award trophy, creating an early sketch on which it was based.

Amazingly, Wilhelm sold the first two science fiction stories she ever wrote. Upon reading an SF anthology from the public library, she thought, "I can do that"; after writing a couple of stories in a notebook, she rented a typewriter and sent them off. Miraculously, both were accepted: "The Pint-Sized Genie" (1956, *Fantastic*) and "The Mile-Long Spaceship" (1957, *Astounding*).

Wilhelm also wrote detective fiction involving women as solvers: her Barbara Holloway series features a female attorney in Oregon who solves mysteries, blending courtroom drama with detective plotlines, and in her Constance Leidl and Charlie Meiklejohn series, Leidl is a psychologist who investigates cases with her retired arson detective husband. Wilhelm released nine collections of her short stories of speculative fiction; in 1980, she also published four volumes of her poetry. Her work has been adapted for TV, film, and theater productions in the US, England, and Germany. Her second marriage, which lasted four decades until her spouse's passing in 2002, was to writer and editor Damon Knight. Along with Knight, Wilhelm played an important part in the creation of the Clarion Workshop for writers. In 2003, she was inducted into the Science Fiction Hall of Fame.

MARION ZIMMER BRADLEY Mists of Avalon *wordsmith*

Marion Zimmer Bradley (1930–1999) was a pioneering author of fantasy, science fiction, and science fantasy. She was most famous for her goddess-centered retelling of the Arthurian legend from a female point of view in her novel *Mists of Avalon*, which spent four months on the *New York Times* bestsellers list; she was also known for her Darkover science fiction/fantasy series, the saga of a planet where human colonists develop ESP powers. Enthusiastic readers saw in her work what essayist Nancy Jesser called "one of the early manifestations of proto-feminist science fiction." Perhaps driven by parenthood's demands on her own life, her fiction often examined women's attempts to find balance between a woman's duty to herself and her obligations to others. She worked in many genres, including Gothic novels, historical fantasy, children's books, teleplays, and lesbian novels, addressing through the characters and worlds she created such issues as gender, androgyny, sexism, homophobia, technology, alienation, and the evolution of cultures and how humans relate. Besides her Darkover and Avalon series, over four decades, she published dozens of stand-alone novels of various kinds. Paradoxically, she often denied possessing any particular talent for writing and said she'd rather edit or teach.

Born Marion Eleanor Zimmer, she grew up on a farm in Albany, New York. She had an early interest in writing and dictated poetry to her mother, historian Evelyn Parkhurst Conklin, before she learned to write; at eleven, when she found her school newspaper not to her taste, she started an alternative school paper, *The Columbia Journal*. In the late 1940s, she did not believe a young woman could make a living out of writing, so in a streak of practicality, she attended the state teachers' college in Albany for a couple of years. But in 1949, she married a railroad man, Robert Alden Bradley, and left college behind. That same year, at age nineteen, she made her first sale via an amateur fiction contest, to *Fantastic/Amazing Stories*. The Bradleys' son was born in 1950; meanwhile, she continued to both write short stories and try her hand at longer works. When she sold another story in 1952, this time to *Vortex Science Fiction*, it kicked off what she saw as her "professional" writing career; she juggled writing with the parenting and homemaking duties expected of women in the 1950s.

The young family moved to Abilene, Texas, in 1959, where Marion went back to school, financing her tuition by writing romances and confessional novels.

In 1961, she was at last able to publish her first novel, *The Door Through Space*, an expansion of her 1957 short SF story "Bird of Prey." 1962 was a banner year for Bradley, one in which she published five different books: three under her own name, including *The Planet Savers*, and two more under various noms de plume. *The Planet Savers*, which had been serialized in *Amazing Science Fiction Stories* in 1959, kicked off her Darkover series, which came to encompass seventeen novels under her sole authorship as well as a couple of collaboratively written works, notably including *Rediscovery*, written with Mercedes Lackey, and a dozen short story anthologies edited by Bradley. The Darkover saga took up much of her time through the sixties and seventies, though she also published a collection of her other short science fiction works, 1964's *The Dark Intruder and Other Stories*, and several volumes of literary criticism.

1964 was the year Bradley finally finished college: She graduated from Texas' Hardin-Simmons University with a triple bachelor's degree in English, Spanish, and psychology; she also gained her teaching credential. But, by that time, her writing was selling sufficiently well that she ended up never using it. The Bradleys divorced; Marion wed again, this time to Walter Breen, an authority on rare coins. They had two children, moving to California in 1965, where she undertook graduate studies at UC Berkeley. She was also an early member of the Society for Creative Anachronism, a historical recreation group focused on the medieval period—in fact, she came up with the name! Fellow F/SF writers Diana Paxson and Poul Anderson were also cofounders of the SCA, which is now a nonprofit with tens of thousands of members in several countries.

In the early 1950s, Bradley began to explore Western esoteric traditions, joining the Rosicrucian Order. In the late 1970s, she was active for a few years in Darkmoon Circle, a women's goddess spirituality group that used to meet in a renovated carriage house at her Berkeley home; it has been described as "part coven, part women's consciousness-raising [group], and part sewing circle." But she left not long after *Mists of Avalon* was published, finding herself beset by people wanting her to give talks on female consciousness and asking her how much of *Mists* had been "channeled"—which was none of it, according to

Bradley. Some members also proposed opening the group to men; she was not keen on that, as she was there in the interest of learning how to better relate to women. She and Breen separated in 1979, the year *Mists of Avalon* was released, but lived on the same street and continued to have business dealings until a decade later, when her former husband was charged with molesting a boy and Bradley obtained an official divorce.

Bradley had long considered telling the tale of Morgan Le Fay, the enchantress sister of King Arthur. When editors Judy and Lester Del Rey asked if she would write an Arthurian novel about Sir Lancelot, she said she would prefer to write about Arthur's sister, whose name she changed to Morgaine. After they agreed to her proposal, Bradley rented a flat in London and visited a number of Arthurian sites in England in preparation for writing *Mists of Avalon*. In *Mists*, the protagonist, a priestess of an ancient Earth-centered religion, is unable to forestall the inexorable expansion of Christianity despite her mystical powers; she watches as women, previously respected in ancient tradition, become oppressed and seen as the source of original sin in patriarchal Christian teachings. In the 1990s, Bradley cowrote two prequels to *Mists* with author Diana Paxson; after Marion's demise, Paxson completed the story with four more prequel volumes.

In her later years, Bradley turned more to fantasy, as in 1980's *The House Between the Worlds*. She'd once trained as a singer and was a self-described "opera nut," so she made use of operatic plotlines in *Night's Daughter* (1985), a retelling of Mozart's *The Magic Flute*, and *The Forest House* (1993), based on Bellini's *Norma*. Besides writing, Bradley edited magazines, including her own *Marion Zimmer Bradley's Fantasy Magazine*, launched in 1988, as well as seventeen years of the annual anthology *Sword and Sorceress*. In these, as well as by licensing anthologies of fan-created stories set in her Darkover universe, Marion encouraged numbers of new writers in the F/SF field, especially women. Her writing output became more sparse due to declining health, though she did still create some new works, like her Gothic parapsychological novels *Ghostlight*, *Witchlight*, *Gravelight*, and *Heartlight*, in the 1990s. She died in Berkeley in 1999, and her ashes were scattered at Glastonbury Tor in Cornwall. Several works by other authors continued the Darkover epic posthumously.

Perennially Praiseworthy Prizewinners of F/SF

CONNIE WILLIS *"none of the things one frets about ever happen"*

Constance Elaine Willis, a.k.a. Connie Willis, is an author who has won more major awards for her work in the science fiction and fantasy genres than any other writer, including numbers of Hugo, Nebula, and Locus Awards, among others. She has also been recognized as a science fiction Grand Master by SFWA (the Science Fiction and Fantasy Writers of America). A number of her stories involve history students of the future at Oxford University who travel in time; the Time Travel series is comprised of both short stories and a few of her prizewinning novels, such as the Nebula and Hugo Award double winners *Doomsday Book* (1992) and *Blackout/All Clear* (2010). She was born in 1945 and graduated with degrees in education and English in 1967, going on to work in the teaching field.

As new writers in the F/SF genres often do, she started out writing short fiction; her first sale was in 1970. She produced seven more stories before publishing *Water Witch*, her first novel, in 1982. That same year she received a grant from the National Endowment for the Arts that allowed her to quit her day job and focus on writing full-time. Willis is known for incorporating 1940s Hollywood movie style screwball comedy, parody, and even romance into her works, as well as writing classic science fiction that explores the possibilities of the hard sciences. She also uses her fiction to look at the implications of psychology, as in *Lincoln's Dreams* (1987) and *Bellwether* (1996). She lives in Colorado with her husband, a retired University of Northern Colorado physics professor, and their daughter Cordelia.

ANNE McCAFFREY *here there be dragons—and more*

Anne McCaffrey was an American writer of Irish descent best known for her science fiction series *The Dragonriders of Pern*, which features many valiant female protagonists in its more than twenty books. She was the first woman ever to win both of the top two prizes for writing science fiction, the Hugo and Nebula awards, for various novellas set on her fictional planet of Pern.

Anne Inez McCaffrey was born April Fool's Day, 1926, in Cambridge, Massachusetts, but she was nobody's fool; she graduated cum laude from Radcliffe in 1947 with a degree in Slavonic languages and literature. She also trained as an opera singer and actress. She married three years later; Horace Wright Johnson worked for DuPont and shared a number of her artistic interests. By the early 1950s, she was writing short stories; she won a hundred dollar prize from a science fiction magazine in 1952 for "Freedom of the Race," the first of her short fiction to see print. Her second published story, "The Lady in the Tower," was reprinted in a *Year's Greatest Science Fiction* anthology.

After relocating to Long Island with her family in 1965, which by then included three children, she started writing full-time. Her first published novel was a satiric science fiction story titled *Restoree* (1967); her first Dragonriders novel, *Dragonflight*, came out the following year. A couple of books, many short stories, and a few years later in 1970, she filed for divorce, packed up her two children who were still under eighteen, and moved to Ireland, where tax policies were very favorable for authors and others working in the arts. Her mother joined the family in Dublin soon afterwards. At first, periods of productivity and the compensation that came with it alternated with times when her writing flow was not adequate to keep the family from struggling to make ends meet, but with the publication of the Harper Hall Trilogy (*Dragonsong*, *Dragonsinger*, and *Dragondrums*) by the end of the 1970s, she was able to purchase a home she named "Dragonhold" for the dragons that had enabled her to buy it, as her son Todd recounts in his biography of his mother.

As well as writing many further tales of the Dragonriders, McCaffrey continued to create other series, notably including her Brain & Brawn ship series, beginning with *The Ship Who Sang*; the Crystal series, starting with the *Crystal Singer* trilogy; the Doona trilogy, kicked off by *Decision at Doona*; the Talents series, which began with *To Ride Pegasus*; and the Freedom or Catteni tetralogy. She later collaborated with other writers on several books and series, including many other female authors such as Elizabeth Moon, Mercedes Lackey, and Elizabeth Ann Scarborough, and worked with her son Todd McCaffrey, who wrote several of the later Dragonrider books with her. McCaffrey was known to tell interviewers that she didn't have time for hobbies, but she did ride and breed horses. She died at home of a stroke in County Wicklow, Ireland, in 2011.

LOIS McMASTER BUJOLD *perennial winner of science fiction awards*

Lois McMaster Bujold is one of the most celebrated authors in the field of science fiction; she is the only writer besides pioneering author Robert Heinlein ever to have won four Hugo Awards during her lifetime (though Heinlein was also awarded two 'Retro-Hugos' posthumously, boosting his ultimate total). Both her novel *Paladin of Souls* (2005) and her novella *The Mountains of Mourning* (1990) also won another top SF prize, the Nebula Award, in addition to each winning a Hugo Award. Her other two Hugo Awards were for entire series she created: the Chalion series and the Vorkosigan Saga (awarded in 2018 and 2017 respectively). Most of her works so far are part of either those two series or her Sharing Knife series.

She was born in 1949 in Columbus, Ohio, the daughter of a noted electrical engineer and professor, and picked up his love of science fiction early; she started reading adult works in the genre at the tender age of nine. She began to write in middle school, and throughout high school, collaborated with her best friend Lillian on creating extended story lines. She attended Ohio State, and after college, worked in the state university hospital system pharmacies as a technician, eventually quitting to start a family. Children Anne and Paul followed in 1979 and 1981. Bujold was inspired to take a second look at writing when her high school best friend, who was by then writing under her married name, Lillian Stewart Carl, made her first sales as a writer; Bujold said of this turning point, "it occurred to me that if she could do it, I could do it too."

Bujold tried her hand at writing but soon discovered that it was too demanding to pursue as a mere hobby. She decided to go pro, putting energy and focus into acquiring and honing the rewriting and editorial skills authors need. In 1983, she completed her first novel, *Shards of Honor*, and soon followed it up with *The Warrior's Apprentice* and *Ethan of Athos*—but *selling* them was a different matter; all three were published, though, by Baen Books in 1986. In *Ethan of Athos*, she used an all-male world where homosexuality is the norm as a narrative setting to demonstrate how what humans presently define as "women's work," including raising children, household maintenance, and emotional bonding, is really *everyone's* work.

Meanwhile, she also wrote and sent out shorter fiction works, making her first sale to *Twilight Zone Magazine*, the short story "Barter," in 1984. After her fourth novel, *Falling Free*, was serialized in *Analog Magazine* in winter 1987–1988, it garnered her first Nebula Award. She continued to create highly acclaimed novels as well as adding anthology editing to her palette of skills when she coedited *Women at War* (1995) with Roland Green, the year she moved from Marion, Ohio, to Minneapolis, following a divorce in the early nineties.

She is best known for her series of Vorkosigan novels, which are set approximately a thousand years in the future and center around Miles Vorkosigan, who despite physical impairments since birth is both a mercenary admiral and an interstellar spy. In the later titles in the series, he has more of a detective aspect, as opposed to the straight-ahead space opera style of the previous stories, which Bujold has said she modeled on the Horatio Hornblower tales, mainly following a single protagonist. She has, however, written in other genres, including epic fantasy, historical fantasy, and romance. Her lucid narrative style and wit have enabled her to infuse even her military science fiction stories with subtle social critiques. Her books have been translated into nineteen languages.

N.K. JEMISIN *next-generation nerd turned pioneering prizewinner*

Nora K. Jemisin is an award-winning writer of speculative fiction (which includes such genre categories as science fiction and fantasy), including both numerous short stories and eight full-length novels. Born in 1972, she started off her writing career with a splash when *The Hundred Thousand Kingdoms* won the Locus Award for Best First Novel in 2011. That same year, she also cowrote a nonfiction work, *Geek Wisdom: The Sacred Teachings of Nerd Culture*. She was a counseling psychologist and educator with degrees from Tulane and the University of Maryland; but via a 2016 Patreon campaign, she was able to raise enough collective funding so that since then, she has been able to focus solely on her writing, exploring themes including cultural conflicts and inequality. Also, from 2016 to 2019, "Otherworldly," her column on science fiction, ran in the *New York Times*; she continues to contribute long-form reviews to that flagship newspaper.

She is the author of the Broken Earth trilogy, consisting of *The Fifth Season* (2015), *The Obelisk Gate* (2016), and *The Stone Sky* (2017); when *The Fifth Season* won a Hugo Award for Best Novel, she became the first African American author to win a Hugo in that category. Then the two sequels each won her another Hugo Award, making her the only author ever to win the Best Novel Hugo in three consecutive years. *The Stone Sky* also won a Nebula Best Novel Award as well as a Locus Best Fantasy Award, and a television adaptation of *The Fifth Season* is planned as of this writing. In 2019, a collection of her short stories entitled *How Long 'til Black Future Month?* won an American Libraries Association Alex Award. Besides her distinguished fiction career, she is also an anti-racist and feminist political blogger. N.K. Jemisin lives in Brooklyn and is just hitting her stride as a writer of note.

Mid-Century Mothers of F/SF Invention

C.J. CHERRYH *from teaching the classics to creating new worlds*

Born Carolyn Jane Cherry, C.J. Cherryh is the author of more than eighty works of science fiction and fantasy from the mid-seventies on, including two

Hugo Award winners, 1981's *Downbelow Station* and 1988's *Cyteen*, both
of which are set in her Alliance-Union universe. Her four-book Morgaine
Cycle books, set in the same fictional universe, have sold over three million
copies in total. In 1975, before the publication of her first novels, she began
to use her first two initials instead of her first name to disguise that she was
female, as most SF/F authors were male at the time; her first editor, Daw's
Don Wollheim, also advised her to alter the spelling of her last name because
he thought the surname "Cherry" made her sound too much like a romance
author. Thus C.J. Cherryh was created.

Born in 1942 in St. Louis, she began to write at age ten out of frustration that
her favorite TV show, *Flash Gordon*, had been canceled, and says she continued
to write "daily" from then on. She went on to major in Latin at the University
of Oklahoma, focusing on mythology, archaeology, and engineering history,
and then earned a master's degree in classics at Johns Hopkins, where she
was awarded a Woodrow Wilson fellowship. Cherryh became a high school
teacher of Latin, ancient Greek, ancient history, and the classics in Oklahoma
City; during the summers, she led tours of ancient ruins in Europe and the
UK. She wrote future fiction in her spare time, incorporating Greco-Roman
mythological material into the plots. In a way atypical of authors in the SF field
at the time, she did not first publish short stories in genre periodicals before
ramping up to writing novels; instead, she began by writing and publishing
several novels before trying her hand at short stories. At first, as for so many
new authors, there were many rejections, and some publishers even lost her
hard-copy manuscript submissions. On these occasions, she had to physically
retype the manuscripts, working from her carbon copies, as photocopying was
expensive at the time.

Finally, Cherryh went through her own library and "investigated who was
the editor who had bought most of [her] favorite books," figuring that their
tastes would match. This led her to specifically reach out to editor Donald A.
Wollheim at Daw Books. In 1975, Wollheim bought the first two books of the
Morgaine Stories, which utilized a set of characters Cherryh had created at the
beginning of her teens; upon seeing print, *Gate of Ivrel* and *Brothers of Earth*
brought her immediate recognition and the John W. Campbell Award for Best
New Writer in 1977. Six more of her books were published in the late 1970s,

and when she won a Hugo Award for Best Short Story for "Cassandra" in 1979, she left teaching to become a full-time writer. Her academic background has contributed to her skill at fictional "world building"; she creates rich realism in her stories by fleshing out the language, history, psychology, and even archaeology of the worlds she invents. One reviewer said of Cherryh, "Her blend of science and folklore gives the novels an intellectual depth comparable to Tolkien or Gene Wolfe." Her novels often include idealistic protagonists striving to uphold the greater good and capable heroines as well as exploring alternatives in gender roles.

Besides creating works in her own fictional universes, Cherryh has written numerous short stories for several shared world anthology series, such as Witch World (created by Andre Norton), Elfquest, Merovingen Nights, and Thieves' World. She lives near Spokane, Washington, with her wife Jane Fancher, who is also a science fiction and fantasy author as well as an artist, and two cats; she enjoys travel and has been most of the way around the world. Interestingly, her brother, David A. Cherry, is an artist who also works in the F/SF field.

If you want to change a culture, you need to transform the role of women.

C.J. Cherryh, in a 1996 interview with *The Camelot Project*

ELIZABETH MOON *writing from experience, including in the Marines*

Elizabeth Moon (née Norris) grew up just a few miles from the US border with Mexico in McAllen, Texas; she credits her experiences there with leaving her with an enduring fascination with cultural differences and how individuals respond to new experiences. She began writing fiction while still in her teens but did not think of it as more than a hobby at the time; little did she know that as a science fiction writer, she would eventually become a winner of the Nebula Award, one of the top two prizes in the field of SF, as well as a Robert Heinlein award for outstanding "writings that inspire the human exploration of space."

She earned a bachelor's degree in history at Rice University in 1968; immediately thereafter, she joined the US Marine Corps as a computer specialist, working with "what were then quite large computers," as she describes them. A year later, she married Richard Sloan Moon, who was also in the military, and continued her active duty military service for two more years, attaining the rank of First Lieutenant. She then returned to academic studies at the University of Texas. After completing a second bachelor's degree in biology, she continued with graduate work in that field at the University of Texas at San Antonio. In her mid-thirties, she began writing professionally, making her first short story sales in 1985 and 1986. One, set in an epic fantasy world, was published in one of the sequence of anthologies titled *Sword and Sorceress* and edited by author Marion Zimmer Bradley; the other, a hard science fiction tale, was purchased by the classic SF monthly *Analog Magazine*, kicking off several years of Moon's short fiction works appearing in its pages. She has continued to write both science fiction and fantasy; to date, she has published nearly thirty novels and dozens of works of short fiction.

Moon's first novel, *Sheepfarmer's Daughter*, came out in 1988, and won the Compton Crook award for best first novel; its story was soon continued in two sequels, forming the Deed of Paksenarrion trilogy. She followed the trilogy with seven other novels set in the same universe. In the midst of writing that fictional series and raising her son Michael, she took the time to write *The Speed of Dark*, a near-future narrative written from the viewpoint of an autistic computer programmer. She drew from her son's experiences growing up with autism in writing the book, which won the 2003 Nebula Award for Best Novel. Moon has also produced several works in her Familias Regnant universe, including a trilogy and four further novels, as well as the seven-book Vatta's War/Vatta's Peace fiction series. She has also collaborated with Anne McCaffrey and Jody Lynn Nye on the Planet Pirates trilogy and has published a number of collections of her short stories. Much of her work contains military SF themes, as well as focusing on politics, human interactions, and biology, drawing on her education.

When not writing, Elizabeth Moon enjoys such pursuits as native plant and wildlife photography, choral singing, and playing music; she also has experience as a paramedic and is an accomplished fencer who captains a group of published SF authors who enjoy swordplay.

TANITH LEE *Gothic mistress of fantasy and horror*

The legendary Tanith Lee was the first woman ever to win a British Fantasy Derleth Award, for 1980's *Death's Master*, which tells the tale of Narasen, "the leopard queen of Merh." She was also the winner of multiple World Fantasy Awards, as well as a World Fantasy Lifetime Achievement Award and the Bram Stoker Award for Lifetime Achievement in Horror. Her style is rich and poetic even in prose, and her work often features creative reinterpretations of such fantastical material as myths, fairytales, and vampire stories, as well as feminist themes and plots exploring alternative sexuality.

She was born in London in 1947 to two professional dancers. Because of her parents' work, they moved frequently. Due to undiagnosed mild dyslexia, young Tanith was not functionally literate until she was about eight, when her father personally taught her to read in about a month; after that, she lost no time before starting to write at age nine. Though not well-to-do, the family maintained a large paperback collection, and she read and discussed classic works such as *Dracula* and *Hamlet* with her parents as well as taking in a great deal of current fantasy fiction. After high school, she spent a year at art school before realizing she would rather express herself through words than pictures. She worked as an assistant librarian and clerk and waited tables before trying her hand at writing professionally. In 1968, she made her first professional sale: a ninety-word vignette. She continued to work at day jobs while mostly collecting rejection slips for several years. But she went on to publish more than three hundred short stories and ninety novels, beginning with *The Dragon's Hoard* (1971), a comic fantasy novel for children.

When *The Birthgrave*, an adult fantasy epic, was rejected by UK publishers in the mid-1970s, Lee sent it across the pond; with its mass-market publication by Daw Books, she was able to transition to full-time writing. She was prolific, producing F/SF novels for both adult and young adult readers, as well as horror, crime and spy fiction, historical fiction, and even erotica. Under the pseudonym Esther Garber, she created lesbian fiction as well. She was also a screenwriter for television and wrote four radio plays for the BBC. Throughout, her writing tended to capture the Goth sensibility of the pursuit of sensuality and freedom to the very edge.

She met writer and artist John Kaiine in 1987, and despite differences (he was nearly two decades younger and sixteen inches taller), the two of them hit it off in short order. In 1992, they married, and they continued on happily in the south of England until she passed away in his arms in 2015 after battling with cancer. She continued to write until her death, and the pair collaborated on many works, including *The Blood of Roses* (1990). Kaiine also created cover art for several of her books.

Due to shifts in the publishing industry, her works had a much harder time finding publishers in the 1990s, partly because they defied strict categorization. She shifted to smaller publishers and tried changing genres, and her works continued to garner positive attention from critics, but even so, the business end of publication was difficult for her until the rise of the small press movement and direct sales via the internet. Daw later undertook a reissue of twenty-two of her books. Perhaps Lee described herself best in a 1998 interview with *Locus Magazine*. "Writers tell stories better, because they've had more practice, but everyone has a book in them—yes, that old cliché. If you gave the most interesting life to a great writer, they could turn it into something wonderful. But all lives are important, all people are important, because everyone is a book. Some people just have easier access to it. We need the expressive arts, the ancient scribes, the storytellers, the priests; and that's where I put myself: as a storyteller; not necessarily a high priestess, but certainly the storyteller."

> *To wake, and not to know where, or even who you are, not even to know what you are—whether a thing with legs and arms, or a brain in the hull of a great fish—that is a strange awakening. But after awhile, uncurling in the darkness, I began to uncover myself, and I was a woman.*
>
> Tanith Lee, from *The Birthgrave* (1975)

PAMELA SARGENT Firebrands *author & Women of Wonder anthologist*

Pamela Sargent is not only a science fiction author who has won both the Nebula and Locus Awards, she is the noted anthology editor who brought us the Women of Wonder series; starting back in 1976, she edited several volumes of science fiction and fantasy stories that were both written by women and featured women as central characters. These were the first collections ever of women writing in these genres—especially fitting considering that the very first science fiction novel, *Frankenstein*, was written by a woman, as is related elsewhere in this book. (See the section on Mary Shelley in Chapter Two for the particulars.)

1976 was a super busy year for this feminist dynamo; besides publishing her first novel, *Cloned Lives*, that same year, she also coauthored *Firebrands: The Heroines of Science Fiction & Fantasy*, an illustrated nonfiction exploration of female characters in the field, and edited an anthology of tales involving biological metamorphosis, *Bio-Futures*. Pamela Sargent sold her first short story while a college senior studying philosophy and ancient history at SUNY Binghamton before going on to earn a master's degree in philosophy.

She is the author of three trilogies—Earthseed, Venus, and Watchstar—and eight other novels, as well as coauthoring four *Star Trek* novelizations. In 2012, the Science Fiction Research Association honored Sargent with the Pilgrim Award for lifetime contribution to scholarship in science fiction and fantasy. *Earthseed*, the first book in the eponymous trilogy, is in development for film adaptation by Paramount Pictures, with scriptwriter Melissa Rosenberg of the *Twilight* series engaged as writer and producer. Pamela Sargent's most recent novel is 2015's *Season of the Cats*.

NANCY KRESS *stories combining rigorous science with humanity's essence*

Nebula and Hugo Award-winning science fiction and fantasy author Nancy Kress (née Koningisor) grew up in upstate New York in a sleepy village where cows graze and apples grow and spent most of her childhood either reading or playing in the woods. She earned a degree in elementary education at SUNY

Plattsburgh and taught fourth-grade students for a few years before leaving the field to marry and start a family in 1973. While pregnant with her second son, she started to write fiction; this had not been her plan, but caring for two infants at home full-time left her with hours in which to experiment. She tried quilting and embroidery first, but found more success with literary creation, selling stories and a first novel, *The Prince of Morning Bells*. During these years, she also furthered her academic pursuits at SUNY Brockport, achieving master's degrees there in the late 1970s in both education and English.

When this first marriage ended in 1984, she went to work writing corporate ad copy at an advertising agency while raising her sons and occasionally teaching at SUNY Brockport. In 1990, she decided to go full-time as a science fiction writer; her first work after taking the plunge was her popular novella *Beggars in Spain*, which went on to win both the Hugo and Nebula awards—a pretty fabulous turn of events, coming right after deciding to leave behind her day job!

She tied the knot a second time with fellow science fiction writer Charles Sheffield in 1998, but tragically lost him only four years later to brain cancer. But the third time seems to have been the charm: she married another writer, Jack Skillingstead, in 2011, and they reside in Seattle, along with, she says, "the world's most spoiled toy poodle," Cosette. Though her early writings leaned toward fantasy, Nancy now writes science fiction, often about genetic engineering, as well as teaching at various institutions, including coteaching the Taos Toolbox writers' intensive workshop with fellow SF writer Walter Jon Williams and writing nonfiction texts about writing itself.

Nancy Kress has won a total of six Nebulas, two Hugos, and a Sturgeon Award for her novellas and short fiction; and her 2003 novel *Probability Space* won a John W. Campbell Award. She is the author of twenty-seven novels, four short story collections, and over a hundred short stories. Her writings have been translated into fourteen Terran languages as well as into Klingon.

JOAN D. VINGE *melder of the mythic with hard science fiction*

Joan Vinge (née Joan Carol Dennison) is a writer of science fiction, poetry, and nonfiction. She is best known for her exceptional novel *The Snow Queen* and its sequels, as well as for her series about a telepath named Cat and her Heaven's Chronicles books, *The Outcasts of Heaven's Belt* (1978) and *Legacy* (1980). She has twice won Hugo Awards for best science fiction, one for her novelette *Eyes of Amber* (1977) and one for her novel *The Snow Queen* (1980), which also won a Locus Award. *Psion* (1982), the first book in her Cat trilogy, won the American Library Association prize for Best Book for Young Adults. Her novels frequently include strong female characters such as the eponymous Snow Queen; and the first Heaven's Chronicles novel tells the tale of a face-off between an egalitarian women's society and collapsing societies dominated by men, set in the various regions of an asteroid belt.

Born in Baltimore in 1948 and inspired by the works of Andre Norton, Joan started to write while still a teenager; her award-winning novel *Psion* was actually an adaptation and expansion of the first long fiction manuscript she created during those years. In college, she studied art before shifting her focus to anthropology, graduating from San Diego State University in 1971. The next year, she married Vernor Vinge, a fellow science fiction writer as well as a young professor of math and computer science at San Diego State. Her first professional sale as a writer was the novella "Tin Soldier," which appeared in *Orbit 14* (1974). She married a second time, the year after her 1979 divorce from Vernor Vinge, and she and second husband James R. Frenkel went on to have two children. *The Snow Queen* (1980), arguably her standout work, draws on the mythopoeic explorations of Robert Graves' *The White Goddess*; its central characterizations are inflected by archetypal echoes of pre-Christian deities in a seamless melding with a science fiction narrative involving a space-going civilization colonizing a planet with two indigenous sentient species. Perhaps it was because of this work that renowned science fiction author Robert Heinlein included her in the dedication page of his novel *Friday* (1982).

In 2002, Vinge was seriously injured in a car accident, resulting in "minor but debilitating" brain damage; at the time, she had been working on *Ladysmith*, a new stand-alone novel set in Europe in the Bronze Age. She was unable to write until early 2007, but then resumed work on the manuscript, which at last saw print in 2012. Also in 2007, a new edition of *Psion* was published in an omnibus edition with *Psiren*, a sequel novella. Her first new novel published after the accident was a novelization of the movie *Cowboys & Aliens* (2011), one of a dozen media novelizations she produced. Vinge has taught science fiction and fantasy writing at both the Clarion East and Clarion West workshops for writers and has published a couple of collections of her original short stories. Besides her literary work, she also creates and sells dolls. She and her husband live in the small town of Green Valley, Arizona.

PAT CADIGAN *the undisputed queen of cyberpunk*

Pat Cadigan is an award-winning science fiction author and editor; though American-born, she lives in the United Kingdom. Her fiction is mostly classified in the cyberpunk subgenre, of which she is considered one of the founders. She has twice won the Arthur C. Clarke Award, for *Synners* (1992) and *Fools* (1995), as well as a 2013 Hugo Award for Best Science Fiction Novelette, a World Fantasy Award, and three Locus Awards. She has also written film novelizations, including one for *Cellular* (2004), which starred Kim Basinger. Her writing is often marked by icy undercurrents of black humor as well as tough-minded vigor, the ingredients of the "punk" part of "cyberpunk." Her works frequently deal with how the human mind relates to technology; she ascribes this to having had the experience of being hooked up to medical machines during recovery from surgery for a congenital heart defect at age five.

Born Patricia Oren Kearney in upstate New York in 1953, she grew up in the small town of Fitchburg, Massachusetts. She pursued theater arts for a time at the University of Massachusetts at Amherst on a scholarship, but went on to study science fiction and science fiction writing with Professor James Gunn at the University of Kansas. She met and married Rufus Cadigan during her college years; shortly after she graduated from the University of Kansas in 1975, they divorced. That same year, she became involved in preparations for the 1976 World Science Fiction Convention (or WorldCon) in Kansas City, Missouri. She ended up serving as liaison with author guest of honor Robert Heinlein; Heinlein later included her in the dedication of his novel *Friday* in recognition of their friendship. In the late 1970s, she had a job at fantasy writer Tom Reamy's graphic design company, and then worked as a writer for Hallmark Cards in Kansas City for ten years. Concurrently, from the late seventies until the early eighties, she and her second husband, Arnie Fenner, edited two small press F/SF magazines, first *Chacal*, and then *Shayol*, which was noted for the quality of its stories.

She sold her first professional science fiction story in 1980 and continued to make short fiction sales and work on longer manuscripts while still working at a full-time day job, and then while also parenting her young son. With the success of her writing in the 1980s, she transitioned to writing full-time in 1987, the year she published her first book, *Mindplayers*; the novel originated in a series of four linked short stories about her heroine Deadpan Allie which Cadigan revised and expanded following their publication earlier in the eighties. In this first novel, she framed the mind as a stage for inner psychodramas in which a healer could intervene using "Dream Hacking" technology. In 1989, *Patterns*, a collection of her short stories, was released; it went on to win a Locus Award the following year. She followed it up with her award-winning second novel *Synners* (1991), and in the next couple years, two more collections of her short fiction as well as the novel *Fools*. *Fools* envisioned a near-future environment in which memories are marketable. *Tea from an Empty Cup* (1998) was again based on two connected novellas she had published in the nineties, and a sequel, *Dervish Is Digital*, was released a couple of years later; these two works comprise the Doré Konstantin series, in which detective Konstantin learns to pursue perpetrators in cyberspace.

While on a short visit to England during the nineties, Cadigan met journalist Christopher Fowler (not to be confused with the noted UK thriller author) when he asked to interview her. He apparently made a good impression; she looked him up after her second divorce, and romance ensued. In 1996, she emigrated to London, England, with her son, Rob Fenner, and she and Fowler were married later that year. After her son had grown to an independent age, her writing took a back seat for several years due to other family obligations, of which Cadigan said in an interview, "I had to look after my elderly mother, and it wasn't easy, even with my husband helping. As a result, for the first dozen years of the century, I could only write short fiction. My mother passed away in late 2012, and I went back to work on a novel in earnest...and then I got cancer. Go figure." In 2014, Pat Cadigan became a citizen of the United Kingdom, where she has been a visiting lecturer on creative writing and science fiction at British universities. *Mad Love* (2019) which tells the origin story of DC Comics' Harley Quinn, is a novelization created by Cadigan in collaboration with Paul Dini, one of the original creators of the character; it is set in the Gotham City of Batman fame, particularly at Arkham Asylum. As of this writing, she is working on a novel that "jumps off from the end" of her Hugo-winning novelette, 2013's "The Girl-Thing Who Went Out for Sushi"; its working title is *See You When You Get There*.

JO WALTON *fan turned world fantasy & science fiction prizewinner*

Jo Walton is a Welsh-born Canadian author of prizewinning science fiction, fantasy, and nonfiction as well as poetry. Born and raised in Aberdare, Wales, in 1964, young Jo started writing at only thirteen, but publication of her creations was still two decades in her future. Meanwhile, she was active in science fiction and fantasy fandom online, notably in Usenet groups, and involved in role-playing game publications. During these years, she attended the University of Lancaster, England; married and had a son in 1990 with first husband Ken Walton; and eventually divorced. She lived in Lancaster in the late 1990s before moving to Swansea.

Her first three published novels, *The King's Peace* (2000), *The King's Name* (2001), and *The Prize in the Game* (2002), though not a trilogy, are all historical fantasies set in the same fictional world of her creation, which draws from legends of Arthurian Britain and the Ireland of the ancient book *The Táin*. In between releases, she married Dr. Emmet A. O'Brien, an Irishman with a bachelor's degree in genetics and a PhD in philosophy, and in 2002, they emigrated to Montreal, Canada. That same year, she also won the John W. Campbell Award for Best New Writer. In 2004, *Tooth and Claw* won both the British and World Fantasy Awards; the author describes it as "a sentimental Victorian novel in which all the characters are dragons who eat each other."

Her first science fiction novel, *Farthing* (2006), was nominated for several awards; in the book's alternate-history version of England and Europe, after the first few years of World War II, Britain becomes an ally of Nazi Germany. Sequels *Ha'penny* and *Half a Crown* followed in 2007 and 2008 to positive reception. Interestingly, when scholar/SF writer Howard V. Hendrix declared in 2007 that professional authors should never publish their own writings online for free because it made them the equivalent of scabs disempowering striking union workers, Walton took the opposite stance: She declared April 23 'International Pixel-Stained Technopeasant Day,' and in 2008, celebrated the occasion by releasing *Those Who Favor Fire* (several chapters of an unfinished sequel to *Tooth and Claw*) online gratis.

Her fantasy novel *Lifelode* (2009) won a Mythopoeic Award; in its world, how magic, thought, and even the flow of time work depends on how far east or west one is. It also features a realistically depicted polyamorous family structure. Walton won both the 2012 Hugo and Nebula awards for *Among Others*, as well as the British Fantasy Award; it tells the story of Morwenna, a young and otherworldly girl trying to deal with having lost her twin sister, set in an alternate-history version of Wales where the fairy folk are drawn to human-built ruins. *My Real Children* (2014), the tale of an aged woman in a nursing home caught between two alternate universes—both of which she remembers—won the Tiptree Award for its handling of a lesbian family in one of the alternate realities. *What Makes This Book So Great*, a book of reviews of classic science fiction works, won a Locus nonfiction award in 2015; she followed it up with her mythic Thessaly trilogy, a fantasy work in which the Greek gods attempt to create an island utopia by having ten thousand human children raised there in the way prescribed in Plato's *Republic*.

Jo Walton says that the reason her books vary so widely is because she "gets bored easily"; her fourteen novels are an array of award-winning ingenuity. She has also published collections of her poetry, essays, and short stories. Her latest novel, *Lent* (2019), takes on the task of reimagining the life of Savonarola in the fifteenth century.

ANN LECKIE *exploring the boundaries of identity*

Ann Leckie hit a science fiction grand slam with her 2013 novel *Ancillary Justice*, winning both the Hugo and Nebula awards for Best Novel, as well as the Arthur C. Clarke and British Science Fiction Association awards. On her way there, having obtained a degree in music from Washington University in 1989, she predictably enough worked in several fields besides music or writing: she did office work, waited tables, and was at various times a sound engineer as well as a "rodman" on a land surveying crew. While an understimulated stay-at-home mom following the births of her two children in 1996 and 2000, in 2002, she tried her hand at NaNoWriMo, a.k.a. National Novel Writing Month, resulting in the first draft of what would eventually become *Ancillary Justice*. She went on to hone her skills under noted science fiction author Octavia Butler at the Clarion West Writers Workshop in 2005, completing her debut novel over the next six years. Concurrently, she wrote and sold over half a dozen works of short fiction to periodicals including *Realms of Fantasy* and *Strange Horizons* as well as editing the online F/SF magazine *Giganotosaurus* from 2010 to 2013.

Ancillary Justice tells the story of Breq, the only survivor of the treacherous destruction of a starship other than the ship's artificial intelligence; as allies, she and the AI essentially merge in their quest for vengeance against an imperial ruler. It was followed by two further works in the trilogy, *Ancillary Sword* (2014) and *Ancillary Mercy* (2015), both of which were well received; the final work earned Leckie another Best Novel Hugo nod. Her speculative fiction works since include 2017's *Provenance*, which was nominated for a Hugo, and in 2019, her debut epic fantasy *The Raven Tower*, which the Kirkus Review describes as "[sharp,] many layered, and as always for Leckie, deeply intelligent." She lives with her family in St. Louis, Missouri.

ELIZABETH BEAR *storyteller of sundry speculative styles*

Elizabeth Bear is the award-winning author of three dozen science fiction and fantasy novels as well as over a hundred short stories. Besides poetry and the odd bit of nonfiction, the genre-hopping Bear has written in myriad speculative fiction subgenres, including cyberpunk, steampunk, classic generation-ship science fiction, space opera, vampire and other paranormal fantasy, epic fantasy, historical fiction, and futuristic mystery, to name a few. Her writing often features strong female characters, such as wizards or special forces warriors who happen to be women. Not infrequently, her works include queer characters and relationships.

Born in 1971 in Hartford, Connecticut, she has said that she is a third-generation science fiction fan on both sides of the family. Bear (née Sarah

Bear Elizabeth Wishnevsky) is of Ukrainian and Swedish descent; she started writing while in grade school, "little stapled 'books' of stories about dinosaurs and race horses and aliens," and then tried her hand at poetry. She went on to be a reporter for her college's five-day-per-week newspaper. Before turning to writing full-time in her mid-thirties, she worked at positions as wide-ranging as stablehand, "media industry professional," and being the person who gets up at three in the morning to bake for a donut shop. She published her first novel, *Hammered*, in early 2005, following it with two sequels, *Scardown* and *Worldwired*, before the end of that year(!); after spending some time living in Las Vegas, she returned to Connecticut in 2006. During that period, she won both the John W. Campbell Award for Best New Writer and the Locus Award for Best First Novel.

She carried on writing at quite a prolific pace, publishing nine more novels in the next five years. Her short story "Tideline" drew major recognition, winning both the Hugo and Sturgeon awards in 2008; she hit Hugo gold again with her novelette "Shoggoths in Bloom" (2009). That same year, she won the Gaylactic Spectrum Award for Best Novel for *The Stratford Man (Ink and Steel* and *Hell and Earth)*. Reviewer Annalee Newitz of *io9* has said that Bear "is famous for combining high-octane military [and] spy tales with eccentric and subversive subplots." Elizabeth Bear has taught at both the Viable Paradise and the Clarion West writers' workshops. She lives in Massachusetts' Pioneer Valley with her spouse, writer Scott Lynch.

> *I think the problem is that some writers (and some readers) have spent a lot of time internalizing our societal narrative that women...just aren't interesting. The things we do and have done don't make good stories, or if they do, those stories are women's stories, and not for general consumption.*
>
> Elizabeth Bear, in her nonfiction "Where Are All the Women?" (Tor publishing blog; 2017 essay on science fiction)

The Beauty of the Otherworld Within Our Own: Magic Realism

JEANETTE WINTERSON *I'd rather be happy than normal*

Author Jeanette Winterson was born in 1959 in Manchester, England, to a seventeen-year-old factory worker. She was adopted by Jack and Constance Winterson and raised Pentecostal in Accrington, near Manchester. The only non-religious book in the house was Mallory's *Morte d'Arthur*. She later claimed it had as much influence on her as the Bible. At age sixteen, while attending Accrington High School for Girls, Jeanette fell in love with a classmate. After she refused her mother's demand that she stop seeing her girlfriend, her mother kicked Jeanette out of her home. She somehow managed to continue her education and went on to study English at Catherine's College, Oxford.

Though Winterson had an undeniable love of literature, she was a philosopher at heart. She worked at the Roundhouse Theatre in London in a variety of positions, including minding the theater concessions and writing playbooks. After that, she applied for a job at Pandora Press. Though she wasn't hired, she told her interviewer, Phillippa Brewster, about a novel she had written called *Oranges Are Not the Only Fruit*; Pandora went on to publish it in 1985. Via word of mouth and local bookshops, the novel garnered publicity and became a success, even winning prizes. Winterson published her second novel, *The Passion*, in 1987.

In 1994, she moved from London to the Cotswolds, where she still resides. She also bought an abandoned 1810 market building in Spitalfields, in London's East End. She took a couple years to remodel the building; on the ground floor, she opened Verde's, a successful market which she still owns. Jeanette says of it, "It is beautiful to look at, and it is an asset to the neighborhood—especially now, when the whole place is becoming a corporate playground." She also grows much of her own food and is part-owner of a herd of rare sheep called the Lions of the Wold.

In 2009, Jeanette met Susie Orbach, psychoanalyst and author of the classics *Fat Is a Feminist Issue* and *The Impossibility of Sex: Stories of the Intimate*

Relationship Between Therapist and Patient; the two married in 2015. Winterson has won numerous awards for her work and is published in eighteen countries. She has written twenty-two books, including her memoir, *Why Be Happy When You Could Be Normal?* She teaches 'New Writing' at the University of Manchester.

AUDREY NIFFENEGGER *her fearful symmetry*

Audrey Niffenegger is an artist, academic, and writer of mystical and mythic speculative fiction. She was born in South Haven, Michigan, and grew up in Evanston, Illinois. Starting in 1978, she studied printmaking at the Art Institute of Chicago and went on to obtain an MFA in 1991 from the Department of Art Theory and Practice at Northwestern University. She has exhibited her artist's books, prints, paintings, comics, and drawings at Chicago's Printworks Gallery since the late 1980s. In 1994, Audrey Niffenegger was one of the book artists, papermakers, and designers who founded the Columbia College Chicago Center for Book and Paper Arts. She went on to teach book arts in the Interdisciplinary Book and Paper Arts MFA program there. She was also a professor on the faculty of its creative writing department until 2015, as well as teaching at the Newberry Library, Penland School of Craft, Haystack, and the University of Illinois at Chicago. In 2013, there was a retrospective of her prints, paintings, and artist's books at the National Museum of Women in the Arts in Washington, DC.

Concurrently, in 1997, she had an idea for a graphic novel about a time traveler and his wife. She eventually decided the project would work better as a novel and published *The Time Traveler's Wife* in 2003 with the independent publisher MacAdam/Cage. It was an international bestseller that went on to be adapted for cinema. In 2008, Niffenegger published *The Night Bookmobile*, a serialized graphic novel for the London Guardian; her second novel, *Her Fearful Symmetry*, was published in 2009. In 2013, her illustrated novella, *Raven Girl*, was released in conjunction with the Royal Opera House Ballet production of the same name. As of this writing, she is working to complete a sequel to *The Time Traveler's Wife* tentatively titled *The Other Husband*, as well as another work entitled *The Chinchilla Girl in Exile*. She is also working on a collection of illustrated adaptations of her short stories with her husband, the artist and writer Eddie Campbell, with whom she lives in Chicago.

JULIA ELLIOTT *the surreal South*

Julia Elliott is a writer of Southern Gothic science fiction. She earned her MFA from Penn State in 1996 and continued on to a PhD from the University of Georgia in 2012. Originally an author of short fiction, her short stories have been published in *Tin House*, the *Georgia Review*, *Conjunctions*, and the *New York Times*, among other publications. She has received a Rona Jaffe Writer's Award, and her stories have been anthologized in *Pushcart Prize: Best of the Small Presses* and *The Best American Short Stories*. Julia's debut story collection, *The Wilds*, was chosen by Kirkus, BuzzFeed, Book Riot, and Electric Literature as one of the best books of 2014, and it was also a *New York Times Book Review* Editors' Choice. *The Wilds* is a combination of genres, including Surrealism, Southern Gothic, fairy tale, and science fiction. Her willingness to experiment with fusing genres has put her on the map.

Julia's debut novel, *The New and Improved Romie Futch*, most of which she wrote while she was pregnant, was published in 2015. The work is about a cybernetically enhanced taxidermist; it is, of course, set in the Deep South. In 2016, she was awarded the Shared Worlds Residency by Amazon.com. She is currently working on a novel about Hamadryas baboons, a species she studied as an amateur primatologist. A lot of the content that informs Elliott's fiction comes from her academic interests; science, gender, and history recombine imaginatively within the pages of her books. Her work is humorous, quirky, speculative, and anachronistic. She lives in Columbia, South Carolina, with her husband and daughter and teaches English, women's studies, and gender studies at the University of South Carolina.

ERIN MORGENSTERN *transcendent magic realism*

Erin Morgenstern is the author of *The Night Circus* (2011) and *The Starless Sea* (2019). After growing up in Massachusetts, she studied theater and studio arts at Smith College. Morgenstern's debut novel began as a National Novel Writing Month project; NaNoWriMo is an annual online challenge which any writer may take up to write 50,000 words during the month of November.

She cites Susanna Clarke's *Jonathan Strange & Mr. Norrell* and both the book and film adaptation of *The Prestige* by Christopher Priest, as well as *Einstein's Dreams* by Alan Lightman, as having influenced *The Night Circus*. It also borrows from classics and children's literature, including works by authors ranging from Shakespeare and Dickens to Roald Dahl, Edward Gorey, and Neil Gaiman. After finishing her first novel, she sent out query letters and sample pages as per agency guidelines; ultimately, she did find an agent to help her publish it. It was rewritten three times and was eventually published by Penguin Random House. Of *The Starless Sea*, her sophomore effort, she says, "It's about stories, and storytelling, and fate, and time, and video games. There is a lot of snow in it. And also bees."

In addition to art and writing, Morgenstern is a practitioner of Tarot reading. She published *The Phantomwise Tarot*, a series of paintings based on the Major Arcana, though only in a very limited printing. Her personal favorite deck is *The Wild Unknown*. Astrology is another favorite divinatory pursuit. She herself is a Cancer with a Leo Moon and Taurus ascendant. She resides in the Berkshires with her husband and their feline companion.

NNEDI OKORAFOR *courageous weaver of cultures*

Nnedi Okorafor is an internationally known award-winning author of science fiction, fantasy, and works of magic realism incorporating African culture, characterization, and settings. She was born in 1974, the daughter of Nigerian Igbo parents who came to the United States to further their educations and were stranded in America when the Nigerian Civil War broke out. Her father was a heart surgeon. From an early age, young Nnedi often visited Nigeria. She went on to become a nationally known track and tennis star for Homewood-Flossmoor High School in Illinois, as well as achieving academic success in science and mathematics; she planned to pursue a career in entomology. But when she was nineteen, a preexisting scoliosis condition worsened, and though surgeons tried to straighten and fuse her spine, she experienced a rare complication following the operation and ended up paralyzed from the waist down.

It was at this point that she began for the first time to write little stories—'little' in a literal sense, as she inscribed them in the margins of one of her science fiction books. With intensive physical therapy the following summer, she was able to literally get back on her feet, but her career as an athlete was finished, as she needed a cane even to walk. A close friend suggested that she take a creative writing course; by the end of the semester, she had begun to write her first novel. She went on to earn a number of writing-related degrees: a master's in journalism from Michigan State, and both a master's and PhD in literature and creative writing from the University of Illinois at Chicago. She also graduated from the Clarion Writers Workshop in Lansing, Michigan, in 2001. During her sophomore undergraduate year, she wrote her first serious story, which she set in Nigeria. She wanted to set stories in Africa because so few stories used it as a setting, and she wanted people of color and girls to play important parts in her narratives, since previously most important characters in speculative fiction had been white and male. She also cites Nigeria itself as her "muse," since she has been deeply influenced by Nigerian folklore, mythology, and mysticism. She also married and had a daughter (Anyaugo, or Anya) during these years of academic study.

In 2001, she received the Hurston-Wright award for her story "Amphibious Green"; since then, many of her short stories have been published in myriad anthologies and magazines, as well as in her own short story collection, *Kabu Kabu* (2013), which includes a foreword written by Whoopi Goldberg. Following her first short story award, she went on to write two prizewinning young adult books, *Zahrah the Windseeker* (2005) and *The Shadow Speaker* (2007), and a children's book, *Long Juju Man* (2009). When she tackled writing a novel for adults after the passing of her father with *Who Fears Death* (2010), the book won the World Fantasy Award for Best Novel for 2011 as well as other accolades; it is currently in development as an HBO drama series with George R.R. Martin of *Game of Thrones* fame on board as executive producer. Her reputation continued to grow with the Akata series for young adults, followed by two novels for adults: *Lagoon* (2014) and *The Book of Phoenix* (2015), a prequel to *Who Fears Death* that the *New York Times* called a "triumph." That same publication once profiled Okorafor's work under the title, "Weapons of Mass Creation."

Okorafor is perhaps best known for her Binti trilogy; it began with the novella *Binti* (2015), which won both the Nebula and Hugo Awards for best novella in 2016. Sequels *Binti: Home* (2017) and *Binti: The Night Masquerade* (2018) were both finalist nominees for the Hugo Award in the same category. Concurrent with these releases, a Nigerian film company optioned a hybrid short story of hers involving both witchcraft and science for adaptation as a short film titled *Hello, Rain,* which premiered at the International Short Film Festival Oberhausen in 2018. She has also written a number of comic books for Marvel based on *Black Panther,* including 2018's *Wakanda Forever* and *Shuri,* focusing on the title character, a princess of the fictional land of Wakanda. *New York Times* writer Alexandra Alter said of Okorafor that her work frequently examines "weighty social issues: racial and gender inequality, political violence, the destruction of the environment, genocide, and corruption" using "the framework of fantasy." Nnedi Okorafor is an associate professor at SUNY in Buffalo, New York, and splits her time between Buffalo and Illinois.

Women in Science Fiction Standing Up for Their Sisters

SHERI S. TEPPER *ecology, equality, theology, and mystery*

Sheri Tepper, née Stewart (1929–2016), was an American author known primarily for her feminist science fiction novels, which explored gender and equality as well as ecology and theology. Though often called an "ecofeminist" science fiction writer, she preferred to describe herself as an eco-humanist. She also wrote mysteries, horror novels, and poetry, and during her life made use of several pen names, including the gender-neutral noms de plume E.E. Horlak, A.J. Orde, and B.J. Oliphant. In all, she published more than forty novels, even though she did not make her first sale until she was over fifty years old. Half her mystery novels feature Shirley McClintock as protagonist, a Colorado ranch woman who solves cases. NPR's Genevieve Valentine said of Tepper's writing: "…her characters can be gripping, especially the women who find themselves in their element somewhere they're expected to wither."

Born in a small town in Colorado in 1929, she started out writing stories for children and poetry under the name Sheri S. Eberhart. After marrying at age twenty and divorcing in her late twenties, she recalls spending "ten years… working all kinds of different jobs" while also the single mother of two children. This included a stint as a clerical worker with the international relief agency CARE. She then worked for Rocky Mountain Planned Parenthood from 1962 to 1986, eventually attaining the position of executive director; one of the tasks at the nonprofit was writing informative pamphlets, notably including *So You Don't Want to Be a Sex Object* (1978).

Meanwhile, her first novel for adults, *King's Blood*, was published in 1982, kicking off her True Game trilogy of trilogies. She wrote a number of fiction series in the eighties as well as her noted stand-alone novel *The Gate to Women's Country* (1988), a post-apocalyptic novel set three hundred years in the American future. She is remembered for her acclaimed novel *Grass* (1989), first in the Arbai trilogy. Her novel *Beauty*, a retelling of the classic fairy tale, won the 1992 Locus Award for Best Fantasy Novel. She lived to be a great-grandmother, residing with her second husband, Gene Tepper, for the last half century of her life in Santa Fe, New Mexico.

MARGE PIERCY *poet, novelist, and activist for a new world*

Marge Piercy is best known for her nearly twenty volumes of poetry and her novels, including *Small Changes, Woman on the Edge of Time*, her cyberpunk novel *He, She and It*, and her sweeping World War II historical novel *Gone to Soldiers*, which was a *New York Times* bestseller. She has received many awards and prizes as well as four honorary doctorates, but the road there was not a smooth one.

She was born in Detroit in 1936; her family, like so many others, was affected by the Depression. Her grandfather Morris was a union organizer who was murdered while organizing bakery workers. His widow, maternal grandmother Hannah, was the daughter of a rabbi and was born in a shtetl in Lithuania; Piercy describes her as having been a great storyteller. Piercy's father went through a period of unemployment but managed to find a job working with heavy machinery at Westinghouse.

Piercy remembers having had a fairly happy early childhood. But halfway through grade school, she almost died from the German measles (for which no effective vaccine existed until the 1960s) and then caught rheumatic fever; this illness transformed young Marge from an attractive, healthy child into a thin and bluish-pale youngster given to fainting. She turned to reading for comfort, following in the footsteps of her mother, an avid reader whom Piercy credits with making her into a poet. But as she grew into more independence, they clashed fiercely, and Marge left the family home and started college at age seventeen; this was made possible by a scholarship she won that paid her tuition at the University of Michigan. She was the first member of her family ever to attend college.

Though the academic work was not exceptionally difficult for her, life as a 1950s college student was far from comfortable in a personal sense for Piercy, whose ambitions and bisexuality were seen as "unwomanly" in a time when conformity was a huge expectation. But she persisted, and in 1957, she won the Hopwood Award for Poetry and Fiction, which greatly improved her financial situation during her senior year and enabled her to travel to France for a time following her graduation. She went on to earn a master's degree at Northwestern University, where she had a fellowship. She was briefly married to an Algerian Jewish French particle physicist, but the union did not last, in part because of his traditionalism. He was unable to understand how much her writing mattered to her. Afterwards, she lived in Chicago and endured very tight financial straits.

While endeavoring to develop herself as a writer of poetry and prose, she worked at all sorts of part-time jobs, ranging from art modeling to low-paid part-time college instructor gigs. She remembers this time as the hardest years of her adult life; fifties society judged her as a failure just for being divorced, and she felt completely invisible as an author, writing novel after novel but receiving only rejection slips. Piercy has said that, like Simone de Beauvoir, who was a major influence, she desired to write fiction that integrated aspects of the political. She wanted real women to be seen in her narratives, people from the working class whose inner lives were not encompassed by a simplistic surface view.

She wed a computer scientist in 1962; it was an unconventional open relationship that by turns enriched and complicated her life. Later, her novels at times explored polyamorous relationships and communal living; *Small Changes* (1973) and *Woman on the Edge of Time* (1976) were ahead of their time in this regard. The couple lived in Cambridge, San Francisco, and New York, eventually settling in Boston; Piercy made frequent visits to Ann Arbor, Michigan, where she was part of organizing the group that would become the Students for a Democratic Society (SDS). She had been active in the civil rights and antiwar movements for some time and became a significant voice for feminist concerns in the SDS and the New Left movement, as well as contributing to the growth of environmental thought.

Her first book of poems, *Breaking Camp*, was published in 1968. In 1971, she was poet in residence at the University of Kansas at Lawrence; later that year, she moved to Cape Cod with her husband. On Cape Cod, she wrote 1973's *Small Changes*, which Myrna Lamb of the *Washington Post* called "groundbreaking," and then *Woman on the Edge of Time* (1976). Piercy has stated that there was a change in her writing and poetry following the move—gardening became a part of her life then, and leaving behind urban environments may have resulted in an experiential shift. She did some teaching stints at other colleges in the following years. Her second marriage ended in the late 1970s.

With *Woman on the Edge of Time*, considered a classic of speculative fiction as well as of feminist literature, Piercy broke into the traditionally male field of dystopian fiction, but fused the novel's dystopian aspects with a contrasting futuristic utopia in the frame of a time travel story. She later wrote that the genesis of the tale was that she "wanted to take what I considered the most fruitful ideas of the various movements for social change and make them vivid and concrete." William Gibson credits this work as the origin of the cyberpunk genre; it is often compared to such classics as Ursula Le Guin's *The Left Hand of Darkness* and *The Dispossessed*, as well as Margaret Atwood's *The Handmaid's Tale*. Piercy later tackled the dystopian genre once more with *He, She and It*, set in a world where ever-expanding megacities have brought about ecological collapse. Again, the human dimension makes the story approachable, as the main character seeks to recover her young son; mystical elements of Judaic tradition, such as the golem, are also intertwined with the narrative.

In 1982, she married Ira Wood; they have written several books together, including the novel *Storm Tide* and a nonfiction text about the writer's craft. In 1993, they started Leapfrog Press, which publishes an eclectic selection of fiction, nonfiction, and poetry. They sold Leapfrog to new owners in 2008.

Piercy is author of nearly twenty volumes of poems, among them *The Moon Is Always Female* (1980, considered a feminist classic) and 1999's *Early Grrrl* and *The Art of Blessing the Day*, as well as eighteen novels, one play in collaboration with her third (and current) husband Ira Wood titled *The Last White Class*, one essay collection, three nonfiction books, and a 2002 memoir, the amusingly named *Sleeping with Cats*. Her most recent collections of poetry include *The Crooked Inheritance* (2006), *The Hunger Moon: New and Selected Poems 1980–2010* (2012), and *Made in Detroit* (2015). She lives on Cape Cod with her husband in a home she designed.

> *Never doubt that you can change history. You already have.*
>
> Marge Piercy

JOANNA RUSS *"I'm not a girl. I'm a genius."*

Joanna Russ was a speculative fiction novelist, reviewer, essayist, and creator of many short stories and nonfiction best known for her landmark feminist science fiction novels *The Female Man* (1975) and *We Who Are About To* (1977). She was born to two school teachers in the Bronx in 1937 and began writing and illustrating her own works of fiction at an early age. She also evinced talent in the sciences, winning a Westinghouse science prize as a high school senior in 1953 for a biology project on the growth of fungi, but later focused on literature at Cornell, where she studied with noted author Vladimir Nabokov. She graduated with a BA in 1957 and went on to Yale Drama School, where she obtained an MFA in playwriting in 1960. She taught at a number of universities including Cornell before teaching at the University of Washington, where she eventually became a full professor.

She had started reading science fiction as a teenager because she was attracted to stories of worlds "where things could be different"; in 1959, she sold her first SF story to the *Magazine of Fantasy and Science Fiction*, where she continued as a reviewer off and on for two decades. She was briefly married to a journalist in the mid-sixties but divorced after four years. Her first novel, 1968's Hugo-nominated *Picnic on Paradise*, was the first in a series depicting Alyx, a female mercenary who became an exemplar for later strong female SF protagonists; it was also some of the earliest time-travel fiction written by a female author. Russ became a leading voice in the New Wave of American science fiction, integrating the political movements of the time into her writing, particularly feminism; her writing is flavored with anger intermixed with humor and irony. Her novel *And Chaos Died* (1970) experimented with portraying telepathy, and she also wrote *The Female Man* in 1970, though it did not see print until 1975, around the time that she began to come out as a lesbian. In 1973, she won a Nebula Award for her short story "When It Changed"; her story "Souls" won both the Hugo and Locus Awards ten years later.

Concurrently, she produced influential literary criticism expressing her political insights, including 1983's *How to Suppress Women's Writing*; 1985's *Magic Mommas, Trembling Sisters, Puritans & Perverts*; *To Write Like a Woman: Essays in Feminism and Science Fiction* (1995); and her 1998 book *What Are We Fighting For? Sex, Race, Class, and the Future of Feminism*. She received retrospective Tiptree Awards in 1995 for "When It Changed" and *The Female Man* (1975) for exploring sex and gender in speculative fiction. In the mid-1990s, she retired from teaching at the University of Washington due to worsening health, and in 2011, she died in Tucson after a series of strokes. Following her death, Russ was named a Science Fiction and Fantasy Writers of America Grand Master and inducted into the Science Fiction and Fantasy Hall of Fame. The University of Oregon maintains an archive of her papers.

There are plenty of images of women in science fiction. There are hardly any women.

Joanna Russ

NICOLA GRIFFITH *"if you wait for the right moment, you'll wait forever"*

Nicola Griffith is an award-winning British-American novelist, essayist, editor, and creative writing teacher born in 1960. While growing up in Yorkshire, at age eleven, she won a BBC student poetry contest; the prize included reading her own winning entry on a radio broadcast. Before her teens, she was aware of her attraction to the same sex, but as her parents had reacted extremely negatively to an older sister acting on similar feelings at age fifteen, young Nicola decided "no hint" of how she felt could be revealed before independent adulthood and immersed herself in a diversity of literature and music. Following a two-year teenage first relationship, in the late seventies, she met Carol Taylor and the two became longtime partners. They moved to Hull, where Griffith got a "real education" from the outlaws as well as the intellectuals and feminists she came to know, though the couple's life there was in some ways marginal. She did find a women's community in Hull and read "earnest feminist fiction" from the library. As lead singer of the band Jane's Plane, founded 1981, she started to write lyrics for the five-woman group; they went on to tour regionally and play on national television.

After the band broke up in 1983, she tried her hand at martial arts and writing fiction; the next year, she smoked her last cigarette, and a month later, left behind hash and speed. Griffith says of this time that she "earned her beer money teaching women's self-defense...and arm-wrestling in bars"; in 1985, she was injured while defending another woman in a bar fight and was even briefly hospitalized. Both her martial arts practice and her writing, as well as seeing her older sister Helena's teenage drug addiction devolve into dealing heroin and meth, led Nicola to quit all recreational use of drugs, even psychedelic mushrooms, which she had explored extensively. In 1987, she sold her first story, "Mirrors and Burnstone," to the enduring F/SF magazine *Interzone*. Though she secured a staff position at a resource center for the unemployed, restlessness spurred her to apply to the Clarion Workshop for science fiction and fantasy writers at Michigan State, which accepted her with a scholarship. At Clarion, while studying with such noted authors as Kim Stanley Robinson, Kate Wilhelm, and Samuel R. Delany, she met fellow writer Kelley Eskridge, an American; they fell in love, and a quarter-million-word correspondence between them ensued.

In 1993, despite a diagnosis of multiple sclerosis, which "slowed her down a bit," Griffith blazed her way into the world of science fiction with her first published full-length book, *Ammonite*; it won both the James Tiptree, Jr. and Lambda awards. That same year, after some challenging wrangles with US immigration about her application for a permanent-resident green card, she and Kelley Eskridge published the announcement of their commitment ceremony in *The Atlanta Journal-Constitution*; it would be two decades before they were at last able to legally wed. Her second novel, 1995's *Slow River*, won the 1996 Nebula Award for best science fiction novel and another Lambda. Since then, Griffith has published several novels, coedited three anthologies of short fiction, both in the F/SF and horror genres, and released a multimedia memoir, *And Now We Are Going to Have a Party: Liner Notes to a Writer's Early Life*.

Besides writing, editing, and teaching, Nicola Griffith has been working toward more just standards for how writing honors are awarded. In 2015, she founded a working group to look at data on literary prizes and get a picture of "how gender bias operates within the trade publishing ecosystem"; this resulted in the founding and funding of the $50,000 Half the World Global Literati Prize. The next year, she began #CripLit, an online community for writers with disabilities which features a regular Twitter chat. As of this writing, Nicola Griffith says she is often "happily lost in the seventh century" while writing the sequel to her 2013 historical fantasy novel *Hild*; titled *Menewood*, it is expected in 2021. Nicola, who now holds dual US/UK citizenship, recently obtained a PhD in Creative Writing from Anglia Ruskin University, and lives on a quiet Seattle cul-de-sac with her wife Kelley.

Science Fiction: The Next Generation

MALKA OLDER *original visions of future societies*

Malka Older is a science fiction writer as well as an academic who also works in humanitarian aid and development, responding to natural disasters and other emergencies in such places as Darfur, Indonesia, Sri Lanka, Uganda, Japan, and Mali. She earned a BA in literature from Harvard and then a master's degree in international relations and economics from the School of Advanced International Studies at Johns Hopkins University, and as of this writing, she is currently a doctoral candidate. She has also conducted research on the human and organizational factors involved in the response to the catastrophic failure of the Fukushima Dai-Ichi nuclear power plant following an earthquake and tsunami in Japan in 2011.

After entering the field of speculative fiction with her short story "Tear Tracks" (2015), Older's first novel, the political science fiction thriller *Infomocracy*, was named one of the best books of 2016 by the *Kirkus Review*. The full Centenal Cycle trilogy, including *Infomocracy*'s two sequels, *Null States* and *State Tectonics*, was nominated for a Hugo Award. The trilogy posits the dissolution of nation-states into "centenals," affinity groups with approximately 100,000 people in each, though as the story unfolds, it becomes clear that this system has not eliminated political infighting. Her first short story collection, *And Other Disasters* published in November 2019. She is also the creator of *Ninth Step Station*, a cyberpunk crime drama serial set in Tokyo.

EMILY ST. JOHN MANDEL *"what tiny thing that you do makes a difference?"*

Emily St. John Mandel is a Canadian-born author of "literary noir" works, and more recently, a prizewinning science fiction novel, *Station Eleven*. The daughter of a social worker and a plumber, she was born and raised on Denman Island off the coast of British Columbia. At eighteen, Emily quit school to study contemporary dance at the School of Toronto Dance Theatre. In an interesting twist of fate, after picking up a free newspaper in Toronto and corresponding with the writer of one of its book reviews, she ended up meeting her future husband, writer Kevin Mandel. While briefly living in Montreal, she refocused her creative goals from dance to literature and began writing her first novel, *Last Night in Montreal* (2009). Its plot was in part inspired by her own rootlessness as she moved around, returning to Toronto before moving to New York City. She now lives in Brooklyn with her husband and daughter. She followed up her debut work with *The Singer's Gun* (2010) and *The Lola Quartet* (2012); though they may be described as suspense thrillers, their narratives cross genre lines.

Mandel hit pay dirt with 2014's *Station Eleven*, which was a finalist for both the National Book Award and the PEN/Faulkner Award; in 2015, it won the Arthur C. Clarke Award and the Toronto Book Award. The novel is set in the near future in a post-apocalyptic version of the Great Lakes region and follows members of a Shakespearian acting troupe as a fictional swine-flu pandemic unfolds. A television series adaptation of *Station Eleven* is currently in development. As of this writing, her fifth novel, *The Glass Hotel*, is expected to be released in 2020; it shares a couple of characters with her acclaimed work *Station Eleven* but is set in the late twentieth century.

CATHERYNNE M. VALENTE *from crowdfunded creation to modern mythmaking*

Cat Valente is not your average bestselling author of poetry and speculative fiction, if there is such a type of person. For starters, she graduated from high school at the age of only fifteen, then continued on to UC San Diego and Edinburgh University, where she received her BA in Classics with an emphasis in Ancient Greek Linguistics. Born in 1979, in 2004, she published a short story, a first poetic volume, and her first two novels, *The Labyrinth* and *The Ice Puzzle*; she has said that she "came to fiction from poetry." Since then, she has produced several novels, numerous novellas, and dozens of short stories, both in her own half-dozen short story collections and in various anthologies, and has published a number of volumes of poetry.

In the midst of this proliferation of literary creation, in 2010, she did something unprecedented. That year, she used crowdfunding to self-publish the first of her series of Fairyland novels, *The Girl Who Circumnavigated Fairyland in a Ship of Her Own Making*; it won the Andre Norton Award for young adult literature before eventually seeing print under the auspices of a publisher, making it the first self-published book ever to win a major literary award. It went on to a more conventional printing the next year and became a national bestseller, and a prequel as well as a number of sequels followed. The Fairyland books have garnered many more awards, including the Prix Imaginales and the Grand Prix de l'Imaginaire for French translations of works in the series. Valente has won the Tiptree, Sturgeon, Eugie Foster Memorial, Mythopoeic, Rhysling, Locus, and Hugo Awards for her writings in fantasy and science fiction; and this is by no means a thorough account of her accolades.

Her full-length novels include *Yume no Hon: The Book of Dreams* (2005), *The Grass-Cutting Sword* (2006), The Orphan's Tales (a duology consisting of 2006's *In the Night Garden* and 2007's *Cities of Coin and Spice*), *Palimpsest* (2009), *The Habitation of the Blessed* (2010), *Deathless* (2011), the previously mentioned Fairyland series (comprised of five books), and in 2015, *Radiance*. *In the Night Garden* won the James Tiptree, Jr. Literary Award for expanding gender and sexuality in science fiction and fantasy; *Palimpsest* won the Lambda Literary Award for LGBT fiction. More recently, she published an illustrated children's book, *The Glass Town Game* (2017); it uses fiction to delve into the inner life of the famed Brontë siblings, in which they stumble upon a fantastical world that reflects their own creations. That same year, her short story "The Future is Blue" took home the Theodore Sturgeon best short science fiction award.

Valente grew up first in Seattle and later in various cities in California. She has since lived in a number of other parts of America and spent a couple years in Japan, but has settled on a small island off the coast of Maine, where she lives with her partner and an array of various animals.

I write about women because I am a woman and I have a voice, just like men have written for millennia about men because they are men themselves, because they believe their experience in the world worth recording. So do I.... I take pleasure and interest in the voices which have not been heard, and more often than not, those voices are female.

Catherynne M. Valente

KAMERON HURLEY *a resistance movement historian writes future fiction*

Kameron Hurley is a science fiction and fantasy author as well as essayist who uses her writing to explore the future of war and resistance to oppression. Her fiction includes vivid female characters such as her 2018 book *Apocalypse Nyx*'s bounty hunter Nyx, who must navigate a dystopian world and deal with challenges like giant bugs and contaminated deserts as she works to survive. Her short fiction was first published in 1998, and she has been writing novels since 2010. She is the author of *The Light Brigade* (2019) and *The Stars are Legion* (2017) as well as two trilogies, the Worldbreaker Saga and the award-winning God's War trilogy.

She was born in the Pacific Northwest and earned a bachelor's degree in historical studies at the University of Alaska at Fairbanks, going on to receive a master's degree in the history of South African resistance movements from the University of Kwa-Zulu Natal in Durban, South Africa. Her nonfiction has been published in journals including *The Atlantic, The Village Voice, Entertainment Weekly*, and *Writers Digest*, and she writes columns about writing and the publishing industry for *Locus Magazine*. In 2014, her essay "We Have Always Fought: Challenging the 'Women, Cattle and Slaves' Narrative" (2013) won a Hugo Award; that same year, she also won the Hugo for Best Fan Writer. Hurley is also the author of the award-winning essay collection *The Geek Feminist Revolution* (2017 Locus and BSFA winner, nonfiction); she is an active blogger who posts reflections on topics including how not to burn out living in a "gig economy" and resisting nihilism. Amusingly, she refers to the sphere of her thought and writing as "the Hurleyverse." She lives in Ohio, where she is cultivating an urban homestead.

BECKY CHAMBERS *self-starting creator of the Galactic Commons*

Becky Chambers literally kickstarted her own writing career; no, really, she used a 2012 Kickstarter campaign to crowdfund her first science fiction novel, *The Long Way to a Small, Angry Planet*, which was not only reissued by publisher Hodder & Stoughton after self-publication, but went on to garner nominations for science fiction literary prizes like the Arthur C. Clarke Award in 2016.

She says of this first work, "*The Long Way* was me trying to write this very accepting, diverse galaxy that I would want to live in." Sequels *A Closed and Common Orbit* (2016) and *Record of a Spaceborn Few* (2018) followed, and in 2019, the Wayfarers trilogy won the Hugo Award for Best Series.

Chambers was born in Southern California in 1985 to parents who worked in aerospace engineering and astrobiology. She grew up outside Los Angeles and went on to pursue studies in theater arts at the University of San Francisco, then spent some time in Iceland and Scotland before returning to California. Having worked on the business side of theaters as well as briefly tending bar, she made her bread and butter money doing technical writing while developing her science fiction writing skills; she used the Kickstarter campaign just to get through the last couple of months of writing her first novel when freelance work slowed down. As of this writing, she is working on a series of "solarpunk" novellas set to debut in 2020. She lives in Northern California with her wife, and when not writing, enjoys pursuits as diverse as gaming, beekeeping, and contemplating the skies through her telescope.

Women of Color in Science Fiction

NISI SHAWL *teaching diversity through her artistry*

Nisi Shawl is an African American journalist and editor who is best known as the author of several dozen science fiction and fantasy short stories. Both in her own writing and as a creative writing teacher, she communicates how speculative fiction can better mirror real-world diversity of not only gender, race, age, and sexual orientation, but also differing levels of physical ability and other socioeconomic variables. With Cynthia Ward, she coauthored the creative writing handbook *Writing the Other: Bridging Cultural Differences for Successful Fiction*, a follow-up to the workshops of the same name, which Shawl has taught for the last decade. *Strange Horizons* reviewer Genevieve Williams said of the handbook, "Much of what Shawl and Ward advocate is, quite simply, good practice: the avoidance of clichés, flat characters, unintended effects, and other hallmarks of lazy writing."

Born in Kalamazoo, Michigan, in 1955, as a small child, young Nisi told fantastical stories of her own invention to her sister. Precociously intelligent, she started college at the University of Michigan College of Literature, Science, and the Arts in Ann Arbor at only sixteen, but feeling alienated, she dropped out two weeks before finals. She moved into Cosmic Plateau, an affordable shared household where her rent was only sixty-five dollars per month, and worked part-time at all sorts of jobs while honing her craft as a writer; she even played in a band for a time as well as doing spoken-word performances of her written works at cafes, parks, and museums.

Her first professional short story sale came in 1989; "I Was a Teenage Genetic Engineer" was published in the literary journal *Semiotext(e)*, alongside works by such authors as Burroughs, William Gibson, J.G. Ballard, and Bruce Sterling. In 1992, in a fateful twist, Shawl went to a cyberpunk symposium in Detroit; because of her story having been published in *Semiotext(e)*, which pioneering cyberpunk author Bruce Sterling thought none of the attendees would have even encountered, she made networking connections with cyberpunk authors Sterling, Pat Cadigan, and John Shirley. Shirley offered to read Shawl's short fiction; he thought that she possessed talent as a writer and advised her to participate in the Clarion West Writers' Workshop, where he and Cadigan were teaching that year. Nisi Shawl later said of the experience, "At Clarion West, I learned in six weeks what six years at the University could never have taught me." Discussions with other workshop participants eventually led her to create a *Writing the Other* essay and class, from which she and Cynthia Ward, whom she met at Clarion West, cocreated the handbook. This, along with positive experiences at another writing program in the Puget Sound area, Cottages at Hedgebrook on Whidbey Island, provided the impetus for Shawl to relocate to Seattle following a divorce. She is now a member of Clarion West's board of directors. She has written dozens of reviews for the *Seattle Times* and *Ms.* magazine and has lectured at Stanford and Duke universities.

Her short story collection *Filter House* was chosen by *Publishers Weekly* as one of their best books of 2008, and won the James Tiptree, Jr. Award for science fiction and fantasy "which expands or explores our understanding of gender," sharing the latter prize for 2008 with Patrick Ness. Shawl has also edited a number of speculative fiction collections; her work as an anthologist has encompassed feminist, Afrofuturist, and LGBT speculative fiction, including twice coediting homages to lesbian and gay novelists of color: *Strange Matings: Science Fiction, Feminism, African American Voices, and Octavia E. Butler* and *Stories for Chip: A Tribute to Samuel R. Delany*, both published in 2015. Shawl herself has stated that she identifies as bisexual. Since then, she has coedited the 2018 collection *Exploring Dark Short Fiction 3* as well as editing *People of Color Take Over Fantastic Stories of the Imagination* (2017) and *New Suns* (2019).

Her 2016 novel *Everfair* broke new ground as well; rather than waxing nostalgic about the colonialist aspects of the Victorian era as many steampunk novels do, it took these issues on, creating an alternate history in which the British Fabian Society decides to create an African sanctuary for those fleeing the tyranny of Belgian King Leopold II, who in the actual nineteenth century brutally enslaved the indigenous people of the Congo in order to profit from the local resource of natural rubber. The new and eponymously named nation of Everfair, like the fictional country of Wakanda, works to develop the technology to protect themselves from rapacious European interests; the novel went on to be nominated for both Hugo and Campbell awards.

MALINDA LO *bringing a wider array of characters into youth literature*

Malinda Lo is a Chinese-born American journalist and the author of several critically acclaimed fantasy and science fiction novels, mostly aimed at the young adult market, as well as an academic researcher on diversity in books for young adults. With fellow YA author Cindy Pon, she is the cofounder of the "Diversity in YA" website and book tour promoting and celebrating representations of diversity in young adult literature. Since 2012, she has analyzed bestselling YA works and published her findings on how many have characters of color, disabled characters, and LGBTQ characters. (Hint: not nearly enough of them is the answer.)

Born in China in 1974, her family moved to the United States when she was three. She earned a bachelor's degree at Wellesley College and went on for a master's degree from Harvard in regional studies concentrating on East Asia, then did graduate work in cultural and social anthropology at Stanford, eventually obtaining a second master's degree there. In 2006, the National

Lesbian & Gay Journalists Association recognized her work at AfterEllen, a queer women's cultural website, with the Sarah Pettit Memorial Award for Excellence in LGBT Journalism. Her nonfiction has run in many media outlets, notably including NPR and *The New York Times Book Review*. Before turning to writing novels as a profession, besides her academic pursuits, Lo worked as an editorial assistant and an entertainment reporter.

Her debut novel *Ash* (2009) is a retelling of the Cinderella story with a lesbian twist; it was nominated for several awards and was a *Kirkus* Best Book for Children and Teens. Interestingly, she hadn't planned on *Ash* being a young adult title, but wrote it "without thinking about what genre it was." Only in the process of working with agents to submit the book to publishers did that genre designation emerge. Lo followed it in 2011 with *Huntress*, a companion novel to *Ash*, which was named Best Book for Young Adults by the American Library Association. *Huntress* features strong female protagonists working to solve an ecological crisis and draws on the I Ching and other Chinese cultural traditions. *Adaptation* (2012) also includes aspects of ecocatastrophe, with flocks of birds flying into airplanes for no apparent reason; this contemporary science fiction thriller was named a Bank Street College Best Children's Book. Its sequel, 2013's *Inheritance*, was the winner of the 2014 Bisexual Book Awards for Bisexual Teen/Young Adult Fiction; it looks at the concept of "the other" both through human sexuality and Terran/alien relations. Lo left the terrain of fantasy and science fiction with the dark psychological thriller *A Line in the Dark*, a contemporary tale of social challenges among young women, again involving alternative sexuality; it was named a *Kirkus* Best YA Book of 2017.

Lo's short story "Don't Speak" appeared in the *New York Times* in 2019, and as of this writing, her novel *Last Night at the Telegraph Club* is expected soon; like *Adaptation*, it is set in San Francisco, but in the 1950s. It explores the intricacies of interactions between the city's queer and Chinese-American communities. Malinda Lo lives in Massachusetts.

OCTAVIA BUTLER *dreaming how humanity can transcend hierarchy*

Octavia E. Butler (1947–2006) was a Black American science fiction author known for her novels, which explored futuristic utopian/dystopian themes.

Young Octavia was the only child of Octavia Guy Butler, a housemaid, and Laurice Butler, a shoeshine man who died when she was seven. She was raised in a strict Baptist household by her grandmother and her mother, whom she often accompanied to her housecleaning work sites, where they were expected to use only the back door to enter the house. Octavia was extremely shy and turned to books for stimulation; after starting with fairy tales and horse stories, she was drawn to science fiction magazines featuring the work of writers including Zenna Henderson, Theodore Sturgeon, and John Brunner. At ten, she pleaded with her mother to buy her a manual Remington typewriter, at which she composed stories for countless hours using two-finger typing; at twelve, she drafted the beginnings of what would later become her Patternist series of science fiction novels. At age thirteen, when her aunt told her that Negroes couldn't be writers, though perhaps temporarily daunted, she persevered. While working days and attending night school as a freshman at Pasadena City College, she earned her first money as a writer by winning a college-wide short story contest.

Butler continued her education at California State University Los Angeles and then at UCLA, where one of her writing instructors was the noted science fiction author Harlan Ellison. Encouraged by Ellison, in 1970, she began her writing career in earnest. In 1976, she published *Patternmaster*, the first of her five-volume Patternist series about an elite group of telepaths governed by Doro, a four-thousand-year-old immortal African man who had to periodically move his consciousness to new bodies to survive. *Patternmaster* was followed by *Mind of My Mind* (1977), *Survivor* (1978), *Wild Seed* (1980), and *Clay's Ark* (1984). While in the midst of producing the Patternist series, Butler released the novel *Kindred* in 1979; it tells the story of a modern Black woman sent back in time to an antebellum plantation, where she poses as a slave in order to carry out the rescue of her own ancestor, a white slave owner. *Kindred* was later adapted as a graphic novel released in 2017.

Later novels included the Xenogenesis trilogy: *Dawn: Xenogenesis* (1987), *Adulthood Rites* (1988), and *Imago* (1989). The trilogy was followed by *The Parable of the Sower* (1993), *The Parable of the Talents* (1998), and *Fledgling* (2005). Butler began to achieve serious recognition when her short story "Speech Sounds" won a Hugo Award in 1984; a year later, her story *Bloodchild*, which told the story of human male slaves who incubated the eggs of their alien masters, won both the Hugo and Nebula awards. In 1995, she became the first science fiction writer ever to be awarded a MacArthur Foundation Fellowship, and she received a PEN Award for lifetime achievement in 2000. Her last book was the science fiction/vampire novel *Fledgling*, the tale of a West Coast vampire community in a state of symbiosis with humans, seen through the eyes of a young female hybrid vampire. Butler's work is associated with the Afrofuturism genre, defined as "speculative fiction that treats African American themes and addresses African American concerns in the context of twentieth century technoculture."

> *Simple peck-order bullying is only the beginning of the kind of hierarchical behavior that can lead to racism, sexism, ethnocentrism, classism, and all the other 'isms' that cause so much suffering in the world.*
>
> Octavia E. Butler

CHAPTER SEVEN

....

Salonists and Culture Makers

Hermeneutic Circles and Human History

A look at cultural turning points throughout history reveals an interesting pattern: often a small circle of friends was the crucial point of origin for a revolutionary change in art, politics, or philosophy. In his definitive study of early modernism, *American Salons*, Robert W. Crunden states that "major changes in human attitude have small beginnings," and indeed, from the pre-Raphaelites to the Romantics, from the Surrealists to the suffragists, and from the Harlem Renaissance to the Beats, intimate gatherings of friends were at the heart of nearly every significant new movement.

The very nature of salons—organic, informal, and relational—made women central to these groupings. Before women could vote or own property, they were part and parcel of this kind of culture making. In Paris, the Surrealists welcomed women as equals, while modernist Gertrude Stein opened her ample home and heart to struggling male artists like Matisse and Picasso, as well as upstart writers like Ernest Hemingway and Paul Bowles. Party girl-intellectual Joan Burroughs hosted a gaggle of charming college dropouts—Allen Ginsberg, William Burroughs, and Jack Kerouac—in her Manhattan apartment, doling out champagne and Spengler in equal servings, as her predecessor Mabel Dodge had in Greenwich Village forty years before.

One writer, Jean Shinoda Bolen, author of *Goddesses in Everywoman*, suggests this phenomenon is no accident. In *The Millionth Circle: How to Change Ourselves and the World*, she proposes that salons, circles, and book discussion groups are actually the key to the evolution of humanity, for "when a critical number of people change how they think and behave, the culture will also, and a new era begins." Think about that when you and your girlfriends sip cappuccinos while chatting about your favorite new novel—you are changing the world!

MADAME ROLAND *priestess of the revolution*

That women intellectuals in turn-of-the-century France suffered during the French Revolution is without a doubt. But while Madame de Staël was exiled for her politics, Madame Jeanne-Marie Roland lost her head entirely.

Roland's father was a laborer, an engraver. Her humble origins, however, did not stop her from becoming one of the pivotal players in the French Revolution, going on to hold great power in the government of her day. While Betsy Ross was sewing stripes onto the flag of the fledgling United States, this French workman's daughter commanded the helm of her country.

Jeanne-Marie Phlipon was politically precocious. Listening raptly while her father waged a verbal war against the French aristocracy, his opinions were engraved upon her sensibility, and she began educating herself for a life of civic action. At the age of nine, she read Plutarch; his *Lives* made her wish she had lived in classical Rome with its senatorial lectures and truth-seeking philosophers. Meanwhile, Jean-Jacques Rousseau was stirring the hearts and minds of his readers with his egalitarian theories, which the young girl devoured as well.

Her idealistic father's fortunes took an unfortunate turn during Jeanne-Marie's adolescence when he lost all his earnings in stock and became a compulsive gambler. Left with nothing but his daughter's dowry, he lived off that, drank himself into dissolution, and refused her hand to Roland de la Platière, whom she met through a convent-school friend. Roland was not the only man in pursuit of the handsome, strong-willed Jeanne-Marie, with her dark, burning eyes and raven hair. However, this suitor was not easily dissuaded and continued his quest for marriage to the bookish girl. De la Platière came from considerable wealth but retained a position as an inspector at a factory. Although he was nearly twice her age, they had quite a bit in common, especially a love of classic literature. In later life, Madame Roland claimed, "He was a man fond of ancient history, and more like the ancients than the modern; about seven and forty years old, stooping and awkward and with manners respectable rather than pleasing."

Their shared life of the mind won out over her other admirers, and they married when she was twenty-five. They began an earnest relationship of respect and erudition. Her feelings about her marriage are indicated in this diary entry from her wedding day: "I could make a model of a man I could love, but it would be shattered the moment he became my master." While theirs was a marriage of minds, Jeanne-Marie eventually found romance elsewhere with Henri Buzot, who was later her companion until her death.

Immediately after her marriage, stirrings of revolution were evident. Madame Roland associated herself with the Girondists, named for the district from which their leaders came, who favored a republic, supported the abolition of the constitutional monarchy, and opposed the violence of the Terror. The Girondists soon became the majority party, dominating the government of France at their height. Led by Jacques Pierre Brissot, they believed in the ownership of private property. The newlyweds both involved themselves deeply in the revolution and opened their home to meetings that rapidly evolved into a salon run by Madame Roland, which she made open to all different elements of revolutionary thinking.

Roland recorded in her journals the fascinating discussions that took place at these events; she also began writing essays and voluminous letters to her fellows. Along with Georges Danton, a member of the Girondists' opposition, the Jacobins, Robespierre frequented the salon and was greatly influenced by Roland, most famously when he made a speech to the National Assembly espousing theories she had taught him, in language she had coached him on. Both husband and wife attended the National Assembly of France, and Madame wrote newspaper articles as well as her husband's speeches and official state documents.

She was a woman who knew the powerful effect her writing could have. When the Austrian army, accompanied by escaped French aristocrats, gathered at the border to invade the weakened, split country, Madame Roland wrote King Louis XVI urging him to declare war in kind; he struck her husband from office. But the consequences of his refusal to do as she suggested ultimately cost the king his crown and his head. The tumult increased; Roland's wealth caused him to be suspected and arrested during the purge of the ruling class. A split between two factions, the Girondists and the Jacobins, occurred when the Jacobins laid blame on the Girondists for the defeats in the war against Austria. The Jacobins' retribution was swift and brutal; they guillotined Brissot and thirty others and arrested the remaining factionalists.

The Girondists had espoused moderation, but conceded in the vote to the executions of King Louis XVI and Marie Antoinette, while fighting against the siege tactics of Marat and Robespierre. Her former salonist and student Robespierre began to plot against the articulate and charismatic Madame Roland and betrayed her, resulting in her imprisonment in a dungeon cell into which the River Seine seeped. Sadly, Robespierre and Madame Roland's relationship, based originally on free exchange, ended tragically out of balance—she saved him from the guillotine, while he gave her up for execution.

The same friend who had introduced Madame Roland to her husband offered to change clothes with her and take her place in prison. Roland's refusal was typically elegant: "Better to suffer a thousand deaths myself than to reproach myself with yours." In prison, she suffered horribly. Sick and wasting, she was thrown in with prostitutes, murderers, and thieves; she used her gift of language to appeal to the doomed women prisoners to stop their riots and cease their violence against each other.

In less than a month's time she wrote her memoirs in prison. The officials presiding over her trial were so afraid of Madame Roland's facility with words that they refused to allow her to "use her wit" and ordered her only to answer the questions put to her with yes or no. She was, of course, convicted and hastened to the guillotine in just twelve hours. One other prisoner was put to the blade that day, a terrified printer for whom she argued for a peculiar kind of mercy; she asked that he be executed first to spare him the awful sight of seeing her head roll. A clay model of the Statue of Liberty was placed near the scaffold to which Madame Roland addressed her famous last words: "O Liberty! What crimes have been committed in thy name!" She died on November 8, 1793, at the age of thirty-nine.

MADAME ROLAND DE LA PLATIÈRE *Jailed and guillotined during the French Revolution's "Reign of Terror"*

JANE WELSH CARLYLE *a life of letters*

Born in Scotland in 1801, Jane Welsh was the daughter of a physician who practiced in London. Her enlightened and intelligent father saw to it that Jane was given the best available education with a grounding in the classics, beginning at the age of five. Her instructor Edward Irving was deeply impressed with Jane's brilliance, and in 1821, introduced her to Thomas Carlyle, an historian and writer of repute. When she turned twenty-five, she married Carlyle; together they were at the center of a circle of English artists, writers, and thinkers. Known for her intelligence and charm, she became fast friends with Geraldine Jewsbury and hosted such luminaries as Charles Dickens, John Stuart Mill, and Lord Tennyson.

Jane was an inveterate letter writer, filling her missives with wit, keen observations, and real feeling. She is viewed as having elevated writing letters to an art form, covering every conceivable topic from travel and books to friends, servants, and acute descriptions of personality. Her letters are published in several volumes, and they reveal the marital dysfunction that pressed enormous strain on Jane. Although her husband had great ambition as a writer, they lived in poverty, with Jane suffering Thomas' neglect and irritability. Though she feared a mental breakdown, she suddenly collapsed and died in 1866 while riding in a carriage.

MERET OPPENHEIM *Surrealist savant*

Paris, the City of Lights, seemed to be the most fertile ground for artists and writers in the early twentieth century. Several salons and schools of thought formed there, leaving an indelible mark upon culture at large. Artist and poet Meret Oppenheim found equal footing for her creativity among the Surrealists.

Meret was born in Germany in 1913, and her family moved from Berlin to Weisenthal, Switzerland, when she was five years old; she was schooled in Germany and Switzerland until she was seventeen. At nineteen, she moved to Paris to attend art school, whereupon she immediately fell in with kindred creatives—dancers, philosophers, painters, and poets—who formed a salon of the first wave of Surrealists, a literary and artistic movement that sought to reveal a reality above or beneath ordinary reality. She was befriended by Hans and Sophie Tauber-Arp, Marcel Duchamp, and Alberto Giacometti, who encouraged her to experiment with different media. In 1933, she was asked to exhibit with the Surrealists at Salon des Surindependents. After a successful debut show, Oppenheim's art was featured in all of this group's important exhibitions, beginning with Cubism-Surrealism in 1935. She tried her hand at jewelry making for the great fashion houses of Paris; she made a copper bracelet lined with sealskin and showed it to Pablo Picasso, who remarked, "Many things could be covered in fur." His remark inspired Meret Oppenheim to do just that.

The following year, Oppenheim's *Dejeuner en fourrure (The Fur Tea Cup)* stunned the art world, set off a scandal with its sexy suggestiveness, and established the twenty-three-year-old as one of the key figures in Surrealism. When the Museum of Modern Art in New York purchased her teacup sculpture, her standing was cemented. Oppenheim felt the Surrealists were more evolved sociologically, and though this school was mainly male, they welcomed her as an artist completely. A muse for Man Ray, his luminous nude photographs of her are now part of the legacy of Surrealism. When she and Max Ernst met and fell in love, she broke off the affair despite the intensity of their feelings for each other. A long time after, she claimed it was an instinct to protect her growth as a fledgling artist from being squelched by him, a fully mature artist of international reputation.

Though she was a fine poet as well, everything else Meret Oppenheim did was overshadowed by *The Fur Tea Cup*, which shot her into stratospheric fame at the very beginning of her career. Finding herself the "darling of the art world" overnight was awkward, and she suffered deep bouts of depression. The next two decades were very difficult for her in terms of her work; after an early and meteoric rise to success, she found herself a "has-been" nearly from the start.

She left Paris for Basel during the aftermath of her sudden fame and undertook years of Jungian analysis to help her understand her depression. In 1949, she married Wolfgang La Roche, a businessman who supported her need for independence, and she spent weekends at her studio in Berne writing, making art, and reading a great deal, particularly the works of Carl Jung, a friend of the family. She maintained some links with friends from her early salon years and designed costumes for a Picasso ballet in 1956. Proving she could still shock, Meret Oppenheim put together the symbolist installation *Banquet* in 1959, featuring a nude woman as the centerpiece for the table. She lived to see herself "rediscovered" in 1967 and enjoyed a retrospective in Stockholm, where she regained her reputation and international standing.

Meret Oppenheim was a deeply sensitive woman who mined her unconscious for inspiration and insight. Both her writing and her art reflected her interest in archetypal imagery. She recorded her dreams for most of her life and strove to prove that art of any kind, whether poetry, painting, or sculpture, should have no gender.

> *During my long crisis, my genius, the animus, the male part of the female soul, that assists the female artist, had abandoned me.... But at the beginning of the fifties, I sensed that things were getting better.*
>
> Meret Oppenheim

SYLVIA BEACH *bookseller extraordinaire*

American Sylvia Beach was captivated by Paris the first time she saw it in the early 1900s. but it wasn't until after World War I, in 1919, that she established her soon-to-be-famous bookshop, Shakespeare and Company, which specialized in American and English books. Quickly it became a haven for American expatriates, including Ernest Hemingway and Gertrude Stein, "the" spot for American tourists to visit, and a place where European scholars became more familiar with American and English literature. In 1922, Beach became a publisher as well, printing James Joyce's *Ulysses* after it had been rejected by a myriad of publishers for being obscene. In 1941, she shut down the store in order to avoid takeover by the Nazis during World War II, and it was never opened again. If you ever travel through Newport, Oregon, stop in at the Sylvia Beach Hotel, named for this great literary patron. It offers three categories of rooms—Bestsellers, Novels, and Classics—each named for a famous writer (Agatha Christie, Herman Melville, and Edgar Allen Poe, to mention just three) and containing a complete set of books by that author. The hotel can be reached at (541) 265-5428 or online: sylviabeachhotel.com.

> *"Fitting people with books is about as difficult as fitting them with shoes."*
>
> Sylvia Beach

GERTRUDE AND ALICE *"the mama of Dada"*

Gertrude Stein was a writer who seems to have been eminently comfortable in her own skin and well aware of her fame. Her wholly original writing style shocked and fascinated readers, prompting some wags to dub her "the mama of Dada" and "the Mother Goose of Montparnasse," but she had her own distinct view: "Einstein was the creative philosophic mind of the century, and I have been the creative literary mind of the century." Her influence is still felt in our culture, and of the modernists, she still seems the most starkly modern.

An American whose German-Jewish family moved to Baltimore from Bavaria, Gertrude Stein's father founded a successful clothing business and moved around a good bit with his wife and young children. The brood lived in Austria and Paris before settling in 1879, when Gertrude was four, in Oakland, California, the home about which she made the famously misunderstood comment, "There's no there there." (She meant that her home as she remembered it wasn't there, but the sentence was bandied about as a put-down of the Northern California city for decades.) The brilliant girl spoke German and French, but quickly made English her first language by voraciously reading England's history, poetry, fiction, and, an odd choice for a young girl, congressional records. Gertrude's mother passed away in 1888 when Gertrude was fourteen, followed by her father in 1891, bonding her and her brother Leo very closely together under the care of their maternal aunt Fannie Bachrach in Baltimore.

Leo Stein was at Harvard; when it came time to go to college, Gertrude studied under special dispensation at Radcliffe College to be near Leo. Among her teachers there were William James, a pioneer in psychology, and philosopher George Santayana. James took Gertrude under his wing and supported her in her desire to study medicine at Johns Hopkins University in Baltimore. She did obstetrical work in addition to her medical training, and she received support from two wealthy friends, Etta and Claribal Cone.

By 1899, she sank into a severe melancholy and abandoned her study of medicine. Her depression was believed by biographers to be a result of the breakup of a love triangle with May Bookstaver and Mabel Haynes, fictionalized in *Q.E.D., OR Things as They Are* (published in 1950, after Stein's death). In 1902 she joined Leo in Italy, where he was pursuing a career in art under the tutelage of Bernard Berenson, and ultimately followed him to Paris. Their flat in the house at 27 rue de Fleurus soon became a famous address in avant-garde circles, with the duo holding regular to which all the art and literature "glitterati" flocked, including Picasso, Juan Gris, and F. Scott Fitzgerald.

Here Gertrude was exposed to the modern art she so loved and began to acquire it at a rapid pace. A story she loved to tell was the memory of seeing Matisse's *La Femme au Chapeau* at a Petit Palais show where enraged patrons heckled the painter and tried to destroy the painting by scraping the paint off the surface. Gertrude acquired a stunning collection of Impressionist and Post-Impressionist art, including works by Renoir, Matisse, Picasso, Rousseau, Braque, and Cézanne. She claimed her attraction to this art was its method of clarification by deformation, an approach some would say she applied to her writing, which was an attempt at a verbal counterpart to Cubism. She eschewed normal punctuation and grammar, and used words associatively and for their sound rather than for meaning. Her goal was to present impressions and states of mind rather than a story.

However, she also undertook *The Making of Americans*, an attempt to record a history of every type of human. Her early work of 1909, *Three Lives*, was written while she sat for Picasso's portrait of her. As usual, modesty was not her strong suit; she proclaimed *Three Lives* to be "the first definite step away from the nineteenth century and into the twentieth century in literature." She asked a new acquaintance, Alice B. Toklas, to proofread the manuscript when she at long last found a publisher. They soon became fast friends and lovers, Alice moving into the atelier once inhabited by Leo Stein. Gertrude's tie to her brother seemed to matter much less with the arrival of San Francisco native

Toklas; Gertrude wrote, "It was I who was the genius, there was no reason for it but I was and he was not."

The union of the two women seemed to be the mating of souls. Toklas founded Plain Edition Press to publish Stein's many unpublished manuscripts, and Stein's writing took on new strength, rhythm, and feeling, with her erotic writings based on their relationship. Popular success evaded Stein, however, until she wrote, in Toklas' voice, *The Autobiography of Alice B. Toklas* in 1933. This charming "autobiography" tells of the salon they hosted—the young writers Stein mentored, Sherwood Anderson and Ernest Hemingway—and discloses delicious gossip about the bevy of artists in their circle. This was less amusing to the artists themselves, prompting *The Testimony Against Gertrude Stein*, a refutation of her comments, wherein Braque accused her of not understanding Cubism, Matisse railed against her lack of taste, and Tristan Tzara decried her "megalomania" and her egotism as evidenced by such statements of Stein's as, "Think of the Bible and Homer, think of Shakespeare and think of me." Among the most fascinating episodes in the *Autobiography* is the ambulance service the two women ran in World War I, which they seemed to regard as high adventure.

Gertrude Stein's reputation as a major influence on new forms in literature was growing. She began to write novels and plays, including *Four Saints in Three Acts*, and she was invited to do lecture tours at the most prestigious venues: Oxford, Cambridge, and in America, with the operatic staging of her play. The Second World War forced Stein and Toklas to leave Paris and set up a more permanent home in the country near Bilignin, France, where they entertained many American soldiers. In 1946, she was diagnosed with an abdominal tumor and was hospitalized at the American Hospital at Neuilly-sur-Seine. Her last words are part of her legacy. She regained consciousness for a few moments after stomach surgery and asked, "What is the answer?" No one responded, and Gertrude Stein answered herself with, "Well, in that case, what is the question?" and immediately lost consciousness and died. Alice B. Toklas died twenty-one years later and lies buried beside her in the cemetery at Père Lachaise in Paris.

Ernest Hemingway once famously said Gertrude Stein looked like a Roman emperor, and indeed, in the portraits by Pavel Tchelitchew and Jacques

Lipchitz, she does rather resemble an ancient noble. Other friends marked her resemblance to a "Jewish Buddha." Partially because she was an amazing looking person and partially because her friends were mostly artists and other writers, she is a very well-documented individual. There are a multitude of portraits of her and many exceptional photographs by the likes of Cecil Beaton and Carl Van Vechten.

During her life, Gertrude Stein authored six hundred novels, poems, essays, plays, opera librettos, and biographies. She influenced generations of writers after her; among those who claim her as inspiration are Edith Sitwell, Samuel Beckett, John Cage, and John Ashbery.

GERTRUDE STEIN *Along with Alice B. Toklas, she hosted Pablo Picasso, Ernest Hemingway, F. Scott Fitzgerald, Paul Bowles, the ladies of the Left Bank, the Impressionists, and the Surrealists in a nonstop salon*

ALICE TOKLAS' LIST OF WIVES OF GENIUSES

In *The Autobiography of Alice B. Toklas*, "Alice" writes, "The geniuses came and talked to Gertrude Stein and the wives sat with me. How they unroll, an endless vista through the years." Here they are. Fernande, the first long-term mistress of Picasso; Madame Matisse; Marcelle Braque; Josette Gris; Eve Picasso; Bridget Gibb; Marjory Gibb; Hadley Hemingway; Pauline Hemingway; Mrs. Sherwood Anderson; Mrs. Bravig Imbs; and Mrs. Ford Madox Ford.

KATHARINE MANSFIELD *driven by duality*

At times, Katharine Mansfield's life story reads like a tale of two women. She is regarded as a great British writer, but she always felt like little Kathleen Beauchamp, the girl from New Zealand. She had a strict and conservative Victorian upbringing, but she was also bohemian. She had a husband and a "wife." Even her reasons for writing, as she explained them, were dual.

Her parents were conventional and proper; her father, Harold Beauchamp, was a Wellington banker, hardworking and ambitious. Daughter Kathleen was born in 1888.

Harold's wife Annie had a delicate constitution, and her sickliness convinced her she couldn't care for Kathleen on her own, so she moved her mother in to take care of her household and daughters. This was a boon for the child and her sisters, as they were given the affection her work-obsessed father and self-obsessed mother were unable to provide. When a son was born, the girls were sent off to several schools until 1903, when the family moved to London and Kathleen enrolled in Queen's College for three years. She became an avid student, her favorite authors being the Brontë sisters, Elizabeth Robins, Leo Tolstoy, and Oscar Wilde. After her taste of the cosmopolitan city, Kathleen dreaded the return to New Zealand, but turned to writing as compensation. Her talent was recognized right away; her pieces were published in the local journal, *The Native Companion*. Her father was so impressed that she received payment for her monographs that he permitted her to go back to the London she loved.

She had a romantic correspondence with Tom Trowell, the son of her
Wellington music instructor, but got engaged to Tom's twin brother Garnet.
She also had a crush on a former schoolmate, Maata Mahupuka, a Maori
heiress, and in college had met a motherless girl, Ida Constance Baker, with
whom she formed a lifelong liaison. (Ida's father was the model for the
overbearing patriarch in Mansfield's *The Daughters of the Late Colonel*.) Ida soon
changed her name to L. M., Leslie Moore, and Kathleen began calling herself
Katharine Mansfield.

Garnet Trowell's parents didn't approve of Katharine, and in a rash move, she
married a man she had just met, George Bowden. She and L. M. went to the
Registry Office for the civil ceremony, the bride clad all in black. That night,
at the beginning of what should have been the honeymoon, she bolted and
ran to L. M. for comfort. Mrs. Beauchamp got wind of her daughter's erratic
antics and installed her in a German resort hotel where she was "treated" for her
lesbian "affliction" with cold baths and spas. Katharine also recovered from a
miscarriage that occurred at the hotel in Germany.

Throughout these romantic adventures, Mansfield wrote. Her first stories were
published in A.R. Orage's New Age; those written from her sanitorium were
published in a 1911 collection, *In a German Pension*. J. Middleton Murry,
editor of a newly established review, *Rhythm*, immediately called her up when
she submitted her story, "The Woman at the Store." In short order, Murry
became a lodger and then lover of this writer, one year his senior. *Rhythm*
was short-lived, but Mansfield continued to earn money for her writing to
add to a tiny stipend from her father, and Murry wrote reviews and critical
essays for pay.

With the onset of World War I, Mansfield's life and loves were pulled apart.
Murry got an assignment for military intelligence, while L. M. became a
machinist in an airplane factory. The Beauchamp family was devastated by
the loss of their only son, who was "blown to bits" in France. *Prelude*, written
in 1917, and *At the Bay*, written in 1921, are Katharine's ruminations about
their time spent together in childhood, written in a style akin to stream
of consciousness.

Her life in London saw Mansfield at the heart of a lively literary circle, with Virginia Woolf and D.H. Lawrence at its epicenter. Mansfield felt a strong kinship, a "sameness" with Lawrence. She saw his disposition as very much like hers and believed they were both attempting to express the erotic in words. She perceived Lawrence's attraction to her lover Murry as an attempt at a "blood brotherhood," and disapproved of his and his wife Frieda's incessant arguing in public—sudden, fierce outbursts that upset everyone around them. While Mansfield was oblivious to Lawrence's portrayal of her and Murry as Gudrun and Gerald in *Women in Love*, she avoided contact with him after he wrote her a nasty, accusing letter in 1920: "You revolt me, stewing in your consumption."

Katharine Mansfield's relationship to Virginia Woolf was equally crucial to her emotional and literary life. Woolf's upper-class, mannered background of comfortable wealth caused her occasionally to reprove Mansfield for her unconventional lifestyle, referring to her as "common." But Woolf liked the younger writer's "inscrutable" intelligence more than she disliked her bohemianism. Mansfield looked up to Woolf and turned to her for comradely support, writing in a letter, "We have the same job, Virginia." Woolf's diaries contain an entry about Mansfield's stories as "the only writing I have ever been jealous of."

Mansfield's relationship with Murry lasted her entire life, but, particularly after she developed tuberculosis, he was not to be relied on. Like Lawrence, he found her tuberculosis repulsive and seemed to feel more sorry for himself than for her. Mansfield's satiric story, "The Man Without a Temperament," depicts his reaction to her illness perfectly. Murry withheld monetary as well as emotional support while she traveled in vain, searching for a place to get well. L. M. was her nurse, cook, valet, and rock, but the unfortunate circumstances of their togetherness eroded the relationship; Mansfield hated losing her independence, referred to L. M. as "The Albatross," and came to see her as a "hysterical ghoul."

Katharine Mansfield's health spiraled downward at a rapid pace, but she refused to let it interfere with her writing. In 1918, she wrote *Bliss and Other Stories* while she suffered constant nausea, insomnia, night terrors, and chest pain; she could barely walk at times. *The Garden Party and Other Stories* was released to high praise; her crisp, precise prose and sharp dialogue won her comparisons

to Anton Chekhov. At the end of her life at age thirty-four, she was introduced
to George Ivanovich Gurdjieff, founder of the Institute for the Harmonious
Development of Man at Fontainebleau. Mansfield entered Gurdjieff's
community unbeknownst to her friends; in an attempt to restore her health,
she undertook the prescribed methods of movement and dance for "centering,"
living in a hayloft where she drank fresh milk and lived above the dairy cows
in a rustic room painted with pastoral scenes of flowers and animals. The night
Murry came to visit her idyll, she hemorrhaged and died immediately.

> *One must be true to one's vision of life—in every single particular.... The only thing to do is to try from tonight to be stronger and better—to be whole.*
>
> **From the expurgated letters of Katharine Mansfield**

THE WOMEN OF THE ROPE *a salon within a salon*

The influence of the enigmatic George Ivanovich Gurdjieff, born George S.
Georgiades in Armenia circa 1872, is global. Judging from the plethora of books
and articles about him and the rapidly expanding popularity of the enneagram,
an ancient wisdom he introduced to the West, today Gurdjieff's star is higher
than ever. A shroud of mystery surrounded him, and details on his early life are
thin. Purportedly, he spent his youth studying world religious traditions while
traveling in India, Africa, Asia, and the Middle East before staking his claim on
Europe, and later, America. Part of his mythology is a tale of stomach illness
while in India, receiving several bullet wounds, passing through revolutions
and wars, and long stays secreted away with assorted mystics, learning their
recondite religious teachings.

Gurdjieff settled in Moscow in 1913 and taught there and in Petrograd,
leaving for the Caucasus as the Russian Revolution swept across the territories
in 1917. He had already attracted followers and founded his Institute for the
Harmonious Development of Man by two years later in what is now Tbilisi,
in the state of Georgia, eventually relocating his center to Fontainebleau,
France, in 1922. His utopian community was ascetic, the hard work and

exercise regimen broken by an occasional feast where the dynamic Gurdjieff held court, lecturing on various themes. His core belief was that humans are "asleep" when they lead an ordinary life, but that through rigorous attention and work, one could "awaken," and enjoy unprecedented awareness and energy. At these banquets, men and women from the community read from the master's writings, and everyone physically able participated in ritual dance and movement to the musical compositions of Gurdjieff and Thomas deHartmann.

Everything about Gurdjieff is profoundly odd, but his relationship with the "Women of the Rope" is perhaps the strangest chapter of all. Paris in the 1930s and subsequent decades was a place of wild experimentation in art, literature, and social mores. The denizens of the Left Bank were especially open-minded and willing to embrace the avant-garde, even spiritually. A group of women well-known in avant-garde literary circles became students of Gurdjieff, calling themselves "The Rope." The Rope included Georgette LeBland, a reputed soprano, accomplished writer of both prose and poetry, and intimate of Jean Cocteau; Dorothy Caruso, the widow of the legendary Enrico Caruso, who became Margaret Anderson's lover after Georgette LeBland's death; Solita Solano, editor extraordinaire, whose secretarial notes from Gurdjieff's sessions provide the best-known records of the man and his methods; Alice Rohrer, a Pennsylvania farm girl who earned wealth from hatmaking, and who was purportedly the most emotional and least intellectual member and thus received the most attention; Kathryn Hulme, author of the award-winning *The Wild Place* and the novel that became an Audrey Hepburn star vehicle, *The Nun's Story*; Jane Heap, cofounder of the history-making *Little Review*, who went on to teach Gurdjieff's beliefs; Louise Davidson, actress and stage manager, who enjoyed the emotive aspect of the sessions; Elisabeth Gordon, the odd woman out, a conservative British spinster Gurdjieff had imprisoned as a "foreign national" during World War II; and Margaret Anderson, publisher with Heap of the *Little Review*, who dared first to publish Ezra Pound, T.S. Eliot, and James Joyce.

Gurdjieff lavished special attention on this lesbian sect of students, who met with him for private lessons. He prepared lavish meals for them at his apartment and treated them to expensive dinners in the finest Parisian bistros. One memorable evening included a very befuddled and cranky Frank Lloyd Wright.

Gurdjieff kept them apart from his other groups and went so far as to give them intensive instruction that sometimes lasted for weeks. Gertrude Stein, their contemporary in both writerly pursuits and lesbianism, would have nothing to do with the mystic, but the others were set on gleaning as much arcane wisdom and insight as possible from their spiritual leader. Kathryn Hulme described in a letter to Jane Heap one bizarre session in which he took her to a bordello, insisting she choose one of the naked dancing women.

Gurdjieff taught that we all have an "inner animal." Each of the women of "The Rope" had a special name expressing this aspect of her nature, by which he referred to each affectionately. They began referring to each other as such as well; in some cases, until the end of their lives:

Kathryn Hulme was Crocodile, pronounced "Krokodeel" by Gurdjieff.

Alice Rohrer, a former San Francisco milliner and companion to Hulme, was Boa Constrictor, or "Theen One," who cried buckets during the teachings.

Solita Solano, editor and writer and longtime partner to Janet Flanner, was Canary. Though initially resistant to Gurdjieff, after his death in 1949, she became the central figure of The Rope.

Margaret Anderson, arrested for first publishing James Joyce's *Ulysses* in *Little Review*, was "Yakina," a Tibetan yak.

Noel Murphy, a later partner of Anderson's after Anderson's breakup with Solita Solano, was Camel.

Gurdjieff's impact on The Rope was lasting; several remained lifelong believers, and all told, they wrote three books about their time with the great spiritualist. As their moniker suggests, the women remained tied together by the experience.

Do not sit too long in the same place.
You are responsible for what you have understood.
Little steps for little feet.
Suppress natural reaction and pay for it later.
We never refuse in the Work.

> *Animals are nature's experiments and embody all*
> *the emotions.*
> *A cat is all essence. Essence remembers.*
> *All that falls from the wagon is lost.*
>
> Gurdjieffian aphorisms from *The Notes of Jane Heap*

VIRGINIA WOOLF *a salon of her own*

One of the leaders of the modern literary movement, Virginia Woolf was born and raised in London to a family of letters; her father had an excellent reputation as a scholar and writer and authored *The Dictionary of English Biography*. Her mother moved in artistic circles and hosted Edward Burne-Jones, William Holman Hunt, G.F. Watts, and stage actress Ellen Terry. Virginia was also accustomed to having literati visit her home; her parents entertained their noteworthy friends Henry James, Lord Tennyson, poet George Meredith, and writer-ambassador James Russell Lowell. In addition to her sister Vanessa, young Virginia Stephen had two natural brothers, Thoby and Adrian, a stepsister, Stella, and two stepbrothers, Gerald and George Duckworth. Though father Leslie Stephen was learned, he was not necessarily socially progressive, believing the girls needed only to be educated at home.

Upon his death in 1905, the Stephen children shocked their relatives by closing the house they were raised in and relocating to Bloomsbury, a poorer neighborhood. There, they began to refashion life in accordance with their needs and interests. Thoby, a student at Cambridge and member of an underground organization, the Apostles, brought his friends over on Thursday evenings. These lively encounters quickly turned into a regular series of salons. This idyllic episode soon came to an end, however, when a group trip to Greece ended in Thoby dying of typhoid. A week later, still in mourning, Vanessa became engaged to Thoby's dear friend Clive Bell and set up a household in a Gordon Square row house. In 1907, Adrian and Virginia also moved, to Fitzroy Square; they took a house formerly occupied by George Bernard Shaw. Brother and sister resumed holding salons in their new home, forming the true beginning of the Bloomsbury group. Virginia keenly enjoyed the high-minded exchanges these evenings afforded her; they were often the highlight of her week.

She was an extremely sensitive person given to occasional depressions and suicidal tendencies. She would go for long periods of time without eating and is thought by some scholars to have been anorexic. An inveterate diarist, we know much about her state of mind and sexual advances by her stepbrothers, as well as her doubts, fears, and dreams. Her diaries also showed the beginnings of her "stream of consciousness" writing technique, an impressionistic, associative style reflecting the outer world through the inner world. She would also gossip about the various members of the salon and its outer circles, the servants, and their extended family.

Her salons were attended by a lively and brilliant group of accomplished poets, artists, and practicing homosexuals—Lytton Strachey, John Maynard Keynes, E.M. Forster, and Duncan Grant. At first, Virginia was puzzled by their lack of interest in courting her, but she soon figured it out. Lytton Strachey developed an affection for Virginia and even went so far as to propose, confessing to his dear friend Leonard Woolf, at the time serving in Ceylon, "It would have been death if she had accepted me." He also had a much-publicized affair with a female artist, Dora Carrington, who committed suicide.

By 1910, the esteemed art critic Roger Fry had joined the group, later embarking on an affair with Vanessa Bell, whose marriage to Clive Bell was strained from raising two sons and from Clive's extramarital affairs. By 1911, Leonard Woolf returned from his India service and joined the Bloomsbury group, now living communally in Fitzroy. Leonard and Virginia married, but soon after the honeymoon period he noticed her bouts of despondency. When she attempted suicide, a frightened, deeply concerned Leonard took on the role of caretaker, watching her eating habits, her menstrual patterns, and her moods. His vigilance worked fairly well to keep her from sinking too low, but the depression she suffered was destined to return.

The members of the Bloomsbury group worked steadily. Virginia, Leonard Woolf, and Forster began writing their first novels. Virginia also became very concerned with feminism and began doing volunteer work for suffragists. To the disgust of British art critics, Roger Fry held two Post-Impressionist exhibits followed by poetry and furniture-craft workshops. Vanessa Bell's skill in painting was developing rapidly, and her friendship with fellow painter Duncan Grant began to take a romantic turn. John Maynard Keynes was teaching his revolutionary economic theory at Cambridge, and Lytton was fast at work on his biographical survey, *Eminent Victorians*. By 1915, however, as their reputations were growing, the salon was held less frequently, and the group gradually began drifting apart.

The Woolfs purchased a printing press and moved to Richmond to found Hogarth Press soon after the publication of Virginia's debut novel, *The Voyage Out*. Hogarth Press published other seminal writers from this time, including Sigmund Freud, Katherine Mansfield, T.S. Eliot, and Gertrude Stein. Virginia Woolf was repulsed by James Joyce's work, however, and refused to publish him. Upon reading *Ulysses*, she recalled feeling as if "her very own pen had been seized from her hands so that someone might scrawl the word 'f' on the seat of a privy."

Vanessa Bell found a great old farmhouse in Sussex, Charleston, and invited the group to visit for parties, feasts, and weekend retreats. She threw Roger Fry over for the openly gay Duncan, with whom she had a baby, Angelica. Upon the baby's birth, the new father proclaimed that moment to be the end of their sexual relationship. One of Duncan Grant's lovers, David Garnett, wrote a letter to Lytton expressing a perverse urge to shock everyone, "I think of marrying it; when she is twenty, I shall be forty-six—will it be scandalous?" The new parents were properly disgusted by this improper sentiment. (When Angelica grew up, she wrote the critically acclaimed book *Deceived by Kindness*.)

Leonard Woolf eventually sold Hogarth Press to Harcourt Brace and carried on as Virginia's editor. Virginia wrote steadily and gained a serious following for her originality and singular style. Leonard Woolf remained vigilant in his self-appointed role as overseer of Virginia's mental and physical health, noting that the publication of each novel brought on one of her great depressions. His loyalty was unswerving, despite her affair with one of the writers they published, Vita Sackville-West, the subject of Virginia's novel *Orlando*.

In 1941, she was at the peak of her career—a critical success with books such as *To the Lighthouse* and *Mrs. Dalloway*, and mentor to a younger generation of writers, including Katherine Mansfield. But her fears for Leonard's and her own safety during World War II brought extreme anxiety; she was convinced they were in grave danger because of Leonard's Jewish heritage and fully expected to be captured and killed in a Nazi invasion. When she could bear it no more, she wrote a note to her beloved sister Vanessa and two notes to her husband: "I don't think two people could have been happier than we've been." She stuffed her pockets with heavy stones and walked into the river.

Against you I will fling myself, unvanquished and unyielding, O Death.

Bernard, from Virginia Woolf's *The Waves*

VIRGINIA WOOLF *Leader of the modernist literary movement and stream-of-consciousness stylist*

VITA SACKVILLE-WEST *the love that cannot be spoken*

Born in Knole, Kent, in 1892, Victoria Mary Sackville is best remembered now as the subject of *Orlando*, Virginia Woolf's 1928 novel (which was made into a critically acclaimed film, with the lead character played by the amazing and award-winning actress Tilda Swinton) about their love affair, told through the adventures of an androgynous and aristocratic heroine. Her father was the third Baron Sackville, and as a child, Vita was afforded the very finest private education and tutors in her ancestral home, which was surrounded by beautiful gardens and grounds. Her interest in writing began as a young girl with poetry, and she completed a history of her family and place, *Knole and the Sackville*, in 1922. She married diplomat and journalist Harold Nicolson, and they traveled extensively, resulting in her *Passenger to Teheran* and her travel fictions, *Heritage* and *The Dark Island*. Vita Sackville-West also wrote several fine biographies of Andrew Marvell, Aphra Behn, and of the saints Joan and Teresa of Avila. She became the subject of another book when her son Nigel Nicolson described his parents' unusual marriage in *Portrait of a Marriage*.

ZORA NEALE HURSTON *her eyes were watching God*

In recent decades, this American folklorist, novelist, and short story writer has received belated acclaim as a chronicler of African American culture. But she was also a major player in the Harlem Renaissance, an artistic and literary movement in the 1920s centered in Harlem, New York.

Born in 1891 (or 1901; Zora played loose with the dates), she was raised by a firebrand of a mother in Eatonville, Florida. After high school she attended Howard University in Atlanta, but soon moved on to Harlem in the early 1920s to become part of the burgeoning scene. The Harlem Renaissance was characterized by nonconformity to white literary standards and a celebration of blackness, particularly the discovery by educated, urban blacks of the vigor, beauty, and honesty of Harlem ghetto life. The leading writers in the movement, aside from Zora, were Langston Hughes, Jean Toomer, Countree Cullen, and Richard Wright. "In effect," writes *Benet's Readers Encyclopedia*, "the Renaissance group consisted of intellectuals in search of an identity; they stood some distance from their own people, yet felt alienated from mainstream American society."

In New York, Zora won a scholarship to Barnard College and later went on to obtain a graduate degree from Columbia, where she studied under the famous anthropologist Franz Boas. Franz encouraged her to study the folklore of the diaspora of African Americans, and that suggestion became her life's passion.

Her first collection of folk stories, *Mules and Men*, came from tales she collected in Alabama and Florida between 1929 and 1931. Its publication was greeted with great enthusiasm by the academic press, but in a theme that would repeat itself throughout her life, she was criticized bitterly by some Black reviewers for painting "too rosy" a picture of African American life and failing to include the degradation and shame of daily existence. (Zora's championing of Black culture would get her into deeper trouble toward the end of her life, when she blasted the Supreme Court's school desegregation decision as an affront to the value of Black institutions.)

Her most noted novel, *Their Eyes Were Watching God* (1937), is a poignant tale of a Black woman's sexual and spiritual yearnings. Her autobiography *Dust Tracks on a Road* was published in 1942, and she also produced a series of short ethnographic films of rural Black existence. The films currently reside in a University of California library and are occasionally exhibited; more information about these films, which are now documented in digital form, can be found on this Columbia University web page: wfpp.cdrs.columbia.edu/pioneer/zora-neale-hurston-2/

Opinionated and single-minded, Hurston was married twice, but both marriages ended in divorce when she refused to give up traveling and collecting folk stories to be a stay-at-home wife. She fell into poverty in the 1950s as book sales fell off, and she died alone and penniless in Fort Pierce, Florida, in 1960. She was buried in a segregated cemetery in a grave that remained unmarked until 1973, when writer Alice Walker erected a stone marker at its site reading: "Zora Neale Hurston, 1901–1960, A Genius of the South, Novelist, Folklorist, Anthropologist." Ironically, in the last twenty-five years, sales of Hurston's works have soared because of the well-publicized interest of others like Alice

Walker and Oprah Winfrey, bringing great acclaim to her and great riches to her estate, both of which she was denied during her lifetime.

> *I do not belong to the sobbing school of Negrohood who hold down that nature somehow has given them a lowdown dirty deal and whose feelings are all hurt about it. Even in the helter-skelter skirmish that is my life, I have seen that the world is to the strong regardless of a little pigmentation more or less. I do not weep at the world—I am too busy sharpening my oyster knife.*
>
> Zora Neale Hurston, from *How It Feels to Be Me*

LITERARY LEGACY

Among many other writers, Maxine Hong Kingston, author of *Woman Warrior* and *Tripmaster Monkey*, credits Virginia Woolf as a major influence on her work. "Virginia Woolf broke through constraints of time, of gender, of culture. Orlando can be a man. Orlando can be a woman." Inspired by Woolf to experiment with point of view along gender and race lines, Kingston has crossed over, she says, to where she "can now write as a man, I can write as a Black person, as a white person; I don't have to be restricted by time and physicality."

DJUNA BARNES *enigma in exile*

While T.S. Eliot and James Joyce are widely heralded as having changed the landscape of twentieth-century literature, American Djuna Barnes, an important player in the same modernist movement, remains fairly obscure. Djuna was a published journalist and saw her plays, short stories, and both her novels greeted by critical praise. Her 1937 novel, *Nightwood*, is considered a classic, and it was met with a clamor of excitement from the literary world of that time. But when the *Little Review* pursued Barnes for an interview, she categorically refused to talk about her life.

Born in upstate New York in 1892, Barnes was homeschooled by her grandmother, Zadel Barnes Budington, a published journalist and feminist who greatly influenced the young writer-to-be. Djuna's father, Wald Barnes, revered his strong-willed, intellectual mother and actually took her surname instead of his father's. Djuna's mother, Elizabeth Chappell Barnes, remains an elusive figure to biographers. The romantic view of Djuna's childhood is of artistic and rustic creativity à la Rousseau. The truth is not nearly so appealing; it seems that young Djuna may have been the recipient of both her grandmother's and her father's unwanted advances, and her father, with the apparent approval of her mother, "gave" Djuna as a mistress to the brother of his live-in mistress.

Nevertheless, the Barnes family still registered socially, and in their home, Wald and Elizabeth Barnes hosted many of the great artists of their day, including Jack London and Franz Liszt. Djuna cherished this aspect of her family heritage throughout her life; she counted among her friends many of the groundbreaking artists and writers of her day. When the Barnes family moved to a 105-acre farm on Long Island, Djuna wasted little time in becoming a part of New York City literary and art circles, studying for a time at Pratt Institute and the Art Students League. Here, she got her first taste of bohemian life and explored both her creativity and her sexuality.

Barnes made a splash almost immediately with a slender volume of poems and drawings, *The Book of Repulsive Women*, published as a chapbook in 1915. Her stories and poetry gained notice in a number of periodicals, and Djuna became a member of the Provincetown Players. Three of Djuna's plays were produced in a single season in the fall of 1919. By 1920, *McCall's* magazine hired her to do interviews of notables of the day and sent her to Europe.

Djuna Barnes pursued her *McCall's* assignment with her typical zeal, producing a memorable interview of filmmaker D.W. Griffith, animated tales of the "Jungle folk" at the circus, and an encounter with James Joyce, who ended up presenting her with the original manuscript for *Ulysses*. Her articles were steeped throughout with wit ("Nothing Amuses Coco Chanel after Midnight" was the title of one) and a disregard for convention that set her apart from her peers. She stayed in Paris for nearly twenty years as a correspondent for *Vanity Fair*, *Charm*, and the *New Yorker*, relishing the modernist scene.

Word of her beauty and appeal to both sexes quickly spread, and she enjoyed numerous affairs with both men and women. She was married, briefly, to writer Courtenay Lemon. She had a famously tempestuous affair with sculptor Thelma Wood, as well as flings with salonist and rival Natalie Barney, and with Janet Heap, coeditor with Margaret Anderson of the *Little Review*. Djuna Barnes attracted friends as well as lovers: poet Mina Loy and affluent art patron Peggy Guggenheim both became quite close associates, and the extended salon included Janet Flanner, Dolly Wild, and Gertrude Stein. This circle of women came to be known as "The Academy of Women" and is now referred to as the literary women of "The Left Bank." Ever irreverent, Djuna Barnes later lampooned this salon scene in the satire *The Ladies Almanack*.

The Ladies Almanack was a skillfully and intricately woven web of puns and fables that also provided a fictionalized portrait of the expatriate writer Natalie Barney and the individuals in her salon. In it, Barnes staked out territory no one else dared dig into, taking an old-fashioned literary model, and although she remained faithful to form, adding dangerously modern literary twists. Though Djuna Barnes attempted to dismiss *The Ladies Almanack* as a "slight satiric wigging" and "jollity" written "in an idle hour" for a "very special audience," namely lover Thelma Wood, she hand-colored fifty copies of the 1,050-copy printing and went as far as to take to the streets of Paris to hawk the book. Sylvia Beach helped Djuna a great deal when she began selling *The Ladies Almanack* in her shop, Shakespeare and Company. Through word of mouth, it became the talk of Paris, with everyone trying to guess who the "Ladies" really were. In *Ryder*, published in 1928, the central character was depicted as a "female Tom Jones" who swaggered through the tale with the comic arrogance of one who wants to rule the world. Both these books gained considerable notice for Barnes' high-spirited and highly skilled use of language, along with an accent on female sexuality.

These same characteristics are true of Barnes' most important work, *Nightwood*, an experimental novel of an affair between two women and the musings of a Doctor O'Connor upon the two lovers. The manuscript racked up a record number of rejections, not even suffering, said biographer Andrew Fields, "the usual agonizing delays but shot in and out of the publishers' offices as though it were being ejected from a greased revolving door in an old silent movie."

Finally, the manuscript made its way into the hands of T.S. Eliot, who, with Barnes' permission, edited the novel as he saw fit, came up with the title, and wrote the introduction, acclaiming it as "so good a novel that only sensibilities trained on poetry can wholly appreciate it." His high praise cemented the importance of the book and catapulted Djuna Barnes into the rarified air of "writers who matter." Some feminist literary historians, however, believe that the relationship between Barnes and Eliot may not have been so benign, focusing on the now-controversial editing of *Nightwood*, a slender 50,000 words in final published form, 15,000 words less than the version Barnes had sent to Eliot, and immensely shorter than the original 190,000. According to scholar Shari Benstock, Eliot reduced the manuscript by two-thirds and cut "among other things—scenes that expressed explicate lesbian rage and virulent anticlerical sentiment."

In the mid-1930s, Barnes suffered a series of breakdowns. In 1939, one year before the Occupation of Paris in World War II, Peggy Guggenheim paid her passage to New York. Barnes lived out the rest of her life in hiding, more than forty years of seclusion broken by an occasional quarrel, illness, or interruption by her neighbor, fellow poet e.e. cummings, yelling out his window, "Are ya still alive, Djuna?" Her impoverished isolation and descent into depression, drugs, drinking, and dementia were relieved slightly by Samuel Beckett, Peggy Guggenheim, and Natalie Barney, who, along with the National Endowment for the Arts, subsidized her scanty income. Sadly, Barnes' avoidance of life outside her apartment door resulted in her obscurity. A handful of writers including Anaïs Nin, Isak Dinesen, Truman Capote, and John Hawkes claimed Barnes as a major influence on their own work. Along with Nathaniel West, best remembered for *The Day of the Locust*, Djuna Barnes has been identified as an innovator of Black comedy; and according to critic Donald J. Greiner, "*Nightwood* stands out among post-World War I American novels as one of the first notable experiments with a type of comedy that makes the reader want to lean forward and laugh with terror."

Red cheeks. Auburn hair. Gray eyes, ever sparkling with delight and mischief. Fantastic earrings in her ears, picturesquely dressed, ever ready to live and to be merry: that's the real Djuna as she walks down Fifth Avenue or sips her black coffee, a cigarette in hand, in the Cafe Lafayette. Her morbidity is not a pose. It is as sincere as she herself.

Guido Bruno, from an interview with Djuna Barnes

POWERFUL PEN PALS

The University of Maryland Libraries are the primary repository for the archive of Djuna Barnes' papers: family and personal correspondence, publications, manuscript drafts, newspaper clippings, serials, photographs, and original artwork. Her correspondents include T.S. Eliot, Emily Coleman, Marianne Moore, Peggy Guggenheim, Dag Hammarskjöld, Kay Boil, Lawrence Ferlinghetti, Robert McAlmon, Lawrence Vial, Allan Ross MacDougall, Allen Tate, e.e. cummings, William Carlos Williams, and Eugene O'Neill.

H. D. (HILDA DOOLITTLE) *the poet's poet*

References to H. D. come up most frequently when modern poets are asked to name their influences. In an odd twist of time and fate, her reputation is ascending, while her fellow poet and mate Ezra Pound is finding less favor in the canonical memory. Previously, she was best remembered for a few poems named by Pound as foundation stones of the modernist movement he called Imagism.

The only daughter in a family of five sons, Hilda Doolittle was born in 1866 and was raised for her first eight years in Bethlehem, Pennsylvania, a community of German immigrants, and then moved to Philadelphia. Her family was socially prominent; her father, Charles Doolittle, was a professor. Hilda's mother, Helen Wolle Doolittle, was a member of the Moravian brotherhood, a rare mystical Hussite sect of Protestantism based on a doctrine of wisdom received directly and bodily from God. H. D. credited this "gift" of spirit and vision passed down generationally among Moravians as an important part of what informed her poetry. Hilda attended the Gordon School, later the Friends Central School, and Bryn Mawr.

A sensitive young woman, she had difficulty living away from home, and after failing English, she left college and suffered a breakdown. H. D.'s fictionalized autobiography, *HERmione*, written in 1923 and unpublished until 1981, examines this period in terms of the relationship between H. D. and her fiancé, Ezra Pound, whom she had met at college, and her beloved friend Frances Gregg. William Carlos Williams admired Hilda as a great beauty, which Pound also celebrated in his *Is-Hilda Book*. In 1911, Hilda, Frances, and chaperone Mrs. Gregg went abroad, and Hilda's extended expatriation began with her reunion with Ezra Pound in London.

H. D. and Pound found like minds in D. H. Lawrence, William Butler Yeats, May Sinclair, and Richard Aldington. Hilda took the excellent advice of her lover and submitted poems to *Poetry* magazine, edited by Harriet Monroe. Her distinct pseudonym began somewhat accidentally when Ezra Pound signed Hilda Doolittle's poems "H. D. Imagiste" in August 1912 in the British Museum's tea room. Pound praised the qualities he saw in H. D.'s verse as essential in imagist poetry—musical rhythm, minimalism, direct approach of the poetry subject. Her first collection, *Sea Garden*, was published a few years later. While their poetic sympathies were perfectly matched, H. D. began to strain against Pound's intransigence and his seeming inability to remain faithful to her. Another mentor took his place both in H. D.'s life and at the landmark literary periodical *The Egoist* (originally *The New Freewoman*): Richard Aldington. Under his influence as a translator, H. D. began to study Greek lyrics, French symbolism, and the romances of medieval troubadours. In 1913, H. D. married her new mentor.

H. D. and her husband made an important new friend in Amy Lowell, a moneyed American poet who published their work in three anthologies as well as a book of literary criticism in which she commended both Imagism, and in particular, H. D.'s poetry.

D. H. and Frieda Lawrence formed a closer bond with the pair, and this foursome shared a great intimacy surrounded by swirling speculation. While H.

D. based characters in *Pilate's Wife* and *Bid Me to Live* on the Lawrences, D. H. Lawrence memorialized H. D. as his bohemian character Julia in *Aaron's Rod*.

H. D. and D. H. shared many things in common, including a loathing for the war that began on the eve of their meeting and a love for esoterica, myth, and the natural world. Their differences were difficult to ignore; H. D. often found Lawrence to be smugly superior and patriarchal, and it is implied in *Bid Me to Live* that she resented it when he withdrew from a sexual relationship with her.

When World War I broke out in 1915, H. D. suffered a miscarriage that she always attributed to the hostilities. Two years later, the Lawrences moved into H. D.'s flat in London, Richard began training as an army officer and, simultaneously, embarked on an affair with a friend of H. D.'s. In 1918, Aldington was sent to the front lines of battle in France, and H. D.'s brother Gilbert died in combat. This tragedy was followed almost immediately by the death of H. D.'s father; soon after, she became pregnant after taking a trip with music critic Cecil Gray. A bout with double pneumonia nearly cost H. D. both her own life and that of her unborn child. H. D. claimed they were saved by a twenty-four-year-old woman, Winifred Ellerman, or "Bryher," who mothered the dangerously ill poet through her sickness.

H. D. retells this very difficult period in her life in her novel *Palimpsest*. Bryher had been born out of wedlock to an enormously wealthy and powerful British shipping magnate; her main ambition in life was to write adventure novels about boys. She was a huge fan of H. D.'s, even going so far as to memorize *Sea Garden*. Bryher paid for the publication of *Hymen* in 1921, paid H. D.'s bills, and adopted H. D.'s daughter, Perdita. In 1919, Bryher took them to Greece, realizing a lifelong dream of H. D.'s of going to the source of inspiration, the home of the Muses, as it were. Here, H. D. experienced her first psychic vision, which she later described as "writing on the wall." It included images of a tripod, a still-helmeted dead soldier, and Niké, the Greek Goddess of victory. Bryher took over for H. D. when she became too fatigued and "channeled" the final vision of winged Niké mating with Helios, the God of the Sun. Together, the women believed they had seen through to an archetypal narrative beyond space and time, a timeless story of female rebirth that recurred in H. D.'s poetry ever after. This auspicious journey led them to further pilgrimages to Paris, Egypt, and America in search of more victorious visions.

This beatific spate of creativity was followed by a dry spell that left H. D. anxious about what she feared was her decline, leading her to seek analysis with Sigmund Freud, as depicted in her critically acclaimed impressionist work *Tribute to Freud*, first published in 1944. Freud's theories regarding H. D. varied from an unresolved attachment to her mother to penis envy in her relationships with the male poets in her life. H. D. countered this with her own belief that she was more spiritually attuned and intuitive than Freud was able to allow with his rigid psychoanalysis.

H. D.'s subsequent works were overtly feminist. She composed two epics about war, *Trilogy* and *Helen in Egypt*, and later wrote a meditation on the role of the sacred prostitute Mary Magdalene in Christ's life. After World War II, H. D. underwent a breakdown and moved from London to Switzerland, but continued to work on *Hermetic Definition*, which was finally published in 1972.

H. D. delved more deeply into mysticism and the occult, working with Tarot cards, astrology, and Moravian ritual. She had several more affairs, including ones with Sir Hugh Carswell Dowding, Chief Air Marshall of the Royal Air Force Fighter Command, and Haitian journalist Lionel Durand, after she turned seventy. In 1960, H. D. came to America one last time to accept the Award of Merit Medal for Poetry from the American Academy of Arts and Letters. Poets like Denise Levertov and Robert Duncan claim her as an influence, but toward the end of her life, H. D. refuted the notion that she was influenced by Pound and Lawrence, counting them as cocreators only. In her poetry, H.D. was in search of "what men say not" and proclaimed, "the mother is the Muse, the Creator."

Take care, do not know me
shun me; for this reality
is infectious—ecstasy!

H. D.

After the invention of the printing press in the fifteenth century, women were often at the helm of these new machines. The most famous was Parisian Yolande Bonhomme, who as both printer and publisher, churned out more than two hundred titles in thirty years between 1500 and 1600.

ROCKING BOTH PAGE & SCREEN: WHEN BOOKS BECOME FILMS

Joan Didion *incisively illuminating undercurrents*

The daughter of an Army Air Corps officer, Joan Didion was born in 1934 in Sacramento, California. As a teenager, she tried to figure out how sentences work by typing out Ernest Hemingway stories; she went on to earn a degree in English from the University of California at Berkeley. Winning an essay contest sponsored by *Vogue* earned her a research assistant job at the magazine. She remained at *Vogue* for more than a decade, eventually working her way up to position as an associate features editor. She also wrote for various other magazines; in 1963, she published *Run, River*, her first novel, a story of murder and betrayal. The following year, she married fellow writer John Gregory Dunne. They moved to Los Angeles and adopted a daughter they named Quintana Roo, after the state in southern Mexico.

Her first volume of essays was published in 1968. Critically acclaimed by the *New York Times, Slouching Towards Bethlehem* expressed her impressions of the 1960s counterculture. Her second novel, *Play It As It Lays* (1970), told the story of a fading starlet whose alienation from Hollywood gradually leads her further from reality; Didion herself lived the Hollywood lifestyle for part of her life. She wrote four screenplays with her husband, in some cases working with other writers: *Panic in Needle Park* (1971), *Play It As It Lays* (1972), the hugely successful *A Star is Born* (1976), and *Up Close and Personal* (1996). In 1979, she produced a second collection of her essays about living in the 1960s and 1970s, *The White Album*.

During her career, Didion has produced collections of essays on many other subjects that drew her attention. Her fascination with America's connections with its neighbors to the south is expressed in *Salvador* (1983) and *Miami* (1987), and her thoughts on American politics and government are revealed in *Political Fictions* (2001). Her observations of New York City infuse *After Henry* (1992), written after she and her family returned to New York. She reflected on the past and present realities of California in *Where I Was From* (2003). After Joan Didion's husband died in 2003, she wrote about her grief in *The Year of Magical Thinking* (2005); the winner of the 2005 National Book Award. The book has been called "a masterpiece of two genres: memoir and investigative journalism." Tragically, the same year Didion won that prize, she also lost her daughter Quintana Roo to a sudden illness; her memoir of that loss is *Blue Nights*, released in 2011.

Her work, thought of as part of the "New Journalism" movement, has earned wide recognition; Didion was awarded the 2005 American Academy of Arts & Letters Gold Medal in Criticism and Belles Letters and the 2007 National Book Foundation's Medal for Distinguished Contribution to American Letters. She has received honorary doctorates from Harvard and Yale. In 2013, she received a National Medal of Arts and Humanities from President Obama and the PEN Center USA's Lifetime Achievement Award.

Jennifer Egan *unpredictably dazzling ingenuity*

Jennifer Egan was born in Chicago and raised in San Francisco. She is the author of *The Invisible Circus*, a novel which in 2001 became a feature film starring Cameron Diaz; she has also written *Look at Me* (2001), *Emerald City and Other Stories*, a short fiction collection, *The Keep* (2006), and 2010's *A Visit From the Goon Squad*. *A Visit From the Goon Squad* won a Pulitzer Prize, an *LA Times* Book Prize, and a National Book Critics Circle Award. She is a recipient of a National Endowment for the Arts Fellowship in Fiction, a Cullman Fellowship at the New York Public Library, and a Guggenheim Fellowship. She is also a journalist who has written frequently for the *New York Times Magazine*.

Egan received a Carroll Kowal Journalism Award for her 2002 cover story on homeless children, and "The Bipolar Kid" won a 2009 Outstanding Media

Award for Science and Health Reporting from the National Alliance on Mental Illness. Her 2017 novel, *Manhattan Beach*, has been awarded the 2018 Andrew Carnegie Medal for Excellence in Fiction.

Alice Sebold *transforming trauma into art*

Born in 1963, Sebold grew up in the suburbs of Philadelphia, near the University of Pennsylvania, where her father taught. In 1981, while attending Syracuse University, she was raped while walking in a park near campus. Though the perpetrator could not immediately be identified, five months later, she recognized him walking down the street. He was arrested, tried, and sent to prison. After graduation, while pursuing a writing career in New York City, she began using heroin recreationally, or perhaps to attempt to medicate her residual trauma, and later said, "I did a lot of things that I am not particularly proud of and that I can't believe that I did." Perhaps these experiences led Sebold to delve into the worldly reality of violence and the seamier side of life, yet she expressed this interest by eloquently juxtaposing the extreme with the everyday. Her first novel, *The Lovely Bones* (2009) focused on the rape and killing of a teenage girl. Despite the darkness of its subject matter, the book was immensely successful, both in the US, where it sold over five million copies, and abroad. A 2009 film adaptation was written and directed by Peter Jackson, and a stage play version of *The Lovely Bones* premiered in London in 2018.

Three months after *The Lovely Bones*, Sebold's memoir *Lucky* (1999) told of the earlier rape she had survived and the trial that followed; it, too, became a bestseller. The title "Lucky" came from a policeman's comment that she was "lucky" to be alive, because another young woman had been killed and dismembered in approximately the same location; of course, Sebold, who had not only been sexually assaulted but beaten bloody, may not have felt terribly fortunate, so the title has an irony about it.

Her provocative second novel, *The Almost Moon* (2007), began with a shocking first sentence: "When all was said and done, killing my mother came easily." Although it, too, became a number one bestseller, it generated quite a bit of critical controversy due to Sebold's diving into the usually avoided territories of mental illness, matricide, and ambivalence about mother/daughter relationships.

Alice Sebold also edited *The Best American Short Stories 2009*, and has contributed to numerous anthologies.

Gillian Flynn *female protagonists, twisty plots*

Gillian Flynn was born in Kansas City, Missouri, to two community-college professors: Her mother taught reading and her father was a film instructor. So she spent many of her youthful hours with her nose in a book or watching movies. She happily recalls having *A Wrinkle in Time* pried from her hands at the dinner table. In high school, she worked truly odd jobs, some of which required her to do things like wrap and unwrap hams or dress up as a giant yogurt cone. She went on to earn undergraduate degrees in English and journalism at the University of Kansas.

After two years of writing about human resources for a trade magazine in California, she moved to Chicago, where she obtained her master's degree in journalism from Northwestern University. But following graduation, she discovered that she did not possess the proper temperament to make it as a crime reporter. She was, however, a film geek with a journalism degree—so she moved to New York City and was hired by *Entertainment Weekly* magazine, where she contentedly wrote for ten years, visiting film sets around the world, traveling to New Zealand for *The Lord of the Rings*, Prague for *The Brothers Grimm*, and somewhere in Florida for *Jackass: The Movie*. During her last four years at *Entertainment Weekly*, Flynn was their resident TV critic.

Her debut novel, a literary mystery titled *Sharp Objects* (2006), won two British Dagger Awards—the first book ever to win more than one Dagger Award in the same year. The book has now been produced as an HBO series starring Amy Adams. Flynn's second novel, *Dark Places* (2009), became a *New York Times* bestseller and drew a great deal of critical acclaim, and in 2015, the novel was adapted as a film starring Charlize Theron. Flynn's 2012 novel, the thriller *Gone Girl*, was a runaway hit that spent more than two years on the *New York Times* bestseller lists. Both *People* Magazine and *New York Times* reviewer Janet Maslin named it one of the best books of the year. Flynn went on to write the screenplay for David Fincher's 2014 cinematic adaptation of *Gone Girl*, which starred Ben Affleck and Rosamund Pike.

Her 2015 release, *The Grownup*, an Edgar Award-winning short story, is an homage to classic ghost tales. Universal has optioned the film rights to the story. Gillian Flynn lives in Chicago with her husband, Brett Nolan, their children, and a giant black cat named Roy. The author says that in theory, she is working on her next novel; but in reality, she may actually be "playing Ms. Pac-Man in her basement lair."

SIMONE DE BEAUVOIR *on her own terms*

Existentialist writer Simone de Beauvoir was the founder of the feminist movement in France. Her book *The Second Sex* immediately took a place of importance in the feminist canon upon its publication in 1949 and established de Beauvoir's reputation as a first-rate thinker. Although her brutally honest examination of the condition of women in the first half of the twentieth century shocked some delicate sensibilities, others were gratified to have someone tell the truth of women's experience as "relative beings."

Born in 1908 to what she characterized as "bourgeois" parents, she met the philosopher Jean-Paul Sartre in her early twenties in a salon study group at Paris' famed university, the Sorbonne. They recognized each other as soulmates immediately and stayed together for fifty-one years in a highly unorthodox partnership, wherein they left openings for "contingent loves" so as not to limit their capacity for enriching experience. She eschewed motherhood and all forms of domesticity; the duo preferred cafés for all their meals. They lived together only very briefly during World War II and had difficulty protecting their privacy as word of the trendy new philosophy they espoused spread and their international prestige heightened.

While Sartre is generally credited as the creator of existentialism, de Beauvoir and the circle of leftist intellectuals that surrounded them were intricately involved in defining the movement. Her treatise *Existentialism and the Wisdom of the Ages* postulates the human condition as neutral, neither inherently good nor evil: "[The individual] is nothing at first," she theorized; "it is up to him to make himself good or bad depending upon whether he assumes his freedom or denies it."

De Beauvoir's first literary efforts were fictional. In 1943's *She Came to Stay*, she fictionalizes the story of Sartre's youthful protégée Olga Kosakiewicz, who entered into a triangular living relationship with the two French intellectuals. Next, she tackled the male point of view in her epic treatment of death, *All Men Are Mortal*, a novel whose central character was an immortal she tracked for seven centuries. In 1954, after the success of *The Second Sex*, de Beauvoir returned to fiction with *The Mandarins*, a novelization of the splintered and disenchanted French intelligentsia, including thinly disguised portrayals of Sartre, Albert Camus, and Nelson Algren, among others, which won the illustrious Goncourt Prize.

She continued to write and publish, creating a weighty body of work. Her penetrating mind is perhaps most evident in the series of five memoirs she wrote, the most famous of which is the first, *Memoirs of a Dutiful Daughter*. She outlived Sartre and died on a Paris summer day in 1986 after a long and thoughtful life, leaving a legacy of significant contributions to gender and identity issues as well as to philosophy and literature.

> *One is not born a woman, one becomes a woman.*
>
> The first line of Simone de Beauvoir's *The Second Sex*

The first novel, The Tale of Genji, was written around 1010 by an aristocratic Japanese woman now known to the world as Lady Murasaki (the name of the heroine of her novel) so that she and the women of the Japanese Court would have something to read. Before this, reading was the province of men in Japan.

THE MABEL DODGE SALON

Anybody who was anybody in the literary and art worlds of the early twentieth century hung out at Mabel's salon; among them: D. H. Lawrence, Gertrude

Stein, Alice B. Toklas, Andrew Dassburg, Georgia O'Keeffe, Leon Gaspard, Ansel Adams, and Robinson Jeffers. Beginning in New York's Greenwich Village after a stint in a Medici villa in Florence, Mabel Dodge worked for her vision of a "New World Plan" to bring together the world's greatest thinkers, writers, artists, musicians, and social reformers to whet each other's minds and create a second renaissance. Lois Palken Rudnick, a historian specializing in this era, says this about Mabel: "When she came back to the States, she landed in New York City amidst America's first great social and political revolution. She became one of the rebels of Greenwich Village and was involved with the Armory Show, the first show of Post-Impressionist art to come to the states. She supported anarchists and socialists and their projects, like Emma Goldman and Margaret Sanger.... She was an artist of life." Dodge was also a member of the Heterodoxy Club, a pioneering feminist group that functioned as a "salon within a salon."

TELLING IT LIKE IT IS THROUGH FICTION

Edwidge Danticat *immigrant author, mother, daughter, lover*

Edwidge Danticat is a Haitian American short story writer and novelist; born in 1969, she started writing while in Haiti before coming to the US at age twelve to live in a Haitian neighborhood in Brooklyn, New York. As a disoriented teenage immigrant, she found solace in literature. At Barnard College in New York City, she originally intended to study nursing, but ended up graduating with a BA in French literature before going on to earn a master's degree in creative writing from Brown University in 1993. Her master's thesis formed the basis for her novel *Breath, Eyes, Memory* (1994), which became an Oprah's Book Club selection in 1998.

Her novels since include *Krik? Krak!, The Farming of Bones, The Dew Breaker, Create Dangerously,* and *Claire of the Sea Light,* as well as her youth fiction works *Anacaona, Behind the Mountains, Eight Days, The Last Mapou, Mama's Nightingale,* and *Untwine.* Her memoir *Brother, I'm Dying* won the National

Book Critics Circle Award for autobiography in 2008. She has edited several collections of essays and authored a travel narrative, *After the Dance: A Walk Through Carnival in Jacmel, Haiti*, which gives readers an inside look at the cultural legacy of the land of her birth. Danticat is best known for her exploration of the developing identity of Haitian immigrants, the politics of the diaspora, especially as related to the experience of women, and mother/daughter relationships. Since the publication of her first novel in 1994, she has consistently won accolades for her literary accomplishments.

Jhumpa Lahiri *"exiled even from the definition of exile"*

Jhumpa Lahiri was born in London in 1967 to Bengali parents, but her family moved to the US when she was three. Her father became a librarian at the University of Rhode Island. Because her mother wanted her children to grow up aware of their cultural heritage, the family often traveled to visit relatives in Calcutta. Her experiences with both cultures led to a conflicted sense of identity, which became grist for her literary mill. Her fiction, which tends to be autobiographical, draws on her experiences as well as those of her relatives and friends, exploring the range of dilemmas facing Indian-Americans. She received a BA from Barnard College of Columbia University, and went on to earn several degrees from Boston University; a master's in English, an MFA in creative writing, a master's in Comparative Literature, and a doctorate in Renaissance Studies. In addition to her writings in English, she has produced both fiction and nonfiction in Italian, and in 2015, she declared that she would only be writing in that language from that time forward.

Lahiri received a Guggenheim Fellowship in 2002; her debut collection of stories, *Interpreter of Maladies* (1999), was awarded the Pulitzer Prize, the PEN/Hemingway Award, and a *New Yorker* Debut of the Year award. Her novel *The Namesake* (2003) was a *New York Times* Notable Book and was selected as one of the best books of the year by *USA Today* and *Entertainment Weekly*. She has been a professor of creative writing at Princeton University since 2015; in 2019, she was named the director of Princeton's Program in Creative Writing, succeeding American Poet Laureate Tracy K. Smith. When not teaching in the United States, she lives in Rome.

Lauren Groff *storyteller of subtle contradictions*

Lauren Groff, a novelist and short fiction author, was born in 1978 and raised in the upstate New York village of Cooperstown. She received an MFA in fiction from the University of Wisconsin at Madison. Her first novel, *The Monsters of Templeton* (2008), is a tale of homecoming set in a fictionalized Cooperstown; her second work of fiction, *Arcadia* (2012), tells the story of the first child born in a fictional hippie commune. It was listed as one of the best books of 2012 by the *New York Times,* the *Washington Post,* NPR, *Vogue,* the *Christian Science Monitor,* and *Kirkus Reviews.*

Her third novel, *Fates and Furies,* was a *New York Times* Notable Book and bestseller as well as Amazon.com's number one book of 2015. The book was also chosen by President Barack Obama as his favorite book of that year. It went on to receive the 2016 American Bookseller Association's Indies' Choice Award for Adult Fiction and a French award, the Madame Figaro Grand Prix de l'Héroïne. Her work has appeared in journals including the *New Yorker,* the *Atlantic Monthly, Harper's,* and *Ploughshares,* and in anthologies such as *The Pushcart Prize: Best of the Small Presses, 100 Years of the Best American Short Stories, PEN/O. Henry Prize Stories,* and in several *Best American Short Stories* collections. In 2018, she was awarded a Guggenheim Fellowship in fiction; her most recent collection of stories, *Florida,* was released that same year. She lives in Gainesville, Florida, with her husband and their two sons.

Roxane Gay *a "bad feminist" takes on sexism, racism, and body prejudice*

Roxane Gay, born in 1974 in Omaha, Nebraska, to a family of Haitian descent, is an American professor, author, editor, and commentator. She began writing essays as a teenager; her writing was sparked by having survived a sexual assault at age twelve. Her higher education was interrupted by a relationship, but she returned to school and went on to receive a master's degree in creative writing from the University of Nebraska at Lincoln and a PhD in rhetoric and communication from Michigan Technological University. She began her academic career teaching English at Eastern Illinois University; while there, she was a contributing editor for *Bluestem* magazine, founded Tiny Hardcore Press, and started to produce short stories, essays, and novels. Her fiction and nonfiction explore a variety of issues and challenges relating to race, gender, and sexual identity, and also delve into privilege, body image, and the immigrant experience.

Gay's fiction works include *Ayiti, An Untamed State* (2014) and her bestselling novel *Difficult Women* (2017), as well as two *New York Times* bestsellers: *Bad Feminist* (2014) and *Hunger: A Memoir of My Body* (2017). Her writings have appeared in such publications as *Best American Mystery Stories 2014, Best American Short Stories 2012, Best Sex Writing 2012, McSweeney's, Tin House,* and *American Short Fiction.* She is an opinion writer for the *New York Times;* she is also the author of the Marvel *Black Panther* spinoff comic series *World of Wakanda.* She is working on several books as well as a number of television and film projects and is a visiting professor at Yale University.

> *Some women being empowered does not prove the patriarchy is dead.*
> *It proves that some of us are lucky.*
>
> Roxane Gay

Zadie Smith *transforming assumptions with her writing*

Born Sadie Smith in 1975 to a Jamaican mother and an English father, at age fourteen, she changed her name to Zadie. An early interest in jazz singing gave way to the pursuit of a career in writing. While studying English literature at King's College, her short stories attracted the attention of a publisher, and her professional career was assured even before she graduated. Her first novel, *White Teeth* (2000), became an immediate bestseller. Since then, she has been a prolific writer of novels, short fiction, and essays. Her novels include *The Autograph Man* (2002), *On Beauty* (2005), *NW* (2012), *Swing Time* (2016), and *The Fraud* (2019); and in 2019, she also published a short fiction collection, *Grand Union: Stories.*

In 2002, Smith was elected a fellow of the Royal Society of Literature. Among her many accolades, her debut novel *White Teeth* received the James Tait Black

Memorial Prize, the Whitbread First Novel Award, and the Guardian First Book Award; her second book, *On Beauty*, won the Orange Prize for Fiction. In 2017, she was awarded the Langston Hughes Medal by the City College of New York. Since 2010, Zadie Smith has been a tenured professor in the creative writing department at New York University.

Ottessa Moshfegh *"Vanity is the enemy"*

Ottessa Moshfegh is a fiction writer from New England who was born in 1981. Her mother was a Croatian immigrant, and her Jewish father was born in Iran; both of her parents were musicians who taught at the New England Conservatory of Music. As a child, she learned to play piano and clarinet. After receiving a BA from Barnard College in 2002, she moved to China, where she taught English and worked in a punk rock bar.

After returning to the US, she worked for a time at Overland Press in New York City, but after catching cat scratch fever from a flea-beset feral cat she took home and tried to bathe, she left the city, going on to earn an MFA at Brown University. Her body of work so far includes three novels, several essays, and many short stories; she is known for stories and characterizations so imaginative they border on the surreal. Her first book, a novella entitled *McGlue* (2014), won the Fence Modern Prize in Prose and the Believer Book Award. Her stories have appeared in the *Paris Review* and the *New Yorker* and have earned a Pushcart Prize, an O' Henry Award, the Plimpton Discovery Prize, and a grant from the National Endowment for the Arts. Her first novel, *Eileen* (2015), won the PEN/Hemingway Award for debut fiction; her second novel, 2018's *My Year of Rest and Relaxation*, was a *New York Times* bestseller.

Angie Thomas *"Be roses that grow in the concrete"*

Angie Thomas was born, raised, and still lives in Jackson, Mississippi, as her accent reveals. She was a rapper as a teenager; her greatest accomplishment was an article about her music with a picture of her in *Right On!* magazine. Besides her skills and experience with hip-hop, she holds a BFA in creative writing from Belhaven University. In 2015, she was the inaugural winner of the Walter Dean Myers Grant, awarded by the children's nonprofit We Need Diverse Books. Her award-winning debut novel, *The Hate U Give*, was on the *New York Times* bestseller list for nearly two years; it was released as a major motion picture in 2018 and was warmly received by both critics and audiences. Her second book, a young adult novel titled *On the Come Up* (2019), tells the story of an aspiring teenage rapper who causes controversy on her road to making it big. As of this writing, it is being adapted for cinematic release after positive reviews from the *New York Times* and *Washington Post*.

> *DeVante's got a point. What makes his name or our names any less normal than yours? Who or what defines "normal" to you? If my pops were here, he'd say you've fallen into the trap of the white standard.*
>
> Angie Thomas, *The Hate U Give*

DOROTHY PARKER *queen of the round table*

The very name of this writer rolls trippingly off the tongue, Dor-o-thy ending with two sonorous, sharp, deliberate syllables, Par-ker. Immediately, a picture forms of high style and hard drinks at the Algonquin Hotel. Deadly wit and comic timing aside, all was not glamour for this highly readable and addictively quotable character. Dorothy's life was hard.

A West End, New Jersey, girl, Dorothy Rothschild's mother was Scottish and her father was Jewish. After Dorothy's birth in 1893, her mother passed away when Dorothy was quite young. She was raised by her father, a garment manufacturer, and her stepmother, who took up residence on New York's Upper West Side and sent her to a convent school and later to Miss Dana's School, an upper-crust girls' school in Morristown, New Jersey. Dorothy regarded her parents as tyrants, alternately fearing and loathing them.

She escaped into writing and discovered she had a way with words. Her first job was writing photograph captions for *Vogue*, where she charmed readers and editors alike with her perfect *bon mots*: "Brevity is the soul of Lingerie" for undergarments was one such nugget. In 1917, Dorothy met and married Wall Street businessman Edwin Pond Parker II. The marriage was rocky, and the young Mrs. Parker despaired over an abortion in 1923 and made her first attempt at suicide. Things completely fell apart when Edwin Parker returned from his tour of duty in World War I, and the couple divorced in 1928.

During this time, Dorothy's sense of drama gained her employment as a theater critic for the magazines *Ainslee's* and *Vanity Fair*. Her first volume of poetry, *Enough Rope*, was published in 1926 and was a triumph. She was chummy with Harold Ross, Robert Sherwood, and Robert Benchley, and was soon ensconced at the Algonquin Hotel's Round Table lunches. Ross and she were utterly simpatico, and he saw her potential to add punch to his new magazine, the *New Yorker*. Ross proved prescient; Dorothy Parker's columns, reviews, and stories helped shape the landmark magazine. Parker quit *Vanity Fair* immediately and basked in the accolades for her intelligent humor and satiric edge.

While popular success was hers, some critics sharpened their pens to match wits with her and dismissed her writing as insubstantial. Parker was very unhappy personally and had a series of messy affairs, drank a lot, and sank into depression. She attempted suicide three times in the '20s, but managed to keep writing even during the desolation. Three more books, *Sunset Gun*, *Death and Taxes*, and *Not So Deep as a Well* were greeted with plaudits.

Her next marriage, to fellow writer Alan Campbell, was even less stable than her first. Campbell was bisexual and eleven years younger than Dorothy Parker. The two worked on screenplays together and collaborated on the fantastic *A Star Is Born*. While marriage wasn't the right fit, there was a strong connection, and they remarried, split up, and got back together several times.

Dorothy Parker's political views were progressive. She was very vocal in her protest of the execution of accused anarchists Sacco and Vanzetti, and she spoke out against fascism during the Spanish Civil War. Hollywood didn't approve of this political activism, and both Dorothy Parker and Alan Campbell were summarily blacklisted in the 1940s, costing them their livelihood of five thousand dollars a week.

Parker's moods swung with the ups and downs of the marriage until Campbell died in 1963. A dispirited Dorothy Parker then spent her remaining years drowning her insecurities in drink. Not unlike the lonely women who inhabited her stories, Parker lived an unconventional life, taking risks and expressing her views even at great personal cost. More than fifty years after her passing, her sensibility still shapes our culture. A truly original mind, she never hesitated to speak it.

Guns aren't lawful; Nooses give; Gas smells awful;
you might as well live.

Dorothy Parker, from "Resume"

DOROTHY PARKER *her rapier wit gave New York its edge*

CHANGING THE WORLD THROUGH NONFICTION AND POETIC PROSE

Rebecca Solnit *"Inside the word 'emergency' is 'emerge' "*

Not only is Rebecca Solnit the author of over twenty books, she is also a historian and activist. Her books range in subject across the realms of "feminism, Western and indigenous history, popular power, social change and insurrection, wandering and walking, hope and disaster." They include a trilogy of atlases plus such titles as *The Mother of All Questions, Hope in the Dark, Men Explain Things to Me,* and *The Faraway Nearby,* as well as *A Paradise Built in Hell: The Extraordinary Communities that Arise in Disaster, A Field Guide to Getting Lost; Wanderlust: A History of Walking,* and *River of Shadows: Eadweard Muybridge and the Technological Wild West,* which received the Guggenheim Award, the National Book Critics Circle Award in criticism, and the Lannan Literary Award. She is also a columnist at *Harper's Magazine.*

Cause-and-effect assumes history marches forward, but history is not an army. It is a crab scuttling sideways, a drip of soft water wearing away stone, an earthquake breaking centuries of tension. Sometimes one person inspires a movement, or her words do decades later; sometimes a few passionate people change the world; sometimes they start a mass movement and millions do; sometimes those millions are stirred by the same outrage or the same ideal, and change comes upon us like a change of weather. All that these transformations have in common is that they begin in the imagination, in hope.

Rebecca Solnit, *Hope in the Dark: Untold Histories, Wild Possibilities*

Gloria Anzaldúa *"a woman who writes has power"*

Gloria E. Anzaldúa (1942–2004) was a writer and scholar of feminist, queer, and Chicana cultural theory. Having grown up on the border between Texas and Mexico, her work was informed by her own experience of identity issues connected to language, culture, color, and gender roles and sexuality.

Her semiautobiographical *Borderlands/La Frontera: The New Mestiza* (1987), a collection of essays and poems, helped establish her authority in Chicana theory. To reflect the multicultural experience, it was written using two variations of English and six of Spanish. She is also known for coediting *This Bridge Called My Back: Writings by Radical Women of Color* (1981) and editing *Making Face, Making Soul/Haciendo Caras: Creative and Critical Perspectives by Women of Color* (1990), as well as for coediting *This Bridge We Call Home: Radical Visions for Transformation* (2002). The greatest development of her philosophy is expressed in the posthumously published book *Light in the Dark* (2004), which was drawn from her unfinished dissertation at the University of California at Santa Cruz. She was awarded a doctorate in literature a year after her death.

One of her greatest contributions was introducing the concept of *mistizaje* to American academic audiences, which expresses a state of being beyond the binary. The "borderlands" that she refers to in her writing extend beyond the geographical to refer to the juxtapositions and contradictions of race, culture, religion, sexuality, and language. Among her many award-winning works, *Borderlands/La Frontera: The New Mestiza* was recognized as one of the thirty-eight best books of 1987 by *Library Journal* and one of the hundred best books of the century by both *Hungry Mind Review* and the *Utne Reader*.

> *A woman who writes has power, and a woman*
> *with power is feared.*
>
> Gloria E. Anzaldúa

Jesmyn Ward *"I burn, and I hope"*

Although Jesmyn Ward was born in 1977 in Berkeley, California, she was raised in DeLisle, Mississippi. She received a BA in 1999, followed in 2000 by an MA in media studies, both from Stanford University. Soon after she received an MFA in creative writing in 2005 from the University of Michigan, she and her family had their home in DeLisle severely damaged by Hurricane Katrina. While working at the University of New Orleans, Ward had to commute daily through neighborhoods that had been destroyed by the hurricane. Continually reminded of the tragedy, she was unable to write creatively for three years; in 2008, just when she was about to give up on writing and enroll in a nursing program, her first novel, *Where the Line Bleeds*, was accepted for publication. It was quickly recognized as significant, and in 2009, it received a Black Caucus of the American Library Association (BCALA) Honor Award. Both her fiction and nonfiction are largely centered around the experience and struggles of Black individuals living in the rural Gulf Coast.

Her two later novels, *Salvage the Bones* (2011) and *Sing, Unburied, Sing* (2017), both won National Book awards for fiction. Between the publication of these two fiction works, her 2013 memoir *Men We Reaped* won the Chicago Tribune Heartland Prize and the Media for a Just Society Award. Other recognition followed, including a MacArthur Genius Grant, a Stegner Fellowship, a John and Renee Grisham Writers Residency, and the Strauss Living Prize, among other accolades. Ward also edited *The Fire This Time: A New Generation Speaks About Race* (2016), a modern analysis that carries into the present the concerns and observations of James Baldwin's classic 1993 examination of racism in America. Ward is currently an associate professor of creative writing at Tulane University and lives in Mississippi.

> *When I was twelve years old, I looked in the mirror and I saw what I perceived to be my faults and my mother's faults. These coalesced into a dark mark that I would carry through my life, a loathing of what I saw, which came from others' hatred of me, and all this fostered a hatred of myself. I thought being unwanted and abandoned and persecuted was the legacy of the poor Southern Black woman. But as an adult, I see my mother's legacy anew. I see how all the burdens she bore, the burdens of her history and identity and of our country's history and identity, enabled her to manifest her greatest gifts. My mother had the courage to look at four hungry children and find a way to fill them. My mother had the strength to work her body to its breaking point to provide for herself and her children. My mother had the residence to cobble together a family from the broken*

bits of another. And my mother's example teaches me other things: This how a transplanted people survived a holocaust and slavery. This is how Black people in the South organized to vote under the shadow of terrorism and the noose. This is how human beings sleep and wake and fight and survive. In the end, this is how a mother teaches her daughter to have courage, to have strength, to be resilient, to open her eyes to what it is, and to make something of it.

Jesmyn Ward, from Men We Reaped: A Memoir

Chimamanda Ngozi Adichie *deconstructing inequality, moving between worlds*

Chimamanda Ngozi Adichie grew up in Nigeria, the fifth of six children of Igbo parents; her father was a statistics professor at the University of Nigeria and her mother was the first ever female registrar at the same university. But during the Nigerian Civil War, the family lost nearly everything, including both Adichie's paternal and maternal grandfathers.

Adichie's work has appeared in publications including the *New Yorker*, the *O. Henry Prize Stories*, and Zoetrope. She is the author of the novels *Purple Hibiscus* (2003), which won the Commonwealth Writers' Prize and the Hurston/Wright Legacy Award; *Half of a Yellow Sun* (2006), which won the Orange Prize and was a *New York Times* Notable Book; and *Americanah*, which won the National Book Critics Circle Award and was named one of the *New York Times* top ten best books of 2013. Adichie has also published a short story collection, 2009's *The Thing Around Your Neck*.

Her 2009 TED Talk, "The Danger of a Single Story," is one of the most viewed TED Talks of all time, and her 2012 TED Talk "We Should All Be Feminists" started a worldwide dialogue on gender dynamics; it was published as a book in 2014. Her most recent book, *Dear Ijeawele, or a Feminist Manifesto in Fifteen Suggestions*, was published in 2017. A past winner of a MacArthur Foundation Fellowship, Chimamanda Adichie splits her time between the United States and Nigeria.

Some people ask: "Why the word feminist? Why not just say you are a believer in human rights, or something like that?" Because that would be dishonest. Feminism is, of course, part of human rights in general—but to choose to use the vague expression "human rights" is to deny the specific and particular problem of gender. It would be a way of pretending that it was not women who have, for centuries, been excluded. It would be a way of denying that the problem of gender targets women—that the problem was not about being human, but specifically about being a female human. For centuries, the world divided human beings into two groups and then proceeded to exclude and oppress one group. It is only fair that the solution to the problem acknowledge that.

Chimamanda Ngozi Adichie, from her 2009 TED Talk

Carmen Maria Machado *writing as activism*

Carmen Maria Machado is an acclaimed short story author, essayist, critic, and memoirist. Her first collection of short stories, *Her Body and Other Parties* (2017), won a Shirley Jackson Award, a Bard Fiction Prize, a Lambda Literary Award for Lesbian Fiction, a Brooklyn Public Library Literature Prize, and a National Book Critics Circle prize. The *New York Times* listed *Her Body and Other Parties* as one of fifteen "remarkable books by women that are shaping the way we read and write fiction in the twenty-first century" in 2018. The author says her stories cover a wide range of topics, including "the oppressed body, gender, sex, and sexuality, media, myths, and legends, and ghosts and the uncanny."

Born in 1986, she was raised in Allentown, a mid-size industrial city an hour north of Philadephia. She went on to obtain an MFA degree from the prestigious Iowa Writers' Workshop at the University of Iowa and has received several fellowships, including one from the Guggenheim Foundation. She has also studied under authors including Ted Chiang at the Clarion Writers' Workshop. She is the Writer in Residence at the University of Pennsylvania; she and her wife reside in Philadelphia. As of this writing, her 2019 memoir *In the Dream House*, described by *Nylon* magazine as "brilliant, twisting, provocative," has just been released.

Something I've struggled with all of my life is this perception of what women are. You hear that a lot: "Women are this. Men are this." And that sentence is never actually true and is always sexist, even if it's well-intentioned. And yet, there is something that binds women together: the oppression of our bodies.

Carmen Maria Machado, in a 2016 interview with *Solstice Literary Magazine*

....

CHAPTER EIGHT

Women Whose Books Are Loved Too Much

Adored Authors

This is a deeply subjective topic, and could, perhaps should, be an entire book. Maybe you hold an undying loyalty to Louisa May Alcott and have read *Little Women* countless times, going through tons of tissues every time you read about Beth dying. Perhaps you have remained enthralled by Jane Austen and know that you could have portrayed Emma much more convincingly than Gwyneth Paltrow did. Maybe you are guilty of rereading your kids' Harry Potter books in secret.

Why do certain books and certain writers inspire such devotion? Maybe it is not best to overanalyze this but simply to indulge and enjoy. Some books should absolutely be read again and again, each time uncovering something new to enjoy. These are not guilty pleasures; these are sacred rites. If Anne Rice's baroque adventures of the undead send shivers up your spine each time, then by all means keep reading. Rice reports that her home in the Garden District of New Orleans has become a site of pilgrimage, and that it is fine with her. I confess I have a photo of myself in a leopard-print raincoat clutching a copy of *Interview with the Vampire* in front of her Gothic manse.

Among my other literary journeys, I tracked down Gertrude Stein's "no there there" childhood home in a forgotten part of Oakland, California, my heart nearly stopping when I saw a huge old rose bush in spectacular full bloom, imagining that was the primordial plant that inspired her immortal "A rose is a rose is a rose" line. That endeavor merely took six months and a furtive favor from a city employee who tracked down the property records. But, I couldn't help myself. I had read her stunning and confounding *How to Write* and a biography of her life with Alice B. Toklas. I felt driven to connect with her in some way, but my budget didn't allow a trip to Paris, the city of her life, love, and interment. Alice Walker's journey to the backwaters of Florida to find Zora Neale Hurston's unmarked grave is a testament to her love of books and to the legacy of a great, and until then, nearly forgotten, writer. Many have trekked to the place where Anne Frank hid behind the walls, writing in the diary that, years after her death, sparkles with the intelligence and spirit of a girl who refused to be doomed.

This section is intended as a tribute to the women whose books incite such fervency and allegiance. Long may their immortal tomes be relished and read, again and again.

> *Bibliophile Ruth M. Baldwin amassed a collection of over 100,000 nineteenth- and twentieth-century children's books which she donated to the University of Florida. But even after the collection was installed there, she controlled access to the books with "an iron hand," recalled a librarian. She set up a desk at the door, "and if she didn't think your reason for wanting to see something was good enough, you were gone."*

JANE AUSTEN *mannered master*

It is hard to believe that Jane Austen, today beloved by readers everywhere and regarded as one of the true masters of the English novel, received little critical or popular attention during her lifetime. Indeed, she spent twenty-five years writing novels—gems that readers now recognize as masterpieces of irony, morality, and vivid characterizations—that were not even published under her own name. Many of her novels center on finding husbands for marriageable daughters, a theme familiar to Jane from her own life.

Born in Hampshire, England, in 1775, she was the seventh child of the Reverend George Austen and his wife, Cassandra. While he had an inherited income that he supplemented by tutoring, his brood of eight children cost a pretty penny; resources were tight. And like Jane's character Mr. Bennet in *Pride and Prejudice*, he didn't have much to give his two daughters to marry on. Jane was educated at home, aside from a short stint at a boarding school. At home she read prodigiously (her father had a library of five hundred books), played the piano, and drew.

As a young adult, she attended many social events, where she trained her witty eye on the comings and goings of the people of her class. Her observations would later inform her novels, including *Northanger Abbey* and *Persuasion* (both 1818), *Sense and Sensibility* (1811), *Mansfield Park* (1814), and *Emma* (1816). She had a flirtation with Tomas Lefroy in 1795, but it didn't come to anything because he couldn't afford to marry her. The family moved to Bath in 1801, and Jane had to go with them—unmarried daughters did *not* live away from home, no matter their age. Here the twenty-seven-year-old apparently fell in love with a mysterious suitor who promised to marry her but died before they could exchange vows. Critics have speculated that she used this personal sorrow to great effect in *Persuasion*. In 1805, her father died, and like the characters in *Pride and Prejudice*, she, her sister, and her mother were left in extreme circumstances, forced to rely on meager help from her brothers. One of the brothers provided a house for the three, and they moved to Chawton.

During all this, Jane was writing and even managed to sell *Northanger Abbey* to a publisher for ten pounds. (They didn't publish it, however, until after her death, fourteen years later.) Refusing to be discouraged, she continued writing. Her first published novel, *Sense and Sensibility*, appeared anonymously ("By a Lady"), and at first, only her family knew it was she who had written it. After *Pride and Prejudice* appeared, even though it too was anonymous, outsiders began to ascertain that she was the author. Even though her books began to appear regularly, she made virtually no money. Her publishers forced her to pay for her own reprints, and she sold the copyright to *Pride and Prejudice* for a small lump sum and therefore received no royalties.

By 1816, she was suffering from ill health, ground down by money troubles. One of her brothers who had helped support her went bankrupt, and another lost a large sum. She died in 1817 at age forty-one. It was only after her death that her books began to identify their author. Today, her novels continue to attract widespread attention, in part due to the series of films that have brought new readers to this beloved author.

> *Those who do not complain are never pitied.*
>
> Jane Austen

JANE AUSTEN *Hollywood's favorite "new screenwriter"*

FUN WITH JANE

Not surprisingly, there exist a number of Jane Austen websites, including the scholarly one of the Jane Austen Society of North America ("a serious but not stuffy group," they maintain) at www.jasna.org, and my personal favorite at www.pemberley.com, which serves up such tasty items as the Jane Austen Punishments List, which includes: relationship advice from Lady Russell; a visit to a library with Miss Bates; a night of babysitting Lady Middleton's children; one day of nursing Mary Musgrove through one of her illnesses; and a weekend in Reno or Las Vegas with Mr. Darcy.

CHRISTINA FOYLE *the lady who lunched*

Christina Foyle was born into the book business. She was the child of William, who in 1904 founded with his brother one of the most famous bookstores of all time: Foyle's, in London. The store was renowned for its layout—books were filed by publisher rather than by author. When Christina was seventeen, she joined the store and began hosting the Foyle's literary luncheons, which brought readers together with the great thinkers and writers of the day, and continued until her death in 1999. During the seven decades she presided over the lunches, she met many of the century's leading writers and politicians, including George Bernard Shaw, Bertrand Russell, and J.B. Priestley.

MARY WEBB AND IVY COMPTON-BURNETT *revivals of the fittest*

Diehard fans of all kinds of authors are filling the internet with their passions, resulting in revivals of a number of writers. Two such women are Britain's Mary Webb and Ivy Compton-Burnett. Webb (1881–1927) is the author of the mystical novels *Precious Bane* (which won the 1924 Prix Femina Vie Heureuse) and *Gone to Earth*, among others. Hailed as a genius by Rebecca West, she remains relatively unknown today, although after her death, Britain's Prime Minister Stanley Baldwin acclaimed her work.

Ivy Compton-Burnett is another figure worthy of book lovers' attention. Born in 1884, she began writing in her forties and penned a series of cool, witty, and ironic novels that sold well through World War II. But unlike her contemporaries Virginia Woolf, D. H. Lawrence, and James Joyce, she is not widely read these days, which is a shame, for she is hailed by critics. In 1996,

A.N. Wilson listed in the *Evening Standard* the hundred books that everyone should read, and Ivy's *More Women Than Men* came right after *Pride and Prejudice* among only twenty English novels.

When her first novel, *Pastors and Masters*, appeared, the *New Statesman* proclaimed, "It is astonishing, amazing. It is like nothing else in the world. It is a work of genius." She was well regarded in avant-garde circles, with her work hailed as "the closest it was possible to come to post-impressionism in fiction," writes her biographer Hilary Spurling. Though avant-garde as a writer, she "dressed and behaved more like a Victorian governess," says Spurling, using Victorian trappings as a "protective cover behind which her penetrating subversive intelligence might operate unsuspected, freely and without constraints."

If you would like to join in on the Compton-Burnett revival, go to: www. brightlightsfilm.com/ivy/

ANNE FRANK *behind the attic wall*

If Anne Frank had lived, what would she think of the fact that her diary of the two years her family spent in hiding from the Nazis would go on to become not only a classic of war literature, but one of the most widely read and loved books of all time? *The Diary of Anne Frank* is now handed down from one generation to the next, and reading the record of Anne's emotions has become a rite of passage for the teens of today. It has been translated into more than fifty languages and made into a play and a movie; a new English version published in 1995 restored one-third more material that had been cut out of the original by her father.

Why such popularity? Anne Frank's diary shows the human face of an inhuman war while it records a young girl's emotional growth with great insight. When she passed through the walls behind the bookcases into the secret rooms of the attic in Amsterdam, she left her real life behind. At thirteen, Anne became a prisoner and fugitive at once. Torn from her friends at the onset of her teens, she poured her heart into the diary she called "Kitty," her imaginary friend and confessor. It's an intense experience for the reader, who knows what Anne couldn't know—she wouldn't survive. Anne believed she would make it and shared her hopes and wishes for the children she would one day have. She died in the concentration camp at Bergen-Belsen at sixteen.

There is heartbreak also in the realization of what a gift for writing Anne had—it is almost unfathomable that some of the passages were written by an adolescent. Her honesty about her feelings, not all of them noble, is the quality that makes Anne's diary eternal. Caged in a hidden world, Anne showed us that a life of the mind could be full, no matter what the circumstances. For her courage and optimism, Anne Frank will always be beloved.

> *The best remedy for those who are afraid, lonely, or unhappy is to go outside, somewhere where they can be quite alone with the heavens, nature, and God…. I firmly believe that nature brings solace in all troubles.*
>
> Anne Frank

ANNE FRANK *The world's most read and beloved diarist*

MARJORIE KINNAN RAWLINGS *life in the backwoods*

What child has not read—and loved—*The Yearling*, Marjorie Kinnan Rawlings's sensitive portrayal of life in the Florida Everglades? It is a schoolroom classic.

Born in 1896, as a girl, Marjorie used to play "Story Lady" in Washington, DC, making up stories to tell the boys from her neighborhood. As an adult, she was a syndicated journalist before she and her husband moved to Cross Creek, Florida. There she fell in love with the unique people of South Florida and their heart in the face of hardship, poverty, and starvation, which she immortalized in her memoir *Cross Creek*.

Through her writings, Rawlings helped focus the nation's attention on an area previously disregarded as a "wasteland." Through her O. Henry Award-winning short stories, like "Gal Young Un" and "The Black Secret," and her novels—*South Moon Under, The Sojourner,* and *The Yearling*—readers came to appreciate the beauty of this unique ecosystem.

The Yearling shows Rawlings at the top of her craft. With a beautifully rendered story and sense of place, the book won a Pulitzer Prize in 1939. *The Yearling* was made into a film that received both critical and popular acclaim, cementing Rawlings' spot in the list of authors of most beloved books.

More recently, Rawlings has gotten a good deal of renewed attention. In 1999, a book of her voluminous correspondence with her editor Max Perkins was published by the University Press of Florida, and Rawlings's maid, Idella Parker, published her autobiography, full of reminiscences of the hard-living writer who smoked nearly six packs of cigarettes a day. In *Max and Marjorie,* Rawlings's and Perkins's remarkable epistolary relationship is revealed. Perkins was her literary champion, offering editorial opinion, a week-by-week critique of her work, and gossip about the other writers he shepherded, particularly Ernest Hemingway, F. Scott Fitzgerald, and Thomas Wolfe.

MARJORIE KINNAN RAWLINGS *Author of* The Yearling *and chronicler of the unique people and region of the Florida Everglades*

AGATHA CHRISTIE *first lady of crime*

Another writer with a devoted following is Agatha Christie, whom many fans think of as their cherished Miss Marple. She was born in 1890 to an upper-class family in comfortable circumstances, surrounded by books, notably Sherlock Holmes. She aroused public interest when she was at the center of a mystery of her own as a young woman. She disappeared and then reemerged, never explaining her whereabouts. (This incident recently became the subject of a novel.)

At the age of thirty, she published her first book, *The Mysterious Affair at Styles*. This was not only Christie's debut but also the first appearance of Hercule Poirot, one of her detective characters. Poirot would go on to incite fierce loyalty from her readers, though the author herself grew rather tired of him and the droves of fan letters she received for him. "Little they know, I can't bear him now," she once remarked. The clever spinster, Miss Marple, actually didn't enter the literary scene until ten years later in 1930, with the release of *The Murder at the Vicarage*.

Christie had invented several other sleuths by the time of her death in 1976, but none so popular as these two key figures. While she sometimes felt confined to the genre (penning more than eighty mysteries) and was generally discouraged by her publishers and fans from writing anything else, she did manage to write romantic fiction under the nom de plume Mary Westmacott. Several of her stories were adapted for the theater, including *Mousetrap*, which for many years held the title of the longest-running play in theater history. Today she remains the most famous author of detective fiction and the most widely translated author in English, who even inspired a fervent fan base in Communist Russia.

> *But of course, detective stories supported me and my daughter for years, and they had to be written.*
>
> Agatha Christie

AGATHA CHRISTIE *Queen of the murder mystery, unbeknownst to many, she authored romance fiction under the pseudonym Mary Westmacott*

SISTERS IN MYSTERY

If you are interested in mystery writing, check out Sisters in Crime. According to their website, "Sisters in Crime exists to combat discrimination against women in the mystery field, educate publishers and the general public as to the inequalities in the treatment of female authors, and raise the level of awareness of their contribution to the field. Today there are nearly fifty chapters across the country and thousands of members both female and male.... This Internet Chapter features chat rooms, message boards, files, research libraries, direct connection to mystery experts, magazine editors, and literary agents as well as virtual writing workshops!" Reach them at www.sistersincrime.org, or if you prefer, you can contact the group by telephone at: (785) 842-1325.

MARGARET MITCHELL *fame in "the wind"*

The fiery, redheaded, Irish Southern belle, whose family typified the antebellum South, went through a terrible war, saw her hometown of Atlanta burned in an uncontrollable conflagration, and lived to see the day when its streets were filled with soldiers. No, it wasn't Scarlett O'Hara, but her creator and alter ego, whose family members were central characters in the history of Georgia.

Born in 1900, Margaret Mitchell came of age during the great mobilization of World War I. Her mother was feminist Maybelle Mitchell, a noted suffragist and founder of the Atlanta Women's Study Club. "Nothing infuriated her so much," reported Margaret later, "as the complacent attitude of other ladies who felt they should let the gentlemen do the voting." She immortalized Mama in her famous novel, modeling the character of Rhett Butler after the tough-minded Maybelle.

A former flapper (who used her maiden name in a manner very uncharacteristic of genteel Southern ladies in the early decades of the century), Margaret began writing her epic novel in 1926 after a serious ankle injury ended her brief career as a columnist for the *Atlanta Journal.* Never intended for publication, *Gone with the Wind* was instead viewed by Margaret as a very private exercise where she could weave together many of the stories that surrounded her. The manuscript evolved over a period of ten years into a massive cluttered stack of disjointed papers. She rarely spoke about it to anyone, although after a while, the existence of this huge pile of words became common knowledge among her friends, one of whom was MacMillan editor Harold Latham. In a 1935 visit to Atlanta, Latham asked Margaret if he could take a look at it.

Impulsively, and in retrospect, surprisingly, for someone who considered herself a poor writer and was extremely private about her writing, Margaret bundled up the huge stack of handwritten pages and dumped them onto his lap. Almost immediately she had second thoughts, and when Latham got back to New York, he found a telegram informing him that she had changed her mind and to send the manuscript back. But by then, he had already become ensnared in the saga (even though at the time, it lacked a first chapter and any semblance of order).

The rest, as they say, is history. *Gone with the Wind* was published in 1936. This huge (over a thousand pages) romantic saga of struggle and perseverance immediately captured the imagination of the Depression-battered public and went on to become a monumental bestseller. It was also the last book Margaret Mitchell would ever write (she had previously written parts of two novellas, *Pansy Hamilton Flapper Heroine* and *Ropa Carmagin*, but both remained unpublished and were destroyed after her death by her family). In 1996, *Lost Laysen*, another lost novella, was published by her estate, but it failed to capture the same attention as her greatest work.

The sheer scope of the impact that *Gone with the Wind* has made on the American cultural landscape is breathtaking. In many respects, due to its incredibly evocative description of the antebellum South, it has come to represent the exact opposite of what Margaret intended. Instead of a simple story about a young girl learning how to grow into a strong woman with her own identity, who is able to rely on her own wits and succeed, it became for many the one-sided symbol of nostalgia for a particular period in history that existed for a small elite group of slave owners, a way of life not at all typical of most Southerners of the time.

When asked her opinion about what made *Gone with the Wind* such a success and her fans so fervent, Margaret opined, "Despite its length and many details, *Gone with the Wind* is basically just a simple yarn of fairly simple people. There's no fine writing; there are no grandiose thoughts; there are no hidden meanings, no symbolism, nothing sensational—nothing, nothing at all that have made other bestsellers. Then how to explain its appeal from the five-year-old to the ninety-five-year-old? I can't figure it out."

Margaret Mitchell, in a fashion true to the free-spirited, strong-willed, independent archetypal female character she created, went on to endow a medical chair providing full scholarships for African American students that has helped to create some of the best doctors in the United States. By the time she was tragically killed by a speeding taxicab on Peachtree Street in Atlanta at the age of forty-eight, Margaret's greatness, on the basis of one book, was cemented forever in history.

The book lives on. The 1939 movie starring Vivien Leigh and Clark Gable only fueled the flames of fame. And while Mitchell's estate's decision to commission a sequel in the 1990s drew controversy, the resulting book, *Scarlett*, had no dearth of readers. At costume parties, there's always bound to be a Scarlett or two; even Mattel has a Scarlett Barbie. The passion and power of Scarlett and the romance between the two firebrands is eternally appealing.

> *The usual masculine disillusionment is in discovering that a woman has a brain.*
>
> Margaret Mitchell, in *Gone with the Wind*

MARGARET MITCHELL *This former flapper set the world (and Atlanta) on fire with the story of Scarlett O'Hara*

THE FEVER CONTINUES

Proof that Margaret Mitchell and her characters continue to be loved can be found in the attendance records of the Margaret Mitchell House and Museum. Upon opening in 1995, it had 45,000 visitors that year; 55,000 in 1998; and 65,000 in 1999. If you want to add yourself to this number, contact the Margaret Mitchell House website for directions, location, tickets, and a calendar of events at: www.exploregeorgia.org/atlanta/arts-culture/museums/margaret-mitchell-house

---

The memory of having been read to is a solace one carries through adulthood. It can wash over a multitude of parental sins.

Kathleen Rockwell Lawrence

LAURA INGALLS WILDER *home on the prairie*

On February 7, 1867, Laura Elizabeth Ingalls was born near Pepin, Wisconsin, the site of *Little House in the Big Woods*, the first of her many beloved books. Laura's pioneer family, her parents Charles and Caroline Ingalls, and sisters Mary, Carrie, and Grace, would be immortalized in Laura's memoirs of her family's travels and adventures. Brother Charles Frederick was never a character in Laura's books, although he was a figure in the television series *Little House on the Prairie*, which was based on the book series.

The family moved from Wisconsin to Missouri, Kansas, Minnesota, and Iowa, finally settling in De Smet, South Dakota. Each move provided more insight into pioneer life in the growing United States. Seven books—*Little House in the Big Woods* (1932), *Little House on the Prairie* (1935), *On the Banks of Plum Creek* (1937), *By the Shores of Silver Lake* (1939), *The Long Winter* (1940), *Little Town on the Prairie* (1941), and *These Happy Golden Years* (1943)—chronicle Laura's journey from a backwoods Wisconsin girl to a woman ready to create her own happiness in the harsh lands of South Dakota.

Wilder would use her life in all of her writing, covering her adulthood, including meeting and marrying Almonzo Wilder in *The First Four Years* (1971), *On the Way Home* (1962), and *West from Home* (1974). *On the Way Home*, edited by Laura's only daughter Rose Wilder Lane, and *West from Home*, edited by Roger Lea McBride, were written after Laura and Almonzo left De Smet and began crisscrossing the United States, finally settling in Mansfield, Missouri, in 1894. *Farmer Boy* (1933) was written about Almonzo's boyhood.

But it was young Laura's recollections of her family's adventures that would stand the test of time and attract a following of devoted young fans from all over the world. Laura's books have been translated into forty languages, including Chinese, Dutch, French, German, Japanese, Spanish, and Swedish.

One fan recounts this story: "My father was in the Army, and moving around was just something my family did. When I was eight, we received moving orders for Germany, and we were to leave halfway through my year in second grade. We had Christmas early so that the presents could be packed with the rest of the household goods and shipped off to our new home. My grandparents, God bless them, gave me the yellow-boxed set of the Little House on the Prairie books. I had never read them before, but I was hooked.

"The box held eight books, one for each of my birthdays, and it was heavy. But I would not let the movers take it; I had to read each one right away. I knew I could never wait for the books to arrive with our furniture. I pleaded, begged, and cajoled my parents—and walked onto the long flight to Germany the happiest little girl in the world, waddling onto the plane with the heaviest package I had ever carried. Those books helped me 'pioneer' my way through many moves. How could I complain? Laura never did about moving. She saw the world as a place to grow and expand. She saw moving as an exciting adventure, an exploration into the unknown. I spent the rest of my time as a 'career army brat' looking forward to the next move, and whatever changes would come."

Laura Ingalls Wilder died February 10, 1957, at age ninety, in Mansfield, Missouri, the last surviving member of her pioneering family.

> *Today our way of living and our schools are much different; so many things have made living and learning easier. But the real things haven't changed. It is still best to be honest and truthful, to make the most of what we have; to be happy with simple pleasures and to be cheerful and have courage when things go wrong. Great improvements in living have been made because every American has always been free to pursue his happiness, and so long as Americans are free, they will continue to make our country even more wonderful.*
>
> Laura Ingalls Wilder

ALICE WALKER *the color of passion*

Though she currently lives in California, Pulitzer Prize-winning author Alice Walker has never forgotten her rural Georgian roots. "You look at old photographs of Southern blacks and you see it—a real determination and proof of a moral center that is absolutely bedrock to the land," she once said.

Certainly that strength, particularly in Southern Black women, is brilliantly displayed in her most famous novel, *The Color Purple*, which also draws on her memories of the landscape and language of the South.

Walker was born in 1944, the eighth child of poor sharecroppers in Eatonton, Georgia. Her mother encouraged her writing, even going so far as to buy her a typewriter, although she herself made less than twenty dollars a week. In 1967, after college, Walker married a white man, and the duo lived in Mississippi as the first legally married interracial couple in the state. Her marriage, she claims, had a negative effect on her career because it angered Black reviewers, who ignored her earlier works, including *In Love and Trouble* and *Meridian*.

It was her third novel, *The Color Purple*, that rocketed her to fame in 1983 (winning both the Pulitzer Prize and the National Book Award) and embroiled her in controversy, particularly with the male members of the African American community, who claimed the work reinforced negative stereotypes about Black men. The subsequent movie by Steven Spielberg in 1985 only fanned the flames of the imbroglio. However, women of all races strongly embraced the novel and identified with Celie, a fourteen-year-old girl who is repeatedly raped by the man she believes to be her father. The children of this union are adopted by a missionary family in Africa. The novel takes the form of letters between Celie and her sister Nettie, who works for the family that has adopted Celie's children.

The literary heir of Zora Neale Hurston and Flannery O'Connor, the prolific "womanist," as she calls herself, has penned novels, short stories, poetry, and essays—seventeen volumes in all so far. Each reveals her deep commitment to social justice, feminism, and particularly, African American women, as seen through her unique inner vision, a vision she has said she began to develop after she became blind in one eye when one of her brothers accidentally shot her with a BB gun. The loss of sight in one eye forced her inward, and she began to carefully observe the people around her. By writing, she has noted, "I'm really paying homage to the people I love, the people who are thought to be dumb and backward but who taught me to see beauty."

She believes strongly in the power of art to help change the world and the artist's responsibility to that power—ideas she expressed in her collection of essays, *In Search of Our Mother's Garden*. In an audiotape entitled *My Life as Myself*, she spoke of her activism: "My way of fighting back is to understand [injustice] and then to create a work that expresses what I understand."

> I think there is hope in the South, not in the North.
>
> Alice Walker

Alice Walker's official website is well named as it is indeed like taking a stroll with this distinctive and rambunctious author—check it out at: alicewalkersgarden.com

ANNE RICE *queen of the damned*

What would make a good Irish Catholic girl write about vampires, modeling her main bloodsucker, Lestat, on a male version of herself, and in her spare time write some of the steamiest sadomasochistic erotica on the market? It might have started as a reaction to being pegged with the name Howard Allen Frances O'Brien by her loving parents, but then again, this was not all that unusual for someone growing up in New Orleans. Before she was ever humiliated on the playground, Anne Rice dumped the 'Howard Allen,' and after a few years of rapid name change experimentation, finally settled on just plain Anne. But since then she's done a fine job of proving there is nothing plain or ordinary about Anne Rice—and there's nothing ordinary about how rabid her fans are, either.

Born in 1941, Anne had the good fortune of being brought up in one of the most uniquely interesting cities in the world, haunted by its charm and mystery. In 1956, when she was just a teenager, her mother died of alcohol abuse. After a brief stay in Texas, where her father had relocated, she met poet Stan Rice, whom she married in 1961. From 1964 through 1988, she lived in the San Francisco Bay Area, alternately writing, working odd jobs, soaking up the West Coast's version of quirk and old-world charm, and going to school.

In 1972, her daughter Michele (affectionately called "Mouse") died of leukemia. During the seven years that followed, Anne worked on *Interview with the Vampire*—a novel featuring child vampire Claudia, a character based on her deceased daughter. After repeated rejection, the novel was finally published in the mid-1970s to wild acclaim. The mix of horror, blood, sexual tension, and romantic settings proved a potent, wealth-producing combination, and the prolific Anne has continued to crank out several bestselling series of books dealing with vampires, witches, demons, mummies, and ghosts. Her books have given her the opportunity to revisit her beloved characters as well as her hometown again and again. In addition, under the pen names Anne Rampling and A.N. Roquelaure, she has also dabbled in erotica, penning such works as *Exit to Eden* (which found its way to the silver screen in 1994 and was well received) and *The Claiming of Sleeping Beauty*.

Her penchant for having a good time has included a season of book-signings where she wore wedding dresses to all of her appearances, including a special affair in New Orleans where she arrived via coffin in an Old Quarter-style jazz funeral procession. But more often than not these shenanigans have resulted in the media's glossing over the deeper, more penetrating and powerful themes found in her work. This distresses her, because as she once pointed out in her fan club newsletter, she uses her "otherworldly characters to delve more deeply into the heart of guilt, love, alienation, bisexuality, loss of grace, [and] terror in a meaningless universe."

Her fame is extraordinary. She created quite a stir a few years ago when she criticized the casting of Tom Cruise as Lestat in the movie version of *Interview with the Vampire* (though she later recanted). Recently, she bought the former St. Elizabeth's Orphanage, a massive old structure that takes up an entire square block in New Orleans, and has brought it back to life in a new incarnation as one part home, one part museum, and one part funhouse.

In 1995, she hosted the annual coven party started by her legion of fans from the Vampire Lestat Fan Club at her "orphanage." With a little luck, inspired by our fascination with the unknown and propelled by a multitude of fans worldwide, Anne Rice will continue to turn out her luminous, demon-filled view of the world for years to come.

GETTING HOOKED UP

For Rice lovers, there's a variety of websites to browse. The two best are Anne's official site, annerice.com, and for vampire fans, the Vampire Lestat Fan Club at www.arvlfc.com/index.html.

J. K. ROWLING *fairy-tale rise to fame*

The life story of Britain's J. K. Rowling is almost as magical as the one she penned for her bestselling character Harry Potter. Divorced, unemployed, and living on welfare with her baby daughter, she took pen in hand, and Harry Potter popped out—an eleven-year-old boy who discovers he is really a wizard and has a series of marvelous adventures while in wizard school. Although she had written two previous books, the blend of fantasy and suspense she created, along with what the Associated Press called "one of the most engaging characters since those Roald Dahl created in *Matilda* and *Charlie and the Chocolate Factory*," spelled instant success. The Harry Potter craze was on, and the former schoolteacher's financial struggles were over. With each volume in the series, Rowling's fame and fortune grew; kids were so eager for the third book that thousands of American parents logged onto British bookstore websites to have copies airmailed to them when the book was released in England before the US version. Rowling is now accounted the wealthiest author on Earth by no less than *Forbes* magazine.

Rowling originally conceived of the story as a seven-book series following Harry through his school days, unfolding seven years of his growth as a wizard and young man, and she has completed all seven plus the "school books," *Quidditch Through the Ages* and *Fantastic Beasts and Where to Find Them*—texts for young wizards. The seven original Potter titles have been made into eight films, with *Harry Potter and the Deathly Hallows* released in two parts in 2010 and 2011; six of the eight were nominated for Academy Awards, for a total of a dozen Oscar nominations. *Harry Potter and the Cursed Child*, a two-part stage play based on a story by Rowling in collaboration with two other writers, opened in London in 2016 before premiering on Broadway in 2018; both the UK and US productions have won numerous awards and been so popular as to set records for ticket sale earnings. It takes place nineteen years after the original book series, and with this addition to the canon, Rowling has declared that the story is complete.

Her magical tales command such a following that you can now visit three-dimensional recreations of their settings; The Wizarding World of Harry Potter has welcomed visitors to Florida at Universal Orlando Resort starting in 2010. It has proved so popular that Wizarding World attractions opened in Japan in 2014 and at Universal Studios Hollywood in 2016. Would-be wizards and witches can wander through the storied village of Hogsmeade, fly with mythical hippogriffs, or visit Ollivander's magic wand emporium.

The millions of copies being sold in English, French, Greek, Italian, Dutch, Danish, Finnish, Spanish, and Swedish aren't all being read by children. Many adults are fans as well, and book groups are even reading them. Rarely have books that kids love so much also received such critical acclaim—the first volume won the British Book Awards Children's Book of the Year and the Smarties Prize; National Public Radio has featured them, and even the *New York Times* raved, "Harry is destined for greatness."

Rowling lived in the English countryside as a girl, wrote her first story when she was six, and attended Exeter University, where she majored in French, worked as a secretary (disastrous, she proclaims), and taught English as a second language in Portugal. Her favorite writer of all time, she says, is Jane Austen, but as a child she loved C.S. Lewis' Narnia books, as well as *Manxmouse* by Paul Gallico. Such acclaim as she has received rarely comes without a price—her books are considered by some to be promoting paganism, and there has been talk of bans. But if anything, that is merely fueling readers' passions—thousands of Potter fans have written web posts in support of Harry.

> *I just wrote the sort of thing I liked reading when I was younger (and still enjoy now!) I didn't expect lots of people to like them, in fact, I never really thought much past getting them published.*
>
> J. K. Rowling

REBECCA WELLS *divine inspiration*

In recent publishing history, nothing, with the exception of the Harry Potter series, has garnered as much enthusiasm and fan devotion as two books about a group of Southern women—*Divine Secrets of the Ya-Ya Sisterhood* and *Little Altars Everywhere*. Inspired by the antics of the group of women in the book, thousands of women across the country formed official Ya-Ya groups to, in the words of author Rebecca Wells on her official website, "eat and drink and dance and scream and squeal and above all: PAINT YOUR TOENAILS!!!!!" Let's hope fans of Liane Moriarty's *Big Little Lies* don't take up all of the habits of the characters from that novel.

And what of the woman who started the ruckus? Rebecca Wells is no ordinary Southern belle. While she was raised in central Louisiana, where her family has been since 1795, as a young adult, she traveled the country. In Colorado, she studied Buddhism with the Tibetan master Chögyam Rinpoche at the Naropa Institute. A lifelong interest in theater led her to pen and perform in a number of very successful plays. Activism in the antinuclear movement took her to Seattle, where she still lives.

But the novels she's written are firmly rooted in the South. Her first novel, *Little Altars Everywhere*, won the Western States Award when it was first published in 1992. It caught on by word of mouth, fueled by both critical and reader acclaim. But it wasn't until *Divine Secrets of the Ya-Ya Sisterhood* that the Ya-Ya craze went full steam ahead. Indeed, many readers began by reading the second novel and then returned to the first. Both books are full of unforgettable characters who know how to have fun and support one another through thick and thin. As Tom Robbins said of *Divine Secrets*, "This is the sweet and sad and goofy monkey-dance of life, as performed by a bevy of unforgettable Southern

belles in a verdant garden of moonlit prose. Poignantly coo-coo, the Ya-Yas…
will prance, priss, ponder, and party their way into your sincere affection."

And indeed they have. Readers love Vivi and her daughter Siddalee and Vivi's
gaggle of girlfriends who've been friends since childhood and carouse through
motherhood, shocking the small community they live in. Wells followed her
first two bestselling titles with 2005's *Ya-Yas in Bloom* and then *The Crowning
Glory of Calla Lily Ponder* in 2009, which is set in the 1960s and introduces a
whole new set of characters.

> *I don't know what will happen to Vivi and Sidda in the next Ya-
> Ya book, any more than I know what my own mother and I will
> do at lunch tomorrow…. My fictional characters…have their own
> rare airwave that, when I'm lucky, I can tune into.*
>
> Rebecca Wells

DONNA TARTT *enigmatic author of cult classics*

Donna Louise Tartt, born in 1963 in Greenwood, Mississippi, is an American
novelist particularly known for her debut novel, 1992's *The Secret History*,
and her third book, *The Goldfinch* (2013), which won the 2014 Pulitzer Prize
for fiction. Tartt grew up as a bookish child in the small town of Grenada,
Mississippi. When she was only five years old, she wrote her first poem, and at
thirteen years of age, she wrote a sonnet which was published.

From 1981 to 1982, Tartt attended the University of Mississippi. Her writing
soon impressed Mississippi writer Willie Morris. Morris recommended her
work to Barry Hannah; at the time, Hannah was writer in residence at the
university. Both writers encouraged her to gain wider experience, and in
1982, she transferred to Vermont's Bennington College, where she befriended
other budding writers, including Bret Easton Ellis, Jonathan Lethem, and Jill
Eisenstadt, while completing a bachelor's degree in 1986. It was there that Tartt
began work on her first novel, *The Secret History*.

Tartt's debut novel was set at a fictional Vermont college and was described as a "murder mystery in reverse," in which the details of the murder were revealed in the early pages of the work. The book was on the *New York Times* bestseller list for three months. It was a decade before Tartt published her eagerly awaited second work, *The Little Friend*; set in the South, it follows a twelve-year-old girl in her quest to avenge the death of her brother. Its feel, setting, and plotline are just about the opposite of her first novel. *The Little Friend* won a WH Smith Literary Award in 2003.

Eleven years later, *The Goldfinch* was released. The title refers to a small but magnificent 1654 painting by the seventeenth century Dutch artist Carel Fabritius; the painting serves as the plot device driving the story. The work was a significant addition to literature concerning trauma and memory as well as a contemplative journey into art itself. The novel won the 2014 Pulitzer Prize for fiction, with the Pulitzer jury acclaiming it as an eloquent coming-of-age story with superbly delineated characters in which a boy mourning a loss encounters a small yet famous painting that had managed to escape destruction. In addition to winning the Pulitzer, that same year, Tartt also won the Andrew Carnegie Medal for Excellence in Fiction for *The Goldfinch*. Despite some critics' dissent with the Pulitzer jury's choice, *The Goldfinch* was adapted for the big screen as a major motion picture released in 2019 starring Nicole Kidman and Ansel Elgort.

AMY TAN *generational and cultural worlds apart, captured*

Amy Tan grew up in the San Francisco Bay Area, the daughter of Chinese immigrant parents; she lived in a dozen different homes before graduating from high school. After her older brother and father both died of brain cancer, her mother, who feared the family was jinxed, moved them to Europe, finally settling in Montreaux, Switzerland. Despite experiencing a number of hair-raising teenage escapades, Amy still managed to complete high school one year early.

Back in the US, Amy attended a succession of colleges, finally earning a BA and then a MA in linguistics from San Jose State University. After college, she worked at county and federal jobs serving developmentally disabled children under six years old. In 1983, she started doing freelance technical writing for companies like AT&T and IBM but soon decided to try writing fiction. She honed that skill via the Squaw Valley Community of Writers and in a writers' group led by author and writing teacher Molly Giles. Her first work was published in 1986, then reprinted by *Seventeen* magazine and *Grazia*. Though literary agent Sandra Dijkstra offered to represent her, Amy was not yet committed to a fiction-writing career.

In 1987, after returning from a visit to China with her mother, Tan discovered that she'd received offers to publish a book of short stories about Chinese immigrants, based on three that she'd already written. This resulted in *The Joy Luck Club* (1989), which remained on the *New York Times* bestseller list for over nine months. She hit the bestseller list again with her novels *The Kitchen God's Wife* (1991), *The Hundred Secret Senses* (1995), *The Bonesetter's Daughter* (2001), *Saving Fish from Drowning* (2005), and *The Valley of Amazement* (2013). She was coproducer and coscreenwriter for the highly successful 1993 film adaptation of *The Joy Luck Club*, and she wrote the libretto for the operatic version of *The Bonesetter's Daughter*. Her other works include two illustrated children's books, *The Moon Lady* (1992) and *Sagwa and The Chinese Siamese Cat* (1994), and two memoirs, *The Opposite of Fate: A Book of Musings* (2003) and *Where the Past Begins: A Writer's Memoir* (2017). Amy Tan lives in New York and California with her husband and their two dogs.

SUZANNE COLLINS *the Mockingjay's maker*

Born in 1962, Suzanne Collins grew up in the Eastern US in a military family that was always moving. She graduated from a theater arts high school and went on to earn a BA with a double major in theater and telecommunications at Indiana University and an MFA in dramatic writing at NYU's Tisch School of the Arts in 1989. She started out as a writer for children's television shows, including several on Nickelodeon. While working on *Generation O!*, a show on Kids WB, she met the children's illustrator and author James Proimos and was inspired to try writing children's books herself. She came up with the idea for *Gregor the Overlander*, the first book in her well-received *Underland Chronicles* series, by considering how a great many people in cities were more likely to tumble down a manhole than down a rabbit hole as in the classic

Alice in Wonderland; between 2003 and 2007, she wrote the five books of the *Underland Chronicles*, as well as a rhyming picture book about a boy obsessed with computer games, *When Charlie McButton Lost Power*.

From there, Collins' writing took an interesting turn: her next book was 2008's *The Hunger Games*, partially inspired by the Greek myth of Ariadne, Theseus, and the Minotaur, and she followed it with two sequels forming the Hunger Games trilogy, *Catching Fire* (2009) and *Mockingjay* (2010). She has said that hearing about her father's military tour of duty to Vietnam when she was six made an impression on her concerning the plight of poor and starving people in a war-torn country; this provided grist for the creative mill when she wrote the trilogy. Writing for young adults was a game changer for her writing career; *The Hunger Games* spent over a year on the *New York Times* bestseller list, and within fourteen months, 1.5 million copies of the first two books in the series were in print in North America alone. When Lionsgate Entertainment acquired the film rights for *The Hunger Games*, as a seasoned writer for the small screen, Collins wrote the film adaptation herself. *Catching Fire* and *Mockingjay* were also adapted into films, with *Mockingjay* split into two separate movie installments.

The cinematic appeal of this young adult series transcended its intended demographic: the 2012 film *The Hunger Games*, starring Jennifer Lawrence as protagonist Katniss Everdeen, broke multiple box office records and went on to become the fourteenth highest-grossing North American release of all time on its way to earning nearly $700 million in international release. *Catching Fire* likewise became the highest-grossing US release of 2013 and the tenth highest-grossing US film release of all time. *Mockingjay Part 1* and *Part 2* each took in gross earnings in excess of half a billion dollars worldwide. The films featured well-known faces including Woody Harrelson, Donald Sutherland, and Lenny Kravitz as supporting actors and launched the careers of several actors of lesser fame into the stratosphere.

In September 2013, Collins released an autobiographical picture book illustrated by James Proimos, the author who had inspired her to write for young people, entitled *Year of the Jungle*; it dealt with the year her father was deployed to Vietnam when Suzanne was six from a child's-eye view. It garnered a positive reception from critics and has been distributed internationally and translated into eleven languages. Her books have sold a total of over a hundred million copies worldwide. As of this writing, Collins has announced that a prequel to the Hunger Games trilogy will be released in 2020. The prequel's plot is based on the failed rebellion that forms the background to the trilogy, and it is set seventy-four years earlier.

MORE ALTERNATE-HISTORY IMAGINARIANS

Samantha Hunt *finding wonder in the ordinary*

Samantha Hunt's novel about the intriguing twentieth-century technologist Nikola Tesla, *The Invention of Everything Else*, won the Bard Fiction Prize. It followed her debut novel, *The Seas*, which was one of the National Book Foundation's Five Under Thirty-Five selections in 2006. Her 2016 novel *Mr. Splitfoot* was an IndieNext Pick; she has also published a 2017 collection of short fiction, *The Dark Dark*. Her work has appeared in the *New Yorker*, the *New York Times Magazine*, *McSweeney's*, and many other publications. Hunt is also a playwright who wrote *The Difference Engine*, a play about the life of pioneering mathematician and inventor Charles Babbage; Babbage is considered by many to be the father of the computer. She lives in upstate New York.

Mary Doria Russell *traveler of conceptual realms*

Mary Doria Russell is an author of works of speculative fiction and historical novels who incorporates elements drawn from other genres as well as from an academic background in anthropology into her stories. She made a splash with her first novel, *The Sparrow* (1996); not only did it win the Arthur C. Clarke Prize, the British Science Fiction Award, and the James Tiptree, Jr. Award for SF works that "explore and expand our understanding of gender," it was selected as one of *Entertainment Weekly's* ten best books of the year. 1998's *Children of God*, the sequel to *The Sparrow*, won the Friends of the Library USA Reader's Choice Award, and she has twice been nominated for the Pulitzer Prize for her stand-alone novels *A Thread of Grace* (2005) and *Doc* (2011).

Mary was born in the suburbs of Chicago in 1950 to parents who were both serving in the military. Her family raised her as a Catholic, but she left the church at age fifteen; her later efforts to sort out what parts of her family of origin's culture to pass along to her own children influenced the focus on questions of spirituality that is found in her fiction. She has said that she was in a way an outsider in her family of birth, as literally "the only Democrat among a hundred or more Republicans!" She earned a BA in cultural anthropology at the University of Illinois, Urbana-Champaign; halfway through her undergraduate studies, she married Don Russell in 1970. She continued on to obtain an MA in social anthropology at Boston's Northeastern University and eventually a doctorate in biological anthropology from the University of Michigan at Ann Arbor in 1983. The areas of focus for her thesis research were in bone biology and paleoanthropology, and she went on to teach graduate courses in osteology at the University of Michigan as well as human anatomy at the Case Western School of Dentistry in Cleveland.

Russell did fieldwork in Australia and in Croatia, where her son Daniel was born in 1985. She also worked for a few years as a technical writer creating computer manuals before she turned to creating literature. She has stated that while in the process of writing her breakthrough first novel, she thought of it as "a historical novel that takes place in the future." After many rejections, her first-contact novel *The Sparrow* at last saw print; in its fictional 2019, the SETI program at Arecibo Observatory detects radio broadcasts of music emanating from near Alpha Centauri. An expedition is launched in secret to the planet Rakhat, the origin point of the signals—a ship full of Jesuits. Holy starfarers, Batman! The novel brought Russell the John W. Campbell Award for Best New Writer in 1998, and its even more philosophical sequel, *Children of God*, was published that year.

A few years later, she published the stand-alone historical novel *A Thread of Grace* (2005), a World War II thriller involving both the plight of Jewish refugees and the Italian resistance to fascism, followed by *Dreamers of the Day* (2008), a historical romance of the early decades of the last century set in both the American Midwest and the Middle East. Russell shifted gears to the nineteenth century with a fictional biography of Doc Holliday and his friendship with Wyatt Earp; *Doc* was named one of the three best novels of

2011 by the *Washington Post*. In its sequel *Epitaph*, she took a look at the way the legendary gunfight at the O.K. Corral became a focal point of mythology about the Old West. She returned to the early 1900s with *The Women of the Copper Country*, the tale of Annie Clements, the young union organizer who was once known as America's Joan of Arc. Russell is recognized for her eloquence, her meticulous research, and the driving flow of her narrative works. She and her husband, retired software engineer Don Russell, live in Cleveland, Ohio, with their two dachshunds.

> [F]irst contact is constant: it's all around you. Watch children! They haven't been on this planet for long, and it's all new to them. Get out of your own culture. Travel. Be confused. Be out of your depth. Be dependent on the kindness of others. Read widely, and read autobiographies of people you loathe. Listen to NPR and AM talk radio. Be revolted. Be thrilled. Be delighted. Pay attention to your own reactions to novel situations, and to the reactions of strangers. It's all grist.
>
> Mary Doria Russell, in *Lightspeed Magazine*, interviewed 2011

SUSANNA CLARKE *alternative history fantasist extraordinaire*

Susanna Clarke, born All Saints' Day, 1959, in Nottingham, England, is best known for her debut novel *Jonathan Strange & Mr. Norrell* (2004), an alternative history/fantasy novel involving competing ideas of magic that won the Hugo, Locus, and World Fantasy Awards, as well as being named *Time* magazine's Best Novel of the Year. In 2015, a highly regarded BBC primetime television adaptation of the novel in seven parts was released in both the US and the UK. In the story, Clarke touches on the edges of reason vs. madness, what it is to be English, and traditional fairy lore; the narrative draws on the styles of nineteenth-century writers like Wilde and Austen with its arch wit and scenes of society manners.

A minister's daughter, Clarke earned a BA in philosophy, politics, and economics from Oxford in 1981. She worked in publishing for several years before teaching English in Italy and Spain for a couple of years. Upon returning to England in 1992, she went to live in a house looking out over the North Sea; soon she began to work on her novel in her spare time while employed as a cookbook editor for Simon & Schuster for ten years. To develop her writing skills, she took a five-day workshop with science fiction and fantasy authors Colin Greenland and Geoff Ryman. Participants were expected to bring an original short story; she extracted a section from her novel for the purpose. Greenland found "The Ladies of Grace Adieu" so inspiring that he secretly sent it to noted fantasy author Neil Gaiman, who later said of it, "It was terrifying from my point of view to read this first short story that had so much assurance…. It was like watching someone sit down to play the piano for the first time and she plays a sonata." Clarke learned of this only when anthology editor Nielsen Hayden rang offering to publish the story in *Starlight 1* (1996), alongside well-known F/SF writers. She agreed to it, and the anthology went on to win a 1997 World Fantasy Award; she published two more original short fiction works in the next two *Starlight* anthologies.

Meanwhile, Clarke tried to keep to a daily schedule of rising at dawn to work on her novel for three hours before beginning her paid editorial labors, but it was a struggle. Along the way, she and Greenland fell in love and moved in together. Eight years on in her writing process, she was beginning to despair, but in 2001, after two rejections, her first literary agent sold the unfinished work to Bloomsbury and even managed to gain a million-pound advance for her. *Jonathan Strange & Mr. Norrell* went on to sell over a million copies, spending eleven weeks on the *New York Times* bestseller list. In 2006, she followed it up with *The Ladies of Grace Adieu and Other Stories*, a collection of her short stories; as with her novel, they are set in an England full of real magic. But while the novel focuses on the relationship of the two male title characters, these stories focus on the power women gain through magic. Ill health has delayed new releases from Susanna Clarke, but as of this writing, there are reports that Clarke's next work, expected in 2020, will be an otherworldly fantasy novel called *Piranesi*; the title character inhabits a

House with a multitude of rooms—and secrets, some of which encompass "a watery labyrinth."

CELESTE NG *little fires of humanity everywhere*

Celeste Ng's first novel, *Everything I Never Told You*, was a *New York Times* bestseller and was named a *New York Times* Notable Book of 2014. It was named best book of the year by over a dozen publications, including *Booklist* and *Entertainment Weekly*, and won the Massachusetts Book Award, the Asian/Pacific American Award for Literature, the ALA's Alex Award, and the Medici Book Club Prize. Her second novel, *Little Fires Everywhere*, was a *New York Times* bestseller and named a best book of the year by over two dozen publications. It won the 2017 Goodreads Readers Choice Award in Fiction and was published abroad in more than twenty countries.

Ng is from Pittsburgh, Pennsylvania, and Shaker Heights, Ohio. She earned a BA from Harvard University and an MFA from the University of Michigan, where she won the Hopwood Award in 2006 for her short story "What Passes Over." Her fiction and essays have appeared in publications including the *New York Times* and the *Guardian*, and she has been honored with the Pushcart Prize and a fellowship from the National Endowment for the Arts.

> *Maybe at birth everyone should be given to a family of a different race to be raised. Maybe that would solve racism once and for all.*
>
> Celeste Ng

AND DON'T FORGET THESE WRITERS WITH RABID FANS

In no particular order:

Ursula Le Guin, V.C. Andrews, Ayn Rand, Jackie Collins, Colleen McCullough, Sheri Tepper, Erica Jong, Jacqueline Susann, Doris Lessing, Marion Zimmer Bradley, Anaïs Nin.

APPENDIX

....

Book Groups: Chatting It Up
Donna Paz

Long before Oprah formed her on-the-air book groups, people gathered in living rooms, libraries, and bookstores to discuss the books they had just read. As the pace of life seems only to increase, the opportunity to take quiet time to savor a book and then to meet with friends and talk about it is a welcome retreat for many; it's no wonder that when Oprah focused on book groups, our whole culture was reminded of the joy and value of reading.

Recently my company sent questionnaires to 1,500 book groups. We discovered that the overwhelming majority of group members are middle-aged, highly educated women in their forties, fifties, and sixties. They're looking for something they find relatable, but also they're looking for reading that stretches their minds.

In 1992, our small firm published our first annual book group resource, *Reading Group Choices: Selections for Lively Book Discussions*. Since that first edition, we've met many book group leaders and members. We've enjoyed talking with them about their groups, what they read, and why many have been successful in meeting month after month, some for decades! While most say they participate in a book group for intellectual stimulation, others join to expand their own reading horizons, meet other book lovers, learn from others, or grow personally. Still others want to meet other people, grow spiritually, or discuss cultural and political issues.

Whether you want to meet interesting people or are simply looking for a good excuse to gather regularly with friends, a book group may be the perfect forum for you. While most people find it easy to establish a group and begin gathering, knowing some of the fundamentals of forming and leading a group can help you avoid common pitfalls. Give these items some prior thought to begin your book group on a positive note.

Find Your Focus

What is your primary purpose in forming the group? If the focus is social interaction, those who want to plunge right into book discussion will become frustrated. If you want a serious discussion of the classics, those who prefer biographies and popular fiction won't be satisfied. Have some ideas of what you want to get out of the book discussion and the kinds of books you'll choose to read.

By Invitation Only?

Think about who will be in the group. Will the group welcome other members? Is participation by invitation from a current member only? How many people would you like in the discussion?

Set Some Ground Rules

It's best to be clear from the beginning about the fundamentals of group interaction. Most groups agree that it's valuable to state the ground rules at the first meeting. No cross-talk (talking over someone else), be open to the opinions of others, respectfully disagree, only whose who have read the book can comment—these are all examples of parameters that help the group function in healthy ways.

Thinking about Logistics

Will you serve food? Is there a host for each meeting? Who leads the discussion? Will you rotate leaders for each meeting? How long will your meetings last? Where will you meet, how often, and when?

What to Read?

Groups generally want books that will affect them personally and that have characters whose actions are discussible. Groups like to compare characters' choices to those they might make themselves. For many groups, developing the discussion topics can be the most challenging thing; after all, how many of us have loads of extra time to conduct research and provide background on the author, an introduction to the work, and questions for discussion? The good news is that there are a number of resources out there to help.

Book Group Resources

Forming a Group

The Reading Group Handbook: Everything You Need to Know from Choosing Members to Leading Discussions by Rachel W. Jacobsohn (Hyperion, ISBN 0-7868-8324-3)

Circles of Sisterhood: A Book Discussion Group Guide for Women of Color by Pat Neblett (Writers & Readers, ISBN 0-8631-6245-2)

The Mother-Daughter Book Club: How Ten Busy Mothers and Daughters Come Together to Talk, Laugh and Learn Through Their Love of Reading by Shireen Dodson and Teresa Barker (HarperCollins, ISBN 0-0609-5242-3)

Book Recommendations and Reading Discussions Guides

Reading Group Choices: Selections for Lively Book Discussions (Paz & Associates, 800-260-865)

Minnesota Women's Press Great Books (Minnesota Women's Press, 612-646-3968)

Reverberations News Journal (Association of Book Group Readers and Leaders, 847-266-0431)

www.readinggroupchoices.com

References all discussion guides known to be currently available from major publishers and independent presses with more than 150 that can be printed directly from the website

www.harpercollins.com/readers/index.htm
Guides available from HarperCollins Publishers

www.penguinputnam.com/clubppi/index.htm
Guides available from the Penguin Putnam imprints

www.randomhouse.com/BB/readerscircle/index.html
Guides available from the Random House imprints

www.SimonSays.com/reading/guides
Guides available from Simon and Schuster imprints

For a listing of online book groups, see the Resource Guide that follows.

Donna Paz is the founder of Paz & Associates, a bookstore training and consulting firm. Her group published Reading Group Choices annually and manages the website www.readinggroupchoices.com, a central online resource for book groups. Donna managed one of the country's leading independent bookstores, is dedicated to fundraising for literacy efforts, and is a past president of the Women's National Book Association. Her favorite T-shirt reads, "Books, Cats. Life is Good!"

Resource Guide

Books, Magazines, Organizations

Poets & Writers Magazine
P.O. Box 422460
Palm Coast, FL 32142
Subscription information: (386) 246-0106
www.pw.org

BookLovers Magazine
www.bookloversmagazine.com

Book Riot—the largest independent editorial North American book site, Book Riot offers a variety of content across genres with an eye to diversity.
bookriot.com

Bustle Books—this media company connected to *Bustle* magazine and other publications also has a book club at: www.bustle.com/bustle-book-club
www.bustle.com/books

Electric Literature—"Get Lit!"
Electric Literature is a nonprofit digital publisher; its mission is to make literature more exciting, relevant, and inclusive, with a commitment to publishing work that is intelligent and unpretentious, elevating new voices, and examining how literature and storytelling can help illuminate social justice issues and current events. Electric Literature has a particular interest in writing that operates at the intersection of different cultures, genres, and media.
www.electricliterature.com

Paz & Associates—the Bookstore Training Group
Resources for the growth and prosperity of independent bookseller businesses, including a free e-newsletter
Paz & Associates

(904) 277-2664 [Eastern US time zone]
www.pazbookbiz.com

The Women's Review of Books, OCP
628 North 2nd Street
Philadelphia, PA 19123
www.wcwonline.org/Women-s-Review-of-Books/womens-review-of-books
Email editor for subscription questions or to submit a book for review:
wrbeditor@oldcitypublishing.com

Great Books Foundation
40 East Huron Street
Chicago, IL 60611
800-222-5870
www.greatbooks.org

Books on Women and Books

500 Great Books by Women: A Reader's Guide
Erica Bauermeister, Jesse Larsen, Holly Smith
Penguin USA; 1994; 425 pp.
ISBN 0-1401-7590-3

Black Women Writing Autobiography: A Tradition Within a Tradition
Joanne M. Braxton
Temple University Press; 1989; 242 pp.
ISBN 0-87722-803-5, $18.95
800-447-1656

The Feminists' Companion to Literature in English: Women Writers from the Middle Ages to the Present
Virginia Blain, Isobel Grundy, Patricia Clements
Yale University Press; 1990; 1,231 pp.
ISBN 0-300-04854-8; $60.00
800-986-7323

Great Women Writers: The Lives and Works of 135 of the World's Most Important Women Writers, from Antiquity to the Present
Frank N. Magill, ed.
Henry Holt & Company; 1994; 611 pp.; $40.00
800-488-5233

The Norton Book of Women's Lives
Phyllis Rose, ed.
W.W. Norton & Co., Inc.; 1993; 826 pp.
ISBN 0-393-31290-9; $17.95
212-354-5500

Radcliffe Biography Series: Contemporary Portraits of Timeless Women
Addison-Wesley Publishing Co.
Free brochure
800-447-2226

The Way of the Woman Writer
Janet Lynn Roseman
Haworth Press; 1995; 156 pp.
ISBN 1-56023-860-7; $12.95
800-342-9678

Women of Words
Janet Bukovinsky, ed., Jenny Powell, illustrator
Running Press; 1994; 176 pp. runningpress.com

The WomenSource Catalog and Review: Tools for Connecting the Community of Women
Ilene Rosof, Editor
Ten Speed Press/Celestial Arts; 1995
ISBN 0-89087-768; $22.95
800-841-2665

Women of the Salons
Evelyn Hill
Ayer Company Publishers; 1926; 235 pp.
ISBN 0-8369-1262-4; $19.00
800-282-5413

Book Groups Online

Canadian Book Clubs—Advice on how to start or join a club and listing of all clubs in Canada, including their book lists: www.canadianbookclubs.com

The Coffee Will Make You Black Reading Group—Part of the African American Literature Book Club: www.aalbc.com

Also: www.aalbc.com/tc/forum/4-black-literature/

Off The Shelf—Simon & Schuster's book page offers a free ebook as of this writing just for signing up: offtheshelf.com

On the Shelf Books: ontheshelfbookblog.wordpress.com

Oprah's Book Club—Features the star's monthly picks and online discussions: www.oprah.com/oprahsbookclub/oprahs-book-club-faq

The Rogue Book Group—Discussions, with smaller subgroups on topics such as Japanese literature: bookgroup.tripod.com

SASIALIT Mailing List—Discusses literature of the Indian and South Asian diaspora: sasialit.org

A Few Newer Book Clubs:

Badass Women's Book Club—a club with "a powerful book" for each month, challenging women to live their best lives: www.badasswomensbookclub.com

Belletrist Book Club—features female fiction authors and an "inspirational" email newsletter: www.belletrist.com

Hello Sunshine—Reese Witherspoon's extremely popular book club features her monthly pick of a personal favorite work of fiction; she frequently ventures far afield from the usual book club fare of already well-known bestsellers and includes many female authors: hello-sunshine.com/book-club

Read It Forward—"At Read It Forward, we have a healthy obsession with authors, stories, and the readers who love them." Our kind of people, for sure: www.readitforward.com/monthly-favorites/

The Rumpus Book Club—an "off the beaten path" subscription fee-based book club where many of the top editorial staff are women, including Editor-In-Chief Marisa Siegel, they strive to be a platform for marginalized voices and writing that might not find a home elsewhere: therumpus.net/bookclub/

Acknowledgments

I have many to thank for this book, many men and women who share a fierce love of books. My gratitude to:

Vesela Simic and her delightful daughter, Jasmine, whose excellent research and gentle hearts took this book from a prayer to a possibility.

Interns extraordinaire Valerie Bantner and Jill Wright, literati who lit up our days and did great work uncovering the obscure.

Donna Paz for her wonderful piece on book groups, and for her unstinting dedication to the cause of books.

Sharon Donovan, Rosie Levy, Betsy Hollwitz, and Annette Madden, public relations power pack and bright spirits.

Heather McArthur, Jenny Collins, Everton Lopez, and Mignon Freeman, who keep the wheels turning in synch.

Claudia Smelser, Suzanne Albertson, and Ame Beanland, whose keen aesthetics helped inspire the whole project.

Will Glennon, for having infinite patience and vision.

Teresa Coronado, who could probably be cashing in at an internet start-up, but gifts us with her presence and excellence each and every day.

And, finally, ultimate thanks to my editor, the indefatigable Mary Jane Ryan, who embodies all the finest qualities of a "Woman Who Loves Books Too Much."

Bibliography

Benet's Reader's Encyclopedia, Third Edition. New York: Harper & Row, 1987.

Crunden, Robert M. *American Salons*. New York: Oxford University Press, 1993.

Dictionary of Literary Biography. Matthew Bruccoli, Editorial Director. Detroit, IL: Gale Research Company, 1980.

Fadiman, Clifton, and John S. Major. *The New Lifetime Reading Plan*. New York: HarperCollins, 1997.

Gilbert, Sandra M. and Susan Gubar, eds. *The Norton Anthology of Literature by Women*. New York: W.W. Norton & Co., 1985.

Goulianos, Joan, ed. *By a Woman Writ*. Baltimore, MD: Penguin Books, 1973.

Hardwick, Elizabeth. *Seduction and Betrayal*. New York: Random House, 1970.

Hirschfield, Jane, ed. *Women in Praise of the Sacred*. New York: HarperCollins, 1994.

Vicki León. *Uppity Women of Ancient Times*. Berkeley, CA: Conari Press, 1997.

_____. *Uppity Women of Medieval Times*. Berkeley, CA: Conari Press, 1997.

_____. *Uppity Women of the Renaissance*. Berkeley, CA: Conari Press, 1999.

Manguel, Alberto. *A History of Reading*. New York: Penguin Books, 1996.

Merriam-Webster's Encyclopedia of Literature. Springfield, MA: Merriam-Webster, 1995.

Moore, Virginia. *Distinguished Women Writers*. Port Washington, NY: Kennikat Press, Inc., 1962.

Nichols, Joan Kane. *Mary Shelley*. Berkeley, CA: Conari Press, 1998.

Petroski, Henry. *The Book on the Bookshelf.* New York: Alfred Knopf, 1999.

Shockley, Ann Allen. *Afro-American Women Writers, 1746–1933: An Anthology and Critical Guide*. Boston: G. K. Hall & Co., 1988.

Sinott, Susan. *Lorraine Hansberry*. Berkeley, CA: Conari Press, 1999.

Snyder, Jane McIntosh. *The Woman and the Lyre: Women Writers in Classical Greece and Rome*. Carbondale, IL: Southern Illinois University Press, 1989.

Shwartz, Ronald B. *For the Love of Books*. New York: Grosset/Putnam, 1999.

Taylor, Jane H. M., and Lesley Smith, eds. *Women and the Book*. Toronto: The British Library and University of Toronto Press, 1996.

Toth, Susan Allen, and John Coughlan, eds. *Reading Rooms*. New York: Doubleday, 1991.

Trager, James. *The Women's Chronology*. New York: Henry Holt, 1994.

Weiser, Marjorie P. K., and Jean S. Arbeiter. *WomanList*. New York: Atheneum, 1981.

Index of Names Cited

Index of Works and Periodicals Cited

Y

Z

General Index

A

Academy of American Poets 87

Academy of Women, The 243

Acmeism 118

African Poetry Prize 84

Algonquin Hotel 260

American Academy of Arts and
Letters 143, 248

American Humane
Association 156

American Library Association
156, 163, 187, 214, 265

Anansi Press 153

Author's Guild 35

B

Beats 126, 217

Black Power 35, 47

Bloomsbury 235–236, 298

Book Critics' Circle Award 47

Bookstores 66, 115,
273, 301, 304

British Book Awards Children's
Book of the Year 289

Buddhism 290

C

Christian Science 79, 257

Columbia University Poetry
Society prize 33

confessional 86, 95, 173

Congress of South African
Writers 132

Cubism 226–227

D

Darkmoon Circle 173

Daw Books 180, 183

E

East and West Association 35

F

Futurians 169

G

Gnome Press 166

Golden Globe 156

Goncourt Prize 254

H

Harcourt Brace 237

Harlem Renaissance 217, 239

Heterodoxy Club 255

Hogarth Press 237

Hugo Award 61, 162, 170, 175,
177, 179–181, 188, 199, 207,
210–211, 215

Humanist of the Year 46

I

Imagism 245–246

Instapoetry 87

Institute for the Harmonious
Development of Man 232

J

James Tait Black Memorial Book
Prize 116

L

League of Nations 38

Leapfrog Press 203

Left Bank 17, 233, 243

Locus Award 59, 179, 187,
189, 193, 200

M

Mañana Literary Society 167

McCarthy era 123

modernism 217

Moravian brotherhood 245

Muses 27, 29, 49, 106, 247

N

NAACP 39

NaNoWriMo 192, 196

National Book Award 43, 66,
101–102, 105, 208, 250, 285

National Committee for the
Prevention of Child Abuse 156

National Endowment for the
Arts 87, 102, 104, 175, 244,
250, 259, 299

Mango Publishing, established in 2014, publishes an eclectic list of books by diverse authors—both new and established voices—on topics ranging from business, personal growth, women's empowerment, LGBTQ studies, health, and spirituality to history, popular culture, time management, decluttering, lifestyle, mental wellness, aging, and sustainable living. We were recently named 2019's #1 fastest growing independent publisher by *Publishers Weekly*. Our success is driven by our main goal, which is to publish high quality books that will entertain readers as well as make a positive difference in their lives.

Our readers are our most important resource; we value your input, suggestions, and ideas. We'd love to hear from you—after all, we are publishing books for you!

Please stay in touch with us and follow us at:

Facebook: Mango Publishing
Twitter: @MangoPublishing
Instagram: @MangoPublishing
LinkedIn: Mango Publishing
Pinterest: Mango Publishing

Sign up for our newsletter at www.mangopublishinggroup.com and receive a free book!

Join us on Mango's journey to reinvent publishing, one book at a time. Lautempo rehendest laborib uscieniatiis quisit es eaturepe ventius seque doluptatibus intinctem quodit voluptur?

CPSIA information can be obtained
at www.ICGtesting.com
Printed in the USA
LVHW012159111220
673993LV00002B/2